STILL COUNTING...

STILL COUNTING...

Biodiversity Exploration for Conservation

The First 20 Years of the Rapid Assessment Program

Edited by
Leeanne E. Alonso, Jessica L. Deichmann, Sheila A. McKenna,
Piotr Naskrecki, and Stephen J. Richards

This book has been published by:
Rapid Assessment Program
Conservation International
2011 Crystal Drive, Suite 500
Arlington, VA 22202
USA

1-703-341-2400 telephone
1-703-979-2980 fax
www.conservation.org

Conservation International is a private, non-profit organization exempt from federal income tax under section 501c(3) of the Internal Revenue Code.

Editors: Leeanne E. Alonso, Jessica L. Deichmann, Sheila A. McKenna, Piotr Naskrecki, and Stephen J. Richards
Design/production: Piotr Naskrecki and Lisa Capon
Map: Jessica L. Deichmann and Piotr Naskrecki
Front and back cover photos: Piotr Naskrecki
Cover design: Piotr Naskrecki

ISBN: 978-1-934151-44-0

The designations of geographical entities in this publication, and the presentation of the material, do not imply the expression of any opinion whatsoever on the part of Conservation International or its supporting organizations concerning the legal status of any country, territory, or area, or of its authorities, or concerning the delimitation of its frontiers or boundaries.

Any opinions expressed in this publication are those of the writers and do not necessarily reflect those of Conservation International.

Citation:
Alonso, L.E., J.L. Deichmann, S.A. McKenna, P. Naskrecki and S.J. Richards (Editors). 2011. Still Counting...Biodiversity Exploration for Conservation – The First 20 Years of the Rapid Assessment Program. Conservation International, Arlington, VA, USA, 316 pp.

An electronic version (pdf) of this book can be downloaded at: www.conservation.org.

 The paper used to print this book is FSC-certified, 55% recycled with 30% post consumer waste. Linemark Printing is 100% wind-powered.

We dedicate this book to the memory of Theodore A. Parker III,
Alwyn H. Gentry, Fonchii Chang, Reynaldo Sandoval,
Henri Blaffart, and Paul Igag

The RAP Katydid *(Brachyamytta rapidoaestima)*
A new species discovered by and named after the Rapid Assessment Program

Contents

Introductory Letter

In 1987 we launched CI with the express purpose of protecting the most important places on earth. As we began to initiate programs in tropical South America, we realized that we faced the challenge of identifying precisely where our ecosystem conservation programs should focus. The information did not exist for us to say one place was more important than another. We just did not know which specific locations had escaped the pressures of modern society and remained the best benchmarks of undisturbed natural systems.

During a late night conversation in my kitchen in Washington DC, Dr. Murray Gellman, the Nobel Prize winning physicist and chair of the John D. and Catherine T. MacArthur Foundation's Resources Committee, suggested to me that we hire a few extraordinary field biologists to find these ecological jewels. He had Louisiana State ornithologist Ted Parker and Missouri Botanical Garden's botanist Al Gentry in mind. These two men were not mere mortals in the world of field biologists. They were legends for their knowledge and their ability to disappear into the wild, only to emerge months later with extraordinary tales of adventure and discovery.

Murray's idea was for us to start with Ted and Al and to build a team of the best field biologists from different disciplines. We could place them in places that we suspected were ecological paradises and then define with precision the highest biodiversity priorities. An ecological SWAT team that could accurately assess the health of an ecosystem in a fraction of the time it would take the normal team of University scientists. Murray was so enthusiastic about the idea and the urgency of the need, that he offered to have the Foundation finance the effort.

Out of this came RAP. Ted Parker and Al Genty had unbridled enthusiasm. I recall a conversation with Ted where he implored me to give him half an hour with the then president of Peru, Alberto Fujimori, so that President Fujimori would know which places in Peru were irreplaceable jewels. The meeting took place. The conversation was a little unusual.

Joined by mammalogist Louise Emmons and forest ecologist Robin Foster, the initial RAP Team emerged. After awful tragedy and extraordinary successes, Leeanne Alonso took over the lead of RAP. Under her clear and strong guidance, RAP has emerged as a high tech, hands on, teaching by experience, tool for identifying and then protecting the most important ecosystems on land, in the oceans and in the water.

This book is a tribute to the ecological warriors who launched RAP and sacrificed their lives doing so.

Peter A. Seligmann
Chairman and CEO, Conservation International

Foreword

Back in the 1970s and 1980s, we were just beginning to understand the great diversity and global importance of tropical forests and other tropical ecosystems. At the same time, we could see that they were under increasing pressure almost everywhere, with land being cleared at unprecedented rates for cattle pasture, large scale monoculture agriculture, huge hydroelectric projects, and large and small scale mining activities. Those of us who had already spent some time carrying out research in these regions had begun to understand their great biological wealth, but what we had seen had made us even more aware of our own ignorance and how much we still needed to learn to understand these places and to effectively engage in their conservation. We were also acutely aware of the time needed to carry out research and exploration in these often remote sites, and, given the growing threats, how little time we had left. What could we do? Was there a way to learn about these wonderful, truly unique storehouses of biological wealth in a much faster way, but a way that was still scientifically rigorous and comprehensive.

These were thoughts that occupied many of us back in those early days, but none of us had an immediate answer. As a result, you can imagine my excitement one day back in early 1990 when my good friend, ornithologist Ted Parker, came into my office, and in his inimitable way told me that he had an offer that I couldn't refuse. Ted, at that time – although he was only in his late 30s – was already acknowledged as the greatest field ornithologist that had ever lived. He had the entire vocal repertoires of more than 4,000 bird species embedded in his brain and he could carry out an inventory of 500 bird species in an Amazonian forest by sound alone. He had even discovered a species new to science simply by hearing it calling in the forest. He was unique, charming, irrepressible, persistent, and endlessly enthusiastic about his passion for birds and for conservation of the natural world.

What Ted told me on that day long ago was that he had been on an expedition to Bolivia, one of his favorite countries for bird-watching, together with Nobel Prize winning physicist Murray Gell-Mann, another avid bird-watcher, and Spencer Beebe, formerly of The Nature Conservancy and one of the co-founders of Conservation International along with Peter Seligmann. They had been sitting around a campfire talking about how little we knew of the tropics and how we needed to learn more as quickly as possible, while there was still time. They had hit upon the idea of using a handful of superstar field biologists like Ted himself to go into remote areas and carry out "quick and dirty" assessments, using their amazing skills to do in a few weeks' time what it would take ordinary mortal Ph.D. level field biologists months or years to do. Aside from Ted, there were only a few people around with such expertise in other groups of organisms such as plants, mammals, and reptiles and amphibians, but there were enough of them to constitute a small team. Ted, Murray, and Spencer came up with the idea of a program for Rapid Assessment of Priority Ecosystems, which was later changed to simply the Rapid Assessment Program or RAP, and Ted wanted to see if the young CI, only three years old, was interested in taking on this challenge.

I had just come to CI as its President a few months earlier, in July of 1989, leaving an 11 year position with the World Wildlife Fund. We were a young, agile, passionate new organization always open to new ideas – even if we had no idea where the resources to pay for them would actually come from. I was immediately thrilled with Ted's proposal, and we bounced around my office like little boys with a new toy, as excited as we could possibly be. What was even more exciting was that there was a potential source of funding for the concept as well. Murray Gell-Mann was then an influential board member of The John D. and Catherine T. MacArthur Foundation, a new foundation that over the past couple of years had shown a strong interest in biodiversity conservation. Murray thought that MacArthur could fund the start-up phase of RAP over perhaps a three year period, and could do so at a scale that was large enough to create a meaningful program.

Right after talking to Ted, I consulted with Peter Seligmann, the Chairman and Co-founder of CI, about this exciting idea. As it turned out, Peter had already had a separate conversation with Murray Gell-Mann, and he was equally enthusiastic about the potential of a RAP Team. As a result, we very quickly put together a proposal, sent it to MacArthur, and had it funded within a few months time. Instrumental in this were two other people who also played key roles. One was Brent Bailey, who was part of CI's Science Program and who put together the original proposal and managed the program in its early days, and the other was Dan Martin, the Director of MacArthur's World Environment and Resources Program, who had already shown great leadership and vision in getting MacArthur to focus its conservation investments on the biodiversity hotspots, an important concept that had just been developed by British ecologist Norman Myers back in 1988. The original grant was for approximately $750,000 over three years.

With this major support – a lot of money in those days, we were off and running. Ted pulled together the initial team, which consisted of botanist Al Gentry from the Missouri Botanical Garden (affectionately referred to as a "perchologist" by avid birdwatcher Murray Gell-Mann because he studied bird's perches), plant ecologist Robin Foster from The Field Museum , and mammalogist Louise Emmons from the Smithsonian Institution in Washington, D.C. Like Ted, Al was a genius. I remember once visiting him in his office at the Missouri Botanical Garden and handing him a stack of unidentified plant specimens pressed in newspaper and fresh from the field. He leafed through them like the pages of a book, unhesitatingly identifying each one in a matter of seconds. He once got lost in a forest in Colombia for three or four days, crawled back into camp on the verge of starvation, grabbed some food from a pot cooking on the campfire, and went right back into the forest to collect a plant specimen that he thought was new to science. Robin Foster was equally amazing. I remember taking a leaf fragment of a forest floor sapling from the mouth of a turtle on Barro Colorado Island in Panama when we were both working there in 1970, bringing it back to him, and having him identify it on the spot. Louise was considered the best field mammalogist working in the Neotropics at that time, and had amazing skills as well.

The location that we chose for the first RAP expedition was the Madidi region of Bolivia, a place that Ted and Al already had some familiarity with. The expedition ran from May 18 – June 15, 1990, and produced amazing results – 403 bird species, nine of which were new for Bolivia and 52 for the department of La Paz, and high plant diversity (204 species in 0.1 hectare). The RAP report was produced very quickly, and was published in 1991. The official launch of the report was held in La Paz, Bolivia, and the then President of Bolivia, Gonzalo Sánchez de Lozada, was so taken with it that he took the report's recommendation that Madidi be set aside as a national park very seriously. Indeed, within a year of the RAP survey, the Bolivian government and the World Bank both ranked Madidi as one of six high-priority sites to receive significant funding and, in 1995, President Sánchez de Lozada declared Madidi as a 1.8 million hectare national park, making it one of the largest then in existence.

This immediate political success demonstrated very clearly to us that RAP was not just going to be an important scientific tool. The romantic adventure-filled nature of the work struck a chord with a wide audience – these, after all, were the true "Indiana Joneses" of the world. Everyone from decision-makers to the media to the general public was taken with the program, and this demonstrated very quickly to us that we had struck upon something very special and that the impact of RAP was going to exceed all of our original expectations. Overnight, RAP became a signature program of the young CI – in many ways it became our most prominent activity in those early years – and it helped to define the character of the program for the remainder of that early critically important decade of the 1990s.

We were also fortunate in that several key media outlets picked up on the program early on. Bill Kurtis, the well-known Chicago journalist and news anchor, had just launched a series called "The New Explorers", and RAP was perfect for his program. *Smithsonian, People* magazine, *National Geographic* and many others covered it, often in considerable depth, and we were off and running.

For the first four years, RAP focused exclusively on tropical rain forest regions, mainly in the Andean countries of Bolivia, Ecuador, and Peru, the heartland of the Tropical Andes Hotspot and the richest and most diverse tropical forest region on Earth. In 1994, with the participation of Bruce Beehler, the world's expert on the birds of New Guinea, we began work in Papua New Guinea, another incredibly rich region and even more poorly known than South America. In 1997, RAP made its first foray into the African region with an expedition to Madagascar, the highest priority biodiversity hotspot on Earth, and in 1998, a trip to Cote d'Ivoire in West Africa, another very high priority, heavily impacted hotspot. The work in Madagascar has been especially productive, with a wide range of new species being discovered on every expedition, in spite of the severe fragmentation in this unique country.

After six years of work in the terrestrial realm, and at the urging of Adrian Forsyth, our first Director of Conservation Biology, and later Jorgen Thomsen, who followed Adrian in this position, we decided to look into freshwater systems as well. With support generously provided by the U.K.–based Rufford Foundation, we were able to move forward with this new dimension, which we called AquaRAP. The first expedition was to the Rio Orthon in the Pando Department of Bolivia in 1996, soon followed by trips to other important rivers in South America and to the Okavango Delta of Botswana.

It was a logical step to add MarineRAP, which officially began in 1997 with an expedition to Milne Bay Province in Papua New Guinea, followed by other expeditions to the Coral Triangle region of the Pacific, by far the richest area on Earth for coral reef diversity. As with Terrestrial RAP, these early marine expeditions had huge impacts, not just on CI's program but on conservation at a global level. Milne Bay became our major focus in Papua New Guinea, our expeditions to the Philippines and Sulawesi laid the groundwork for our major Sulu-Seascape Program, and, most impressive of all, our 2001 RAP expeditions to the Raja Ampat Islands of Papua Province in Indonesian New Guinea discovered the richest coral reef system known to date. This expedition resulted in an intense focus on Raja Ampat, and the creation of 1.7 million ha of new marine protected areas in what we are now calling the Bird's Head Seascape. Indeed, in many ways, these early MarineRAP expeditions were responsible for the great global interest in the Coral Triangle, which has now become one of the largest conservation programs in the world, the six-nation Coral Triangle initiative.

By the end of the 1990s, we knew that we had something very special. Not only had our RAP program succeeded in achieving its original goals, it had developed a methodology that had been replicated by a number of other institutions and had become a mainstream element of the biodiversity conservation business. What is more, since we knew that RAP would have to be fully-owned by the countries of the tropics where so much of the world's biodiversity resides, we began early on to train field biologists from these countries so that they could become the super-stars of the future. This has worked particularly well, to the point that the vast majority of RAP work is now done by researchers from the tropical countries themselves. This was something envisioned by Parker, Gentry, Foster, and Emmons in the early days, and it has come to fruition in a major way.

Sadly, the work of RAP has come at a high cost. When we began the program in 1990, we all knew that there were great risks involved. Reaching the remote areas of greatest interest required travelling by small plane, helicopter, or boat in often precarious conditions, and the risks of disease, snakebite, guerrillas, and drug-dealers were ever-present – regardless of how well one prepared for a given expedition. We all took them for granted, and still do – an accepted occupational hazard, and it has never prevented any of us from carrying out our life's work. But the risks are real, as became painfully evident in August, 1993, when two of our RAP founders, and perhaps the two greatest field biologists that ever lived – Ted Parker and Al Gentry, died in a plane crash in the mountains outside of Guayaquil, Ecuador. Ironically, they were not actually on a RAP expedition. They had just completed an expedition, had missed their flight to the U.S., and were occupying their time by taking a scouting trip with a local conservation NGO. We are all shocked and greatly saddened by this loss, but, as both Ted and Al would have wanted, their untimely deaths only strengthened our resolve to continue the work that had been such an integral part of their lives.

Six years later, disaster struck again, this time during an AquaRAP expedition in Peru's Rio Pastaza. The expedition boat was trawling for fish when it got stuck on a submerged log, dragging the boat under water. Two people perished in this accident, Fonchii Chang, a promising young Peruvian ichthyologist, and Reynaldo Sandoval, a local boat driver. As sad as these tragic accidents were, we never thought of ending the program because of them. Rather, we always felt that the best thing that we could do to honor the memory of these committed pioneers who gave their lives for conservation was to increase our efforts and do even more than we had done before.

Now, as I look back at the past 20 years, I am extremely proud of what RAP has accomplished and how important it has been to CI and to the conservation world in general. Indeed, it is fair to say that CI would not be where it is today without the sound science and great visibility that RAP provided for us in those early years. We have carried out an amazing 80 expeditions, 51 terrestrial, 13 freshwater, and 16 marine. We have discovered more than 1,300 species previously unknown to science and have gathered vast amounts of data on poorly known species, adding greatly to our knowledge of the tropical world. The new protected areas created as a result of RAP expeditions have been of global significance, and have led to major global programs extending far beyond CI's own activities. In several cases, our expeditions have laid the foundation for land claims by indigenous people, resulting in the creation of special community conservation areas for them. Our methodology is even being used in a program called IBAT (Integrative Biodiversity Assessment Tool) to inform businesses on where to site their extractive industries. And perhaps most important of all, by training hundreds of students from tropical countries, we have truly laid the groundwork for the future and created constituencies that are already carrying the cause of conservation forward.

Nonetheless, in spite of all that we have learned, there is still much to do. The pressures on the countries richest in biodiversity have not diminished, and many regions still remain unexplored. Knowledge has already helped to conserve some of the world's highest priority sites and regions, and knowledge will continue to be our strongest tool in ensuring the future of life on our planet. RAP has been critical in providing us with such knowledge, and we look forward to the next 20 years and the many challenges and the exciting new discoveries that lie ahead.

Russell A. Mittermeier
President, Conservation International

Read Spencer Beebe's account of the trip
to Bolivia that inspired the creation of the
RAP program on page 126

For the past 20 years, RAP has played a catalytic role in many of CI's successful conservation actions in the field. RAP teams have exemplified CI's values of courage, passion, and integrity as they explore the far reaches of our planet to document and assess the value of the natural world. We are counting on RAP to continue to provide the essential data on natural capital that will guide CI's new mission of green economies and spatial planning.

- Niels Crone, Chief Operating Officer, Conservation International

Preface

If you ask different people "What is RAP?" you will likely get many different answers. Aside from the obvious answer that it's a type of music with rhyming lyrics, "RAP" has become a well-known acronym for Conservation International's Rapid Assessment Program (RAP). Some familiar with the roots of the RAP program may reply that it's a small team of expert field biologists swooping in to rapidly collect data for conservation. The general public who has seen recent media may state that it's a bunch of scientists discovering new species. Scientists may reply that it's a way to quickly collect data to complete their taxonomic revisions and ecological studies. Students may say that it's an opportunity to gain field experience and learn from scientific experts. Local communities may reply that it's a means of learning more about what's in their backyard and how to protect and sustainably use it. NGOs and governments may say that it's a way to obtain information they need to make informed decisions about conservation or development. All of these views are correct and collectively they provide a picture of what RAP is all about.

Rapid biodiversity assessment is a means of quickly collecting information on the species present in a given area. Rapid biodiversity assessment differs from other biodiversity assessment approaches because it is done quickly with the aim of providing information to guide conservation action. Conservation decision-making is usually done on a time frame that is much more urgent than many scientific studies and thus data needed to inform these decisions must be made available as quickly as possible. The typical time frame for RAP is: field survey of 4-6 weeks, with 5-7 days/nights surveying per site; preliminary report published within 2 months of field survey; final report (with species lists) published about one year after field survey in the *RAP Bulletin of Biological Assessment*; and utilization of the RAP data for follow-up conservation action taken by CI field programs and partners.

At the core of RAP is the collaboration between expert scientists (collaborators from universities and museums) who specialize in the taxonomy and identification of multiple taxonomic groups – birds, mammals, reptiles, amphibians, plants, and select insect groups – and a wide range of folks from other CI programs and outside partners, including local communities, government, NGOs, development agencies etc. The biodiversity surveys carried out by RAP are not, and cannot, be done by CI alone – it takes a team of devoted people with many diverse skills to make it work. In the NGO world, keeping a program funded for this long is not easy. RAP's longevity is a testament to the dedication of RAP staff and collaborators, as well as to the appeal of the RAP concept as a means of attracting and motivating funders and the general public for biodiversity conservation.

I first learned about CI's RAP program in 1992, when as a graduate student I became interested in measuring species richness in tropical ecosystems. I took a discussion course on conservation biology with Dr. Edward O. Wilson who encouraged me to investigate how species data can guide conservation decision making. For my class project, I compared various aspects of species inventory programs from universities and museums and concluded that the RAP program was the best at directly applying the survey data into conservation planning. Other programs surveyed mostly for scientific purposes. Of course this piqued my interest in getting involved in RAP so when Dr. Wilson was invited to collect ants on a RAP survey to Peru but could not go, I heartily volunteered to go in his stead. I was disappointed that they didn't take me along then but was delighted six years later when an even greater opportunity came along and I landed my dream job of running the RAP program. The last 12 years have been an incredible adventure for me - I have had the pleasure of working with brilliant collaborators to make amazing discoveries leading to conservation action all over the world.

This book is a celebration of a multitude of accomplishments by many people the world over during the first 20 years of the RAP program (1990-2010). In preparing this book, our first goal was to have a written history of the RAP program, which has been a central part of CI's work for most of the organization's history. We also wanted to show highlights of the 80 RAP surveys, emphasizing the many ways that the RAP data have been used to catalyze follow-up action at the RAP survey sites. While all RAP surveys have had multiple impacts, the RAP profiles in the book are categorized based on the central objective and outcome of each survey, principally related to: Protected Areas, Species New to Science, Capacity Building, Spatial Planning, and Human Well-being.

There are two messages that I hope come through to readers of this book. The first is that the applications of rapid biodiversity assessment reach far beyond the collection of scientific data and the discovery of species new to science. The second is that species data are essential for any conservation and development planning or action, as species are the building blocks of all our natural ecosystems. We know so little about each species and the roles they play in keeping our planet functioning. Conservation legend Aldo Leopold once said "To keep every cog and wheel is the first precaution of intelligent tinkering." RAP aims to find and study species to guide mankind toward the sustainable management of natural resources to benefit all creatures on Earth. That's why we're still counting...

Leeanne E. Alonso
Director of the Rapid Assessment Program

Acknowledgments

RAP is, first and foremost, a collaboration among many talented and dedicated people. Over these past 20 years we have had the honor and pleasure to work with and be supported by so many who have contributed in ways as diverse as the species we study. We thank all collaborating scientists, who take time out from their research projects and teaching schedules to lend their expertise to conservation. We thank all CI staff and partners who help plan and coordinate the extremely complicated logistics involved in getting to remote field sites. We thank all the authors, editors, designers, printers, publishers, communicators, and media who help us to get our RAP results distributed around the world. We thank all partner NGOs, academic institutions, museums and government agencies, who take the RAP data and turn it into conservation action. We thank all the local people and communities who surely wonder why we chase after small creatures in the forest but who open up their homes and land to us and share with us their traditional knowledge. We thank the senior leadership of Conservation International for being supportive of the RAP program for two decades. We thank all the individuals, foundations, and organizations who understand the importance of documenting biodiversity and have financially supported our RAP work.

We look forward to another 20 years of collaborating with all of you!

RAP at a Glance
Leeanne E. Alonso and Piotr Naskrecki

What is RAP?

Conservation International's Rapid Assessment Program (RAP) was created in 1990 to address the lack of biological information needed to make quick but sound conservation decisions in the developing world. RAP puts together teams of international and host-country expert scientists to conduct rapid first-cut assessments of the biological value of little-known and unexplored areas. RAP field surveys generally last three to four weeks, focused on taxonomic groups that can give an indication of the health of the ecosystem and its conservation value. Preliminary RAP results and conservation recommendations are made available immediately to local decision-makers with a final report and species lists published in the *RAP Bulletin of Biological Assessment* series.

RAP serves as an important catalyst for conservation action. Data collected during RAP surveys form an essential scientific baseline from which conservation priorities can be derived and recommendations for conservation action made. Exciting discoveries of species new to science and the documentation of threatened species help draw attention to the unique biological resources of a site and raise awareness of its conservation importance.

What is Rapid Biodiversity Assessment?

At its most basic, biodiversity assessment (survey/inventory/etc.) can be viewed as an evaluation of biological diversity – a scientific study of the species present at a site. This involves making a list of the species observed, sometimes with information about abundance, and analyzing the data in relation to species lists from other sites. Multi-taxa biodiversity surveys were once a major preoccupation of museums and universities in the 19th and early 20th centuries, but are less common today, due to funding constraints and increasing difficulties in obtaining proper permits to conduct fieldwork in many countries.

Rapid biodiversity assessment aims to collect biodiversity data quickly so that they can be available to meet the needs of urgent conservation challenges. An assessment may focus on one taxonomic group, such as birds or vascular plants, or on multiple taxa. In addition to the species list, scientists can also collect information on habitat condition, extent of disturbance to the habitat, and details on the biology of the species (e.g., nesting sites, habitat, diet, etc.).

Rapid biodiversity assessment is not an exhaustive inventory and will not record every species in an area. A longer-term inventory or monitoring program will add more species to the list. Careful thought must go into planning and implementing an assessment. Like any biodiversity assessment, rapid biodiversity assessment can only report what species have been detected and recorded as present in the area. It cannot tell you what species are definitely not there.

Who is RAP?

At the core of the RAP team are experienced field biologists, primarily taxonomists, who specialize in finding, collecting, and identifying species of a particular group of animals or plants. Ecologists and socioeconomic specialists are also often part of the RAP team. The scientific experts on the RAP team are not usually staff of RAP or CI, but are collaborators from universities, museums, government agencies, other NGOs, etc. Whenever local experts are available, the RAP team preferably includes scientists from the host countries. Scientists are the core of RAP, without them there would be no exciting RAP results to report. The relationship between the RAP program and the RAP scientists is a mutualism, a relationship in which both parties benefit. RAP provides the logistical support for accessing remote, unexplored regions of the world of interest to collaborating scientists,

What makes RAP an effective conservation tool?

RAP is above all a pragmatic methodology designed to provide a species-driven basis for the formulation of conservation policies and action. RAP has a wide taxonomic scope, speedy data processing, and swift and broad data dissemination. RAP involves government, local counterparts and stakeholders to actively participate at all stages of the surveys. RAP's approach involves a team of both international and national experts combined with training of local scientists to build scientific capacity for biodiversity assessment and conservation.

The RAP methodology is primarily designed to quickly collect data on species richness and composition, compare the data on a global and regional scale, and make conservation recommendations. These recommendations may range from identifying priority sites and taxa for conservation, to informing and designing management and monitoring plans for the area, to designing conservation strategies for particular taxa. RAP often includes a social science component to address the challenge of how to use the RAP results to influence conservation policy and action. Combined with the species information, data on local natural resource-use and livelihoods provide a rough characterization of the importance of the forests for local people, a history of anthropogenic disturbance, and the likely changes in scale of resource use in the near future.

RAP is..... supporting targeted rapid tough flexible catalytic surprising news breaking engaging impactful science-based exciting

whose job is usually to collect and study specimens of their target group. The scientists also provide an evaluation of the threats and conservation status of the species they document and thus contribute to conservation recommendations for the species and the sites.

In addition to the core scientific RAP team, RAP is a collaboration of many people and organizations. RAP works closely with CI's regional and country programs to identify the need for a RAP survey in areas for which biodiversity information is required to guide conservation priorities or management strategies. RAP works together and with other CI programs to raise the funds needed to carry out the survey. Local, scientific, non-governmental and government, as well as private sector partners, are then involved to help with logistics planning for the RAP – everything from food, to helicopters, to research permits. Local communities are an essential part of the team since they have a lot of tradi-

Required qualifications of core RAP team members

- Recognized experts in their field
- Ability to identify observed species and collected specimens to species level
- Field experience: able to live cooperatively under primitive, remote field conditions
- Time available to produce a scientific report with species lists within one year of the RAP survey
- Ability to analyze the RAP data in a regional and global context to make conservation recommendations

tional knowledge and are the beneficiaries of the data collected and the follow-up conservation activities. RAP works closely with these communities to understand their needs, to obtain approval to work on their land, and to learn from their knowledge of the site and of the local biodiversity. The RAP team grows to include partners, students, governmental and community trainees, local field guides, and field support personnel. Immediately after a survey, RAP scientists provide preliminary conservation recommendations to local governmental agencies, environmental groups, and other stakeholders based on their observations. RAP teams have ranged in size from 3-29 expert scientists (average 10-15) from a wide variety of governmental, NGO, and academic institutions around the world.

Reasons to RAP

The rapid loss of natural ecosystems around the world drives the need to collect biodiversity data that can be used to prioritize and protect areas that are threatened. Pristine, remote, unexplored ecosystems are becoming fewer and more endangered every day. Documenting the species from these sites provides the scientific baseline to guide conservation efforts at the site level as well as the global scale as the species data are fed into global datasets such as the IUCN Red List and the Global Biodiversity Information Facility (GBIF).

It is also clear that a staggering number of species worldwide falls victim to a tragic process known as the Centinelan extinction – disappearance of species before science even had a chance to recognize and formally described them. It was named after the Centinela ridge

in Ecuador, where, in 1978, RAP founder Alwyn Gentry and botanist Caraway Dodson discovered 90 previously unknown plant species. Within a few years, before many of them could be scientifically described, the ridge was converted into a plantation, and all its newly discovered species became extinct. By conducting RAP surveys in places under immediate threat of industrial development, as we often do, we create a record of species that otherwise could have lived and disappeared without anybody's knowledge, and by publicizing their existence we dramatically increase their chances of survival.

The objectives of each RAP survey are unique, designed to meet the data and conservation needs of the area surveyed. However, the principal objective of RAP has always been, and continues to be, to quickly collect biodiversity data for unexplored areas to guide conservation decision making.

RAP surveys are a field biologist's dream!

The hardships of living and working in mud and rain without the basic comforts of home and the dangers of tropical diseases are easily forgotten when you get a chance to explore a remote, unknown area where no scientist and few humans have ever set foot. The scientific treasures and discoveries of species new to science are more than worth the minor risks and lack of comfort.

The principal objectives of RAP surveys are:

- Derive a brief but thorough overview of species diversity at the survey sites.
- Evaluate the area's conservation importance to identify conservation priorities.
- Offer recommendations for sustainable management and research.
- Increase awareness in local communities (and national and global communities) of the value of the species and ecosystem services provided by the natural ecosystem surveyed
- Build local scientific capacity for biodiversity assessment and conservation planning through training.
- Guide private sector activities such as mining and energy activities, ecotourism, and fishing
- Evaluate human and natural disturbances to the ecosystem.
- Contribute the scientific baseline for spatial planning and long-term monitoring.
- Provide scientific justification for creating, expanding, and strengthening protected areas.

While long-term scientific studies are critically important, decision-makers often need information quickly in order to determine biodiversity priorities, manage natural resources, and avoid negatively impacting the environment. Rapid biological assessments provide the baseline data that decision-makers need. These short, intense, and focused studies help to answer the following three fundamental biological questions that are important for the conservation of biodiversity:

1. What organisms live in a specific area? In other words, what plants and animals will be affected by decisions regarding land use? If we don't know what organisms depend upon a piece of land, we can't possibly assess the potential impacts of modifications to that land.

The Diversity of a RAP Team

The motivation and benefits of participation in a RAP survey varies for the many different participants. Take for example the 2010 RAP survey of southwestern Suriname around the Indigenous Trio village of Kwamalasamutu. The team consisted of the following, each of whom had their own motivation for joining the RAP survey, and different expectations of how the experience and data would benefit them:

- 16 international and Surinamese scientists: Collect data for scientific research and specimens for their museum/university collection, opportunity to explore remote field site
- 7 students and recent graduates from Anton de Kom University of Suriname and Advanced Teachers Training Institute: Obtain field experience and learn from expert scientists
- 3 representatives from the Government of Suriname's Nature Conservation Division: Obtain field experience and learn from expert scientists
- 6 forest rangers from Amazon Conservation Team: Learn new field techniques from expert scientists, assist team with their local knowledge
- 18 Trio field assistants from Kwamalasamutu: Employment, assist team with their local knowledge, learn new techniques for long-term monitoring of biodiversity
- Community of Kwamalasamutu: obtain an evaluation of their natural resources and recommendations for sustainable use of freshwater, wildlife, fisheries and other forest products, obtain information and products to promote ecotourism to their village
- Conservation International - Suriname staff: Obtain data to guide creation of nature reserve, help develop ecotourism in the area, and raise awareness of the importance of biological resources in southwestern Suriname.

2. Do the organisms living in a specific area differ from those living in other areas? How distinct is the community of organisms in one area when compared to other areas? We might wish to take special care of species or groups of species that are rare or restricted in their distribution, whereas we might be less concerned about a species that is wide-spread and abundant. To answer this question, analytical procedures must be applied to the field data.

3. Will a certain use of land or resources (or did a previous use) negatively or positively affect specific organisms? This can be a very complicated question to answer confidently, but rapid biological assessment can collect the basic data to begin answering this question.

Places to RAP

Geographic Priorities. All of the 80 RAP surveys conducted during RAP's first 20 years - 51 terrestrial, 13 freshwater, and 16 marine - have been conducted in tropical regions of the world (see Map 1 on p. 92). RAP sites have all been located within Biodiversity Hotspots, regions of high diversity, endemism, and threat, or within High Biodiversity Wilderness Areas, regions of high diversity and endemism but with lower threat, and more expansive natural habitat for exploration. These regions harbor the highest species diversity and number of endemic species in the world, so they are of interest to RAP scientists as potential sites for rare and new species and to CI as conservation priorities.

RAP may be best known for getting into the most remote, hard-to-reach places on earth that have the potential for new, surprising discoveries. Tropical mountain areas and remote islands are examples of such places because they tend to have a high degree of endemism i.e., each mountain/island has a different array of unique species found nowhere else on Earth. Other sites of interest include habitats that require special adaptations for species to survive, such as areas with low oxygen levels (e.g., swamps) and limestone caves. Sites with high rainfall, long geological history, and unique environmental conditions all have high potential for the discovery of new and rare species.

See the RAP History Chapters (pages 56, 74 and 80) for details on geographic priorities for RAP surveys.

RAP Survey Site selection. Characteristics of sites of interest for RAP surveys include:

- high species richness
- high endemism
- threat of habitat conversion and ecosystem degradation
- lack of ecosystem representation in protected area systems
- absence of adequate biological inventory
- significant potential for biodiversity conservation
- existence of large areas of potentially intact habitat

The presence of large areas of intact habitat is crucial to the long term ecological viability of tropical ecosystem functions because it allows for the maintenance of critical ecosystem services and species, such as viable seed dispersal systems and keystone predators. Studies of tropical forest fragments reveal that the prospects of ecosystem viability are substantially and negatively impacted by fragmentation and reduction of habitat. Accordingly, RAP places particular emphasis on selection of sites that are potentially large enough to remain ecologically viable.

Specific site selection is based on the analysis of satellite images, aerial photographs, and over-flights. About six months prior to a RAP survey the team consults remote-sensing imagery to determine the extent of forest cover and best areas for exploration. Fortunately, with online tools such as Google Maps (http://maps.google.com) and Microsoft Live (http://maps.live.com) quality satellite imagery is available to anyone with a computer and an internet connection. When searching for potential study sites, RAP scientists look for any hills, gradients, or mountain peaks and any obvious changes in forest or savanna habitat and plant composition. Geological maps are also a good source of information on what may make an area distinct, and therefore especially important for conservation. Detailed local maps are extremely useful to identify potential camp sites and access points.

Sites for rapid biological assessment are selected primarily based on habitat type and condition. Because the objectives of a RAP survey include documentation of any rare, endemic or threatened species in the area, as well as documentation of as much of the diversity as possible, a representative of all habitat types in the area should be surveyed. If the area of interest has a wide range of elevations, sites should be located along this gradient in order to cover as much of the range as possible. Surveys should be done in the habitats that are in the best condition. If some of the target sites of interest to the RAP survey are not in good condition, these may be surveyed, but additional sites in better forest should also be included.

In the surveyed country, the scientists conduct aerial reconnaissance in small planes or helicopters to identify and verify forest types, access routes, and potential campsites. Local people are consulted about the vegetation and fauna of the planned survey sites as they often know the local terrain better than anyone. Once key habitats are identified, two to four RAP target areas are usually selected within the study area and their precise geographic coordinates are recorded. A field reconnaissance team, consisting of a few RAP scientists and the logistical coordinators, then goes into the area to try to get to the desired survey site and select an area for the RAP camp. Ideally, the recon team is able to reach all the target RAP sites and set up the infrastructure for a RAP camp prior to the RAP survey. Sometimes this is not possible if the RAP sites are far apart or particularly difficult to access. In those cases, the first RAP camp is set up then while the RAP scientists work at the first RAP camp, a camp set-up team of local field assistants and RAP coordinators travels to the area of the second RAP target site to set up a camp that will be ready when the scientific team is ready to move on.

Conducting a RAP Survey

The RAP Logistics. During RAP surveys, scientists spend three-to-four weeks deep in remote forests, river systems, coral reefs or other wild places, looking for species. The logistics required to undertake such trips often takes as much planning and work as the expedition itself. The process of planning a RAP survey is outlined on the RAP Biodiversity Survey Network website (https://learning.conservation.org/biosurvey/Pages/default.aspx) and in the RAP logistics manual available at https://learning.conservation.org/biosurvey/RAP/Toolkit/Pages/SurveyCoordinating.aspx.

There are many steps involved in planning and organizing a rapid biodiversity survey, including the following, listed in order:
- Identify need and objective for the survey.
- Choose survey area.
- Obtain all available biodiversity information for the area/region.
- Determine number and location of sampling sites.
- Set survey dates based on climate and season.
- Determine appropriate taxonomic groups.
- Determine appropriate survey team members.

- Logistical planning (transport, camps, equipment, contracts, food, etc.).
- Organize and purchase equipment and supplies.

Getting to the field sites is one of RAP's biggest challenges. After all, they wouldn't be remote and unexplored if they were easy to access! RAP teams utilize many different modes of transportation, depending on the remoteness of the site, its terrain, and whether there is access by river or by land. The purpose of RAP is not adventure travel or extreme sports. The goal is to spend as much time conducting the scientific survey work as possible and to minimize time spent getting to and from the sites. Thus small planes and helicopters are used whenever possible to get the RAP team quickly into remote areas. If there is river access, motor boats or dugout canoes are used to get to the site.

Ground travel is more difficult: often a combination of vehicles, boats, pack animals, and foot travel is required to get the team to remote sites where few, if any, roads exist. The most remote and difficult RAP surveys may require several days of hiking, usually up steep mountainsides. The RAP team surveying in the Foja Mountains of Papua, Indonesia (November 2008) faced constant torrential rains, repeatedly crossed streams at flood tide, and constantly worked in wet clothes. It is tough work to reach places where undescribed species are found, but well worth the effort to these scientists whose dream is to discover and document life on Earth.

RAP employs people from local communities to help porter all the scientific equipment, food, camp gear, and personal gear of the RAP team, which can together be quite heavy. The cargo weight on the recent RAP survey to the Muller Range Mountains in Papua New Guinea was probably in excess of 1,000 kilos – it had to be delivered to the vicinity of the camp by a helicopter, but fortunately not carried far from the landing pad. Similarly, the cargo weight for the RAP survey of southwest Suriname around Kwamalasamutu was over 2,000 kilos – all of which was flown down to Kwamalasamutu in small charter planes and then taken by dugout canoes (with outboard motors, fortunately) six hours down river to reach the first RAP camp site.

Taxonomic groups surveyed. While many people may think of mammals and birds when they think of biodiversity, these groups constitute less than 1% of known life (approx. 15,000 species of the 1.9 million documented species of animals). The majority of species are invertebrates, which includes arthropods (insects, spiders, and relatives), mollusks (snails, mussels etc.), echinoderms (starfish, sea urchins etc.), platyhelminths (flat worms), and many others. It is estimated that as many as 10-30 million species of organisms are yet to be discovered and scientifically described. It is important to consider all of biodiversity when conducting a RAP survey, especially since it is these smaller organisms that are often both the principal ecosystem engineers and keystone species, and at the same time face a greater risk of becoming threatened or extinct than the larger, warm-blooded species.

However, it is impossible to survey all species during a rapid biological assessment. We therefore concentrate efforts on surveying focal taxonomic groups, or focal taxa. Focal taxa must meet three criteria:

1. The group can be fairly easily sampled in the field in order to obtain a good picture of species richness in a short time.
2. The taxonomy of the group is worked out well enough so that species-level identification can be made.
3. There are adequate identification guides with which to identify specimens and sightings of the group to species level, or there are specialists willing to devote their time and expertise to participate in the survey and perform the identification.

Focal taxonomic groups surveyed most often during rapid assessment include vascular plants, mammals, birds, reptiles, and amphibians. More recently, the taxonomy of many invertebrate groups has improved so that they can also be included in biological assessment. Invertebrate groups surveyed include several insect groups: ants, orthopterans (grasshoppers, crickets and katydids), termites, dung beetles, butterflies, and dragonflies, as well as a few other invertebrate groups such as mollusks, crabs and spiders. For most groups of invertebrates there are only a few experts for each region, thus the selection of invertebrate groups for inclusion in a particular RAP survey depends on the existence of an expert and their availability for the RAP survey. For AquaRAP surveys, fishes, aquatic plants, aquatic invertebrates, and water quality are sampled. Corals, marine invertebrates, and fishes are the focus of coastal MarineRAP surveys.

Rapid biological assessment also relies on indicator species, which are species whose presence (or absence) is also an indicator of a particular aspect of the environment, such as closed canopy or good quality forest, disturbance, or the presence of other species. For example, certain bird species require closed canopy forest and thus their presence indicates good forest quality. Likewise, some amphibian and insect species are more typical of open areas and thus can indicate if there has been disturbance to the area. Species and broader taxonomic groups that respond quickly to small changes in microclimate, such as moisture and heat regimes, are best at detecting disturbance, such as fire and habitat conversion, and also best suited to monitor restoration efforts. Large mammal species richness and composition are usually good indicators of the extent of hunting pressure in an area.

It is important to choose the right target taxa so that the objectives of the project can be met. These are some of the things to consider when deciding which groups to survey:

- Do the data collected for the taxon address the objectives and questions of the study?
- Well-known taxa have more experts and resources. Poorly known groups have fewer experts and can have disputed taxonomy delaying final determinations.
- What level of taxonomic accuracy and precision is needed? Is a list of morphospecies sufficient or are species names needed? Are there taxonomic references for species identification?
- How difficult is it to make species determinations? Can enough useful data be collected on this group in the allotted period in the field? Can specimens be identified within eight months?
- Which groups will have most species new to science? The likelihood of discovery of new or very significant taxa (i.e., rare birds) helps to generate public interest and awareness.

RAP data. The types of RAP data collected must meet the objectives and goals of the survey.

Data collected during RAP usually include:
- List of species by site.
- Total number of species for each site and for entire assessment (if multiple sites).
- Comparisons between sites (as appropriate) in terms of species richness and important species.
- List of important species including threatened, endemic, restricted range, indicator, introduced, and other key species.
- Ecological information about each of the important species, including what type of habitat they require, what they feed on, where they live/nest, their population size (if possible), and their role in ecosystem processes/services.

RAP data collected in the field fall into the following categories:

- Species check-lists
- Habitat where each species is found
- GPS location for each species and individual recorded
- Additional biological notes on species records (e.g., diet, nesting site, number of individuals)
- Habitat heterogeneity (identify different habitat types)
- Use of particular species by local people (interviews)
- Habitat condition
- Threats – observed and future

Field Survey Methods

RAP survey methods need to be *fast*, because time is of the essence. They should be *reliable*, because diverse people need to apply them in a variety of areas to generate comparable data. They should also be *simple* and *inexpensive* because species diversity is highest in developing tropical countries where the scientific and museum infrastructure is often still rudimentary.

Each RAP survey is individually designed to meet specific objectives, with distinct team size, members, focal taxa, length of survey, etc. However, there is one aspect that we try to keep constant across all RAP surveys: *a minimum of five nights per site.* Each site should have the same sampling effort if possible. This allows for some degree of comparison among thoroughly surveyed sites globally, and for most taxa will allow RAP team members to obtain a good impression of the biodiversity at the site.

RAP scientists have been at the forefront of novel, cutting-edge methodologies for detecting and recording species in tropical forests and technology has played an increasingly larger role in this process. Some examples include the use of heat-in-motion camera traps for mammals, sound recording and playbacks for birds using iPods, and digital recording devices for other acoustic animals. DNA analysis has also become important for identification of species that are indistinguishable morphologically and for determining evolutionary relationships among the species. Online identification aids featuring high magnification photography of small organisms has greatly advanced scientists' abilities to identify organisms to species level and are valuable as a training tool. As technology advances even more rapidly in the next decade, new methods of species detection and rapid identification of species are sure to be developed.

Although some groups of organisms can be documented in the field by simple observations and non-invasive methods (sound recordings, camera traps, bird watching), for many taxonomic groups scientists must collect and preserve physical specimens in order to perform definite identifications. For example, nearly all ants look similar when seen scurrying on the forest floor, but reveal amazing differences in the morphology of their bodies when examined under a microscope. Sometimes minute, seemingly trivial differences in the details of their bodies carry significant information – the shape of the abdomen, impossible to see in an active, live insect, can tell the scientist whether this ant is an invasive pest, indicative of habitat disturbance, or a species new to science. While RAP scientists always strive to minimize their impact on the environment they are surveying, and this includes collecting only the absolute minimum number of specimens, trapping and preserving specimens is a critically important part of the RAP methodology. Without physical, preserved specimens scientists would neither be able to describe the many species new to science found during the RAP survey, nor study their genetics. It also must be stressed that RAP scientists never trap or collect species that are known to be threatened (such as those on the IUCN Red List) or species whose populations, due to their relatively small size, may be impacted by collecting (such as those of many birds, mammals, or reptiles). Conversely, species whose populations are known to be very large, such as those of many insects, will never be imperiled by RAP scientists collecting a handful of specimens. (An average insect-eating bird probably consumes more insects in a day than a RAP scientist collects during a week-long survey.)

Searching for Species. Each RAP scientist searches extensively in the micro-habitats where they are most likely to find interesting species from their group. For example, bird experts walk trails through the forest, especially along edges where a mixture of forest and open field birds can be found and where the birds can be better seen than in the dense forest. Mammal experts seek out areas where mammals find water, salt or prey. Ant experts search through leaf litter and soil for tiny species that have been overlooked by others. Of course, species are sometimes found in unexpected places, such as your own tent or around the lights of the field kitchen!

For organisms that use songs and other sounds to communicate, sound detection and recording is a good way to recognize and document something different. Virtually all birds, frogs, many insects, and, surprisingly, many fish produce distinct calls, each unique to a particular species. By recording all sounds in a specific environment, such as the forest canopy or a coral reef, and using sound analysis software to assess the data, scientists can quickly pinpoint those elements of the sound spectrum that are different from all known animal songs. Often such songs are not audible to the human ear because they use frequencies that are too low (infrasounds) or too high (ultrasounds) for us to perceive. In such instances special recording equipment must be used. In Ghana RAP researchers have already discovered a number of katydid species new to science by tracking never-before-heard ultrasonic sounds.

Many unnamed species are very shy or live in places that are virtually inaccessible to researchers. In such cases we often use traps or remote recording devices. Pitfall traps left on the forest floor or hung in the canopy attract and capture many small organisms that are active only at night or are particularly cryptic. Sometimes traps are baited with a broad spectrum of artificial pheromones, chemical attractants that mimic the scent of a mating partner. Nocturnal flying insects can be lured to traps equipped with ultraviolet light.

For particularly shy animals, such as most mammals, remote camera traps sometimes help document never-before-seen species of rodents or occasionally deer. Such traps consist of a well-camouflaged camera, which will take a photo if the animal trips an invisible infrared or laser beam. Some traps will also detect the body heat of an approaching animal or react to the sound of it, taking a photograph that otherwise would be impossible to get.

Surveys of the marine life of coral reefs generally involve scuba diving and snorkeling along transect routes among the coral, recording all species of invertebrates, corals and fishes observed. Old fashioned hard work and determination is still often the best way to find interesting species. Scientists spend long hours, often all night in the rain, or all day in the hot sun, to find species they suspect should be there, or to find undescribed species that had eluded other scientists. True dedication is required.

Field scientists generally use a set of standard methods for rapid biological assessment. A manual of field methods specifically for rapid biological assessment is in preparation by CI's RAP program. For now, drafts of RAP field methods are available on RAP's Biodiversity Survey Network website: https://learning. conservation.org/biosurvey/RAP/Toolkit/ Pages/SurveyCoordinating.aspx. There are many sources of information for specific field methods for surveying each taxonomic group including Heyer et al. (1994), Wilson et al. (1996), Agosti et al. (2000), and Rödel and Ernst (2004). Some general descriptions of the field methods are listed below.

Vascular plants: One hundred meter transects are established and all tree species within 10 meters of the transect are identified. Plots are set up and all trees and shrubs in the plot are identified. Visual searches for rare, endemic and threatened species are conducted in a variety of habitats. In some places, grasses and herbs may also need to be surveyed because tree diversity may not be high. Specimens of plants that

Tetraponera rufonigra – a beautiful ant from Cambodia

cannot be identified in the field are collected and deposited in herbaria (museum or university collections of dried and pressed plants).

Ants: Field sampling methods include targeted searches within three strata where ants are commonly found: leaf litter and soil, lower arboreal, and high arboreal. Collecting from leaf litter includes examining rotting logs and branches, looking under stones, locating nests in soil and between rotting leaves, searching for individuals and foraging columns, and also some limited litter and extraction using Winkler sacs. Collections from the lower arboreal strata include looking under loose bark, in myrmecophilous plants, in epiphytic root masses, and in leaf litter trapped in arboreal vegetation. Ants from the higher arboreal strata are more difficult to collect, but can be found when they descend from the canopy to forage and nest in branches, old termite nests, and epiphytes that have fallen from the canopy as well as on freshly fallen trees. An extensive area need not be sampled, as many ant species can be found within a small area (e.g., 254 species from an area less than 1 km^2 in Papua New Guinea).

The presence of introduced species, such as the Tropical Fire Ant, *Solenopsis geminata*, should be documented in order to evaluate the level of disturbance to the area. Data on nesting sites and food habits are noted whenever possible. Basic data on the micro-habitat environment (temperature, humidity, leaf litter depth, and canopy cover) are also recorded for each major sample. The status of the survey sites in terms of ant diversity is evaluated with respect to the level of ant species richness compared to that expected, the status of the micro and general habitats for ants and other insects, and the presence of invasive species, rare or new species, mutualistic species (with plants, etc.), species that perform key functions in the ecosystem, and species that may be restricted to particular microhabitats. Specimens are collected for each species that cannot be identified in the field.

Katydids and relatives: Three main methods are used to collect the Orthoptera (grasshoppers, crickets and katydids): (1) sweeping, (2) UV-light trapping, and (3) visual and acoustic searches. Sweeping includes standardized sweeping of grass and low vegetation with a durable insect net.

It is usually conducted in a series of 6-10 forceful sweeps within a series of parallel transects 20-30 m long, depending on the type of vegetation. Collected insects are immediately sorted to family and preserved in 70% ethanol or preserved dry on silica gel in glassine or paper envelopes. A portion of specimens is retained live for subsequent photographic documentation. UV (=blacklight) trapping involves collecting all insects attracted to light at night within a designated period of time. In most cases UV-trapping is done between dusk until 23:00 or midnight. Attracted insects are collected by hand or with a small aspirator, and preserved in 70% ethanol.

Visual and acoustic searching is employed mostly in habitats with dense vegetation cover where sweeping is impossible. It involves collecting individuals noticed or heard on their calling perches, and is usually conducted at night when most species are active. In addition to the collection of physical specimens, acoustically signaling species (most katydids and some grasshoppers of the family Acrididae) are recorded. Such recordings are often the only reliable characters that allow for positive identification of species. Specimens are collected for each species that cannot be identified in the field.

Butterflies: Butterflies are surveyed by catching or identifying butterflies along transects through different habitats, particularly open fields and areas with nectar plants. Baited traps are put out for five days (with rotting fruit) to attract forest butterflies. Visual searches are made diurnally in all habitat types. Specimens are collected for each species that cannot be identified in the field.

Freshwater fishes: Fishes are surveyed using a variety of net sizes and types (seine and gill nets) according to habitat type, water depth, and water flow rate. Rapids and rocks are inspected and sampled using hand nets when possible. Water quality parameters such as temperature, pH, oxygen levels, and turbidity will also be recorded. Specimens are collected for species that cannot be identified in the field.

Amphibians and reptiles: Visual searches of aquatic and terrestrial habitats are done both during night and day. All specimens are photographed to insure that later identification of problematic species will be possible. Calling frog species are recorded at night with a portable sound recorder. Nocturnal and diurnal searches include checking under rocks and logs in the forest, and raking through leaf litter on the forest floor. Snakes are captured with snake tongs or a snake stick. The appropriate terrestrial habitat is searched for tortoises, and turtle traps are set in aquatic habitats. Dip nets are used to sample amphibians and tadpoles in aquatic habitats. Pitfall traps are set in the ground and drift fences (metal flashing) are set up between pitfall traps to lead animals into the pitfalls during the night. Specimens are collected for reference and positive identification by comparison with museum specimens.

Mammals: Tracks, sounds, evidence of feeding sites, and direct observations are recorded. In addition, 20 camera traps are set within 10 km of the base camp at each site. The traps are motion-sensitive and thus automatically take photographs of any animal that comes in front of the camera. Camera traps are set to run continuously. A 20 second delay between pictures is programmed. Scent and visual lures are sometimes used to attract mammals to the camera traps. The cameras are left in place and not checked until we move to a different location. If the locations are close, some of the cameras are left in place and a subset of the cameras are moved to the next location.

RAP scientists preparing a camera trap in Botswana

A relative abundance index for each confirmed species can sometimes be calculated. A photo-trapping rate that allows comparison of camera photo-trap effort between sites is also computed. RAP scientists generally try to survey beyond the area where other RAP team members collect their data. Day and night surveys are made to collect information on large mammals. Transects are walked for primates and other diurnal mammals.

Birds: The widest range of natural habitats in the area should be surveyed, with a more intense focus in specific habitats for species of interest. Transects are walked at dawn and in the early evening and all birds observed and heard are noted. Bird calls are recorded for later identification. Mist nets are set up for catching and identifying understory birds. Survey results include species lists and estimates of the relative abundance of species.

See page 74 for details of MarineRAP Methods.

Training Local Scientists

The best way to do rapid biological assessment is to make use of the best available scientific expertise. An interdisciplinary scientific team comprised of experienced, highly respected, field scientists can collect a significant amount of high-quality biodiversity data in a short time period. Taxonomic experts from the area or region of the rapid assessment are essential since they are familiar with the species of the region. However, in many of the highly diverse countries where rapid assessment will be required, there are not many taxonomic experts and the general scientific capacity of the country or region may be poor. Therefore, RAP promotes collaboration between expert scientists from scientific institutions worldwide and local scientists, and places particular emphasis on training local students in modern research and conservation methodology.

Building local capacity for biodiversity research and assessment involves training local students and scientists to increase their skills in biological assessment, taxonomy, data analysis, and report preparation. Throughout the past 20 years, RAP has developed and implemented a well-established training program designed to build up expertise in these areas. RAP training includes building a local team of scientists who will develop the skills to conduct rapid biological assessment in their country or region. Once local scientists are trained, it is important that opportunities exist for them to use their skills to conduct biodiversity research. Therefore, RAP also aims to include trainees in RAP surveys in order to give them field experience and opportunities for further collaborations with international experts. RAP's Biodiversity Survey Network website provides many materials useful to anyone seeking to learn more about rapid biodiversity surveys (https://learning.conservation.org/biosurvey/Pages/default.aspx).

Data Analysis

Knowledge of the species richness of a variety of taxa can provide a great deal of useful information for conservation planning. First of all, an inventory of the species in an area will provide data on the distributions of species and will document the presence of any rare, threatened or ecologically important species, such as introduced species or species found only in particular habitat types. The number of species and the species composition in an area can indicate the health of an ecosystem and can provide insight into the presence of other organisms or habitat changes (indicator species). Data on species richness and composition provide the baseline needed for using various taxa to monitor environmental change or recovery. While many taxa are capable of living in a wide range of habitats, some species have narrow ecological requirements, and thus can be used as indicators of habitat change or restoration success.

Many developing countries with high biodiversity lack the scientific capacity to collect and analyze biodiversity data needed to make sound conservation decisions for the country. It is important to build local scientific capacity by training local students and scientists in biodiversity research, assessment, and monitoring. Such efforts are vital for decisions to be made about the long-term management of the country's resources, which involves both conserving biodiversity as well as benefiting local people.

The first step for the RAP team is to identify and list the species recorded at each site. From this list, species of particular interest (threatened, endemic, or new to science) are identified and studied to reveal patterns of distribution and habitat preferences. For most analyses, specimens must be identified to species level. If just a total count of the number of species in an area is needed, perhaps to compare with other areas, then identification to the morphospecies level may be satisfactory.

Careful consideration is given to which methods of data analysis will best address the questions of each particular study. The relevant analytical tools and their use varies for each taxonomic group (Magurran 1988, Krebs 2002). Statistical analyses will depend on the research objectives and questions. Some questions that are often asked and the statistical tools that can be used to address them include:

1. What is the estimated species richness based on the available data? EstimateS (Colwell 2004) is a widely used, freely available online program, which allows to compute a number of indices (Chao, ACE, ICE, etc.).
2. What is the diversity at a site? Several diversity measures are available including Shannon index (H), alpha index (α), the Simpson index (D), and the Berger-Parker index (d).
3. Does one site or transect have higher diversity than another? Compare the diversity indices using a t-test or Mann-Whitney U test.
4. What are the patterns of association among samples or sites? Indices of similarity such as Jaccard's index and indices of complementarity such as the Marczewski-Steinhaus distance measure, ordination and classification procedures can be used.

Data that are particularly useful to biodiversity conservation and project planning include:

A. Global/regional importance of each species and taxonomic group including:
 • Species ranges and distributions (local, regional and global), especially for species listed on the IUCN Red List of Threatened Species.
 • Identification and data for endemic, rare, commercial and invasive species.
 • Species used by local human communities (for food, building, cultural ceremonies, etc.).

B. Habitat condition and its regional/global conservation value, comparisons between sites as appropriate, threats observed (roads, hunting, logging, etc.).

C. Comparisons between survey sites and other areas or regions – evaluation of sites as priorities for global or local conservation based on presence of key species and habitat condition; analysis of sites for designation as conservation priority areas, such as an Important Bird Area (IBA), Key Biodiversity Area (KBA), etc.

D. Specific recommendations to illustrate what is needed to protect key species and their habitats, including:
 • What specific habitat and sites within the survey area does the species need to survive?
 • How large is the range of the species and how much area is needed to protect it?
 • Do the food sources for this species need protection as well?
 • If the area is impacted, can this species move to a nearby area (e.g., is it mobile), and if so, is there sufficient habitat nearby to sustain it?
 • What specific human impacts will affect these species most and how?
 • What measures should be taken to protect these species?

E. Presence of species that indicate the status of the ecosystem's health. Evidence of species known to be invasive or common in disturbed areas can indicate that the ecosystem has been impacted. Similarly, the presence of species known to survive only in healthy, dense natural forest or savanna can indicate a healthy ecosystem.

In most cases, data from different RAP surveys cannot be directly compared because they were collected using different methods, by different people, over different time frames, and for different objectives. In some cases, RAP surveys are conducted at more than one site by the same RAP team and thus RAP data can then be directly compared. The RAP data for all the taxonomic groups can be evaluated together to develop a picture of the status of the ecosystem and to prioritize sites for conservation based on the health of the habitat and species groups, as well as the extent of threats documented during the RAP survey. See Table 1 for an example from southeast Guinea.

Discovering Species New to Science

It is not easy to determine whether a species is different from those already described and named. Imagine the expertise needed to differentiate among species from large taxonomic groups like birds (10,000 species) and ants (>12,000 species). But in tropical regions, scientists often come across a species they do not recognize and cannot identify – these are referred to as "undescribed" (or "unnamed") species that are considered potentially new to science.

To verify that a species is indeed undescribed, scientists collect a small series of specimens (these are needed to evaluate morphological variation, and sexual and age dimorphism within the species) and compare their characteristics to specimens of related species already known. They compare many different features, including things such as the number of hairs or spines on the legs, the texture of the body, the shape of the bones, or the number of scales on the head. Characteristics that are used to define a species new to science vary from group to group, but generally involve a few key morphological characters, often related to reproduction. Unique features – like the shape of reproductive organs or coloration of body parts used in a courtship display – not only prevent species from unsuccessful mating, but also provide useful traits for scientific differentiation.

Similarly, behavioral traits, such as vocalizations or courtship displays, provide very good clues to a species' identity. This principle is well known to ornithologists, who are often capable of instantly recognizing hundreds of different species of birds based on a single note. Entomologists also use sounds produced by insects such as cicadas, crickets, or katydids to tell species apart, and sometimes describe new discoveries based solely on the characteristics of the song. The pattern of flashes produced by lightning bugs, the rhythm of claw waving in mud crabs, or the shape of an orb spun by a spider are other examples of behavioral characters that can be used to identify species, and pinpoint those that are different. During RAP surveys, scientists often make sound or video recordings of animal behavior, and these data help confirm the new status of documented species. For example, the first indication that a katydid found during a RAP survey in Guinea in 2003 was potentially new to science was its song which was very different from that of any other species known from Africa.

Table 1. Comparison of species, threats and habitat condition between five sites in southeast Guinea. The sites were prioritized for conservation value based on species and habitat data

Site	Elevation/ Habitat	Degree of habitat degradation	Logging	Hunting	Agriculture	Groups indicating healthy ecosystem	Groups indicating unhealthy ecosystem	Priority for biodiversity conservation
Déré (8,920 ha)	360-750 m flood-plains, RAP camp at 440 m, lowland forest, foothills of Mt. Nimba	90%	High intensity, cleared for agri-culture	Active hunting; evidence of snares, car-tridges & hunting trails	High degree of degrada-tion and cultivated land	Birds, Am-phibians	Plants, Small & Large Mammals, Primates, Reptiles, Katydids, Bats	Lower Priority (site degraded but harbors key habitat and species)
Diécké (59,143 ha)	400-595 m, RAP camp at 450 m lowland humid forest	30%	Selective log-ging for fuelwood and potential com-mercial logging	Moderate hunting; evidence of hunt-ing trails, car-tridges	Moderate degree of agricultural encroach-ment	Plants, Small & Large Mammals, Primates, Rep-tiles, Katydids, Bats, Birds, Amphibians	None	Highest Priority
Mt. Béro (26,850 ha)	600-1210m, RAP camp at 620 m, semi-deciduous forest and savanna	75%	Moderate logging and clearing for agri-culture	High hunting pressure: greatest # of car-tridges found here	Moderate degree of habitat degrada-tion and cultivated land	Plants, Small Mammals, Primates, Katydids, Bats, Birds, Amphibians	Large, Mammals, Reptiles	High Priority
Pic de Fon (25,600 ha)	600-1656m, RAP camps at 600m and 1000-1600m, humid forest, savanna, montane forest and grassland	30-35%	Signifi-cant log-ging for fuelwood and construc-tion	Moderate hunting pressure: snares, trails car-tridges	Moderate degree of agricultural encroach-ment	Plants, Small & Large Mammals, Primates, Rep-tiles, Katydids, Bats, Birds, Amphibians	None	Highest Priority
Ziama* (116,1703 ha)	500-1387m, montane forest and savanna	Current status unknown	Logging conces-sion per-mitted in 30,000 ha (27% of re-serve)	Over-hunted with >750 animals taken per year	56,170 ha multiple use zone, current status unknown	Plants, Small & Large Mam-mals, Reptiles, Amphibians, Birds	None	Biosphere Reserve, Highest priority to pro-tect the 42,547 ha core zone

* Data for Ziama from literature not from RAP survey

A different behavior is a very good indication of a species' distinctness, but additional proof is often needed to declare a species new to science. These can usually be found among the morphological or molecular characteristics of an organism. Molecular and other genetic characters, such as certain DNA sequences or shapes and numbers of chromosomes, often provide very reliable indicators of a species' uniqueness. Genetic barcoding, a fast and easy genetic screening process that allows scientists to compare a key fragment of mitochondrial DNA among thousands of species at once, has recently begun to play an important role in identifying both known and as yet unnamed species. RAP scientists routinely collect DNA samples from species, which in some cases leads to the discovery of new species, like new species of frogs described in West Africa in 2005.

RAP Audiences and Presentation of Results

Each RAP scientist makes conservation recommendations for their taxonomic group and the survey sites based on their RAP data. These recommendations form the basis for follow-up conservation action that can be pursued by CI field programs and partners, other NGOs, governments, etc. The audience for the RAP results must always be considered carefully so that the RAP results and recommendations are presented in a way that is useful, understandable and informative for their decision-making.

Some of the key audiences of RAP data and recommendations include:

- Governments - decisions on conservation priorities and management.
- NGOs - data to support conservation action and set global priorities.
- Local communities - to raise awareness of the value their biodiversity, to develop plans for sustainable use of natural resources, and to support conservation efforts.
- Ecotourism - development of sustainable practices and promotion of species attractions
- Private sector - guiding mining, energy, agriculture and other activities that may impact natural resources.
- Conservation community - evaluation of threatened species (IUCN), identification of priority sites such as Important Bird Areas (IBAs, Birdlife International) and Key Biodiversity Areas (KBAs), etc.
- Scientific community - taxonomic, ecological, distribution data to inform research.

RAP works with CI field programs and partners to get the RAP data to these key audiences. Immediately following each RAP survey, the RAP team makes a presentation of the preliminary results to local communities and partners. The preliminary RAP report is then distributed among key stakeholders about one month later. The final RAP report and other products are delivered to all stakeholders often accompanied by a book launch/press release. When appropriate, local and global media has effectively been used by CI to publicize the RAP results and to draw attention to conservation needs.

Products

RAP publications. One of the strong points of RAP is that there is always a concrete product at the end of the RAP surveys that is a clear indication of the completion of the RAP project and successful data collection. Although it has been suggested that RAP should only produce electronic versions of the RAP reports, we have found that printed publications are needed as they can have a great impact when delivered to government officials and partners in support of conservation recommendations.

RAP database. In addition to printed publications, RAP has developed an online database into which all the species data are entered and displayed (rap.conservation.org). Users can search for specific species records by taxonomic group, site, or RAP survey. The RAP database is linked with the Global Biodiversity Information Facility (GBIF) and thus RAP data feed into a large global dataset and can be searched through GBIF as well.

Media. Species new to science are particularly valuable as a tool for raising global interest in biodiversity conservation. RAP and CI have been very successful at using the exciting RAP survey results to raise awareness of interesting species and the need to conserve them and their habitats. The discovery of species new to science peaks the interest of people the world over and engages them in ways that other aspects of conservation cannot. Local, national and global media coverage of a RAP survey help to bring attention to conservation needs at the RAP survey site. Thus, whenever there are exciting RAP results, CI prepares and releases a press release, usually about discoveries of species new to science, which is most effective. The press release may go out immediately after a RAP survey if the results are especially novel or at the time of the publication of the final RAP report, which may include important information about the health of the ecosystem surveyed and an urgent call for conservation action.

Several types of publications result from each RAP survey:

- Preliminary report of RAP results produced 1-2 months after RAP survey, presented to local partners, communities and government officials; PDFs available online
- Final RAP report published in the *RAP Bulletin of Biological Assessment* (formerly *RAP Working Papers*) series about a year after each RAP survey; PDFs available online (conservation.org)
- Biodiversity booklets for local communities to illustrate the importance and beauty of biodiversity in their area, including photographs of species documented during the RAP survey
- Peer-reviewed papers in scientific journals

CI's website is currently featuring and tracking RAP's new species discoveries at
http://www.conservation.org/explore/discoveries/Pages/expeditions_discovery.aspx

Impacts

As should be evident throughout this book, RAP surveys have many different impacts over a wide range of scales. These impacts have been measurable and RAP is able to report on metrics related to most of them. The principal categories of RAP impacts and the metrics used to measure them are presented in Table 2. While each RAP survey has multiple impacts, the RAP survey profiles presented in this book are ordered according to their principal impacts.

Scientific impacts. As the biodiversity of our planet diminishes at an alarming rate (scientific estimates put the rate of species loss at one species every 20 minutes!), the time to document and save it is quickly running out. There is no question that future generations will inherit a world that harbors but a fraction of the richness of species and natural ecosystems ours is still privileged to enjoy. The RAP program, in collaboration with other conservation initiatives at CI and elsewhere, is often the first and most important step in trying to protect particularly valuable fragments of the

Table 2. Principal categories of RAP impacts and their metrics	
Protected Areas	Number of hectares of new, expanded or improved protected areas for biodiversity conservation
Species New to Science	Number of species new to science discovered
Capacity Building	Number of local students, scientists, land managers, and conservationists trained
Spatial Planning	Amount of globally threatened species distribution data recorded, number of corridors developed, guidance provided to private sector
Human Well-being	Number of communities provided with RAP data for use in developing sustainable use of natural resources
Scientific impact	Number of RAP volumes of the *RAP Bulletin of Biological Assessment* published, number of peer-reviewed papers published

world's biodiversity. The data collected during RAP surveys serve not only to document the current distribution of species, both already known and those new to science, but they also allow scientists to examine conservation issues on multiple scales – from the effects of bushmeat hunting on a local mammalian population to global trends affecting entire classes of organisms. Each survey provides thousands of data points that help model and predict the impact of human activities on the natural world, and develop strategies to minimize its negative results. RAP data have been used to assess species conservation status for both the IUCN Red List and local conservation ranking systems, such as the "star" ranking system of plant species in Ghana.

Information on species behavior and ecology gathered during RAP surveys is often the very first and only such information available for many tropical animals and plants. It is not uncommon for RAP scientists to be the first ones to see alive species previously known only from singular, preserved specimens collected over a century ago, and record their ecological preferences, feeding behavior, courtship habits, or relationships with other organisms. Such observations give us not only priceless insight into the evolution of life on Earth, but also arm conservationists with information that may be critical in designing strategies for those species' preservation.

RAP surveys have led to the collection of over 1,300 never-before-seen species new to science. Over 500 of these have already been formally described by taxonomists, but many more are currently being processed. (Unfortunately, in some particularly poorly known groups of animals and plants this process may take several years.) The ability to collect fresh samples and specimens during RAP surveys allows scientists to use modern, genetic tools to look into the species' relationships and population structure, something that cannot be done using existing museum specimens. Ecological data, sound recordings, and photographs of live organisms taken in their natural environments have also been used by RAP scientists to publish field guides and identification keys to animals and plants that are used by local conservation authorities, students, and scientists, leading to more effective efforts to protect them.

Local economic impacts. Over the past 20 years, RAP surveys have contributed significantly to the national and local economies of the countries where RAP surveys have taken place. The average RAP survey costs about US$100,000. Estimating that two-thirds of this amount is spent within the

Ricinoides atewa – an ancient, relict species of arachnid discovered during a RAP survey in Ghana

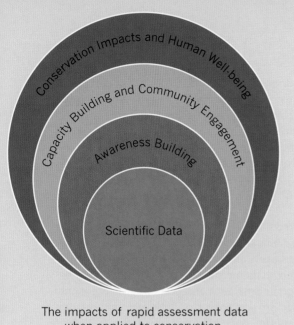

The impacts of rapid assessment data when applied to conservation.

country where the RAP survey has taken place, an average of US$67,000 is spent in country for each RAP survey. Expenses include payments to local contractors for logistical planning; payments to local community members who assist the RAP team as field assistants, guides, boat drivers, and cooks; field supplies including camping equipment, food, and communications; domestic flights; boat rental from local communities; charter flights and helicopters. Totaling over the 80 RAP surveys conducted, at least US $5,340,000 has been invested in local communities and national economies through RAP surveys.

RAP amplifies and catalyzes. RAP surveys provide essential baseline data on biodiversity, ecosystem health, and natural resource use that are amplified as they are used by a wide variety of stakeholders. RAP surveys may often serve as the beginning of data collection in an area, but are never the end of data collection or of conservation action. RAP is a catalyst: collecting the first round of data, training a new generation of scientists, engaging communities in biological exploration, and enticing the global public with amazing discoveries.

Read more about RAP online at:

http://www.conservation.org/explore/discoveries/Pages/expeditions_discovery.aspx
https://learning.conservation.org/biosurvey/Pages/default.aspx

References

Agosti D., J.D. Majer, L.E. Alonso, T. R. Schultz (eds). 2000. Ants: Standard Methods for Measuring and Monitoring Biological Diversity. Smithsonian Institution Press. Washington, D.C.

Colwell R.K. 2004. EstimateS, Version 7: Statistical Estimation of Species Richness and Shared Species from Samples (Software and User's Guide). Freeware for Windows and Mac OS (http://viceroy.eeb.uconn.edu/estimates).

Heyer W.R., M.A. Donnelly, R.W. McDiarmid, L.C. Hayek and M.S. Foster (eds). 1994. Measuring and Monitoring Biological Diversity. Standard Methods for Amphibians. Smithsonian Institution Press, Washington, D.C.

Krebs C.J. 2002. Program for Ecological Methodology 2nd ed. (version 6.1). Web site: zoology.ubc.ca/kebs

Magurran A.E. 1988. Ecological Diversity and its Measurement. Princeton University Press, Princeton.

Rödel M.-O. and Ernst R. 2004. Measuring and monitoring amphibian diversity in tropical forests. I. An evaluation of methods with recommendations for standardization. Ecotropica 10:1-14.

Wilson D.E., R.F. Cole, J.D. Nichols, R. Rudran and M.S. Foster. 1996. Measuring and Monitoring Biological Diversity. Standard Methods for Mammals. Smithsonian Institution Press, Washington, DC.

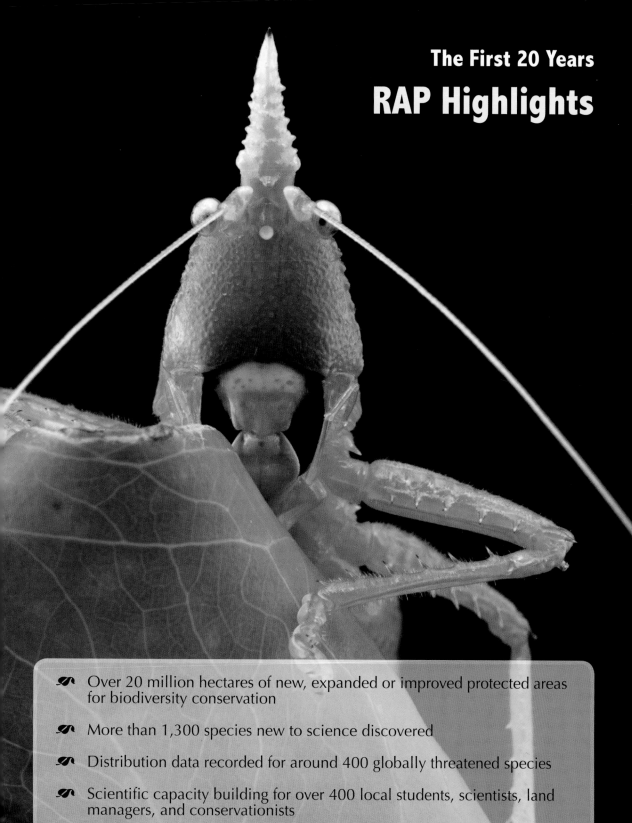

- ✍ Over 20 million hectares of new, expanded or improved protected areas for biodiversity conservation

- ✍ More than 1,300 species new to science discovered

- ✍ Distribution data recorded for around 400 globally threatened species

- ✍ Scientific capacity building for over 400 local students, scientists, land managers, and conservationists

- ✍ 58 volumes of the *RAP Bulletin of Biological Assessment* published

© Piotr Naskrecki

© Andre Baertschi

Madidi, Bolivia

RAP data from the very first RAP survey helped create Madidi National Park, 1.8 million hectares.

© Conservation International/photo by Sterling Zumbrunn

Bird's Head Seascape, Indonesia

Amazing marine discoveries, including 76 species new to science, contributed to the creation of 1.7 million hectares of new marine protected areas.

© Conservation International/photo by Haroldo Castro

Vilcabamba, Peru

RAP data supported efforts by CI-Peru and many partners to establish two indigenous reserves and a national park totaling 700,000 hectares.

SPECIES NEW TO SCIENCE

Foja Mountains, Papua, Indonesia

The mountains of New Guinea have a seemingly unlimited number of species unknown to science. This "Lost World" revealed many new species including two new birds, five new mammals, and over 20 new frogs.

© Bruce Beehler

Rio Orthon, Bolivia

The first AquaRAP team found over 93 species new to science in this large river basin, with an amazingly high – 45 – new fish species.

© Theresa Bert

Nakanai and Muller Ranges, Papua New Guinea

Over 200 species new to science in just eight weeks at two sites. Enough said!

RAP data are currently supporting a bid to designate these sites as World Heritage Sites.

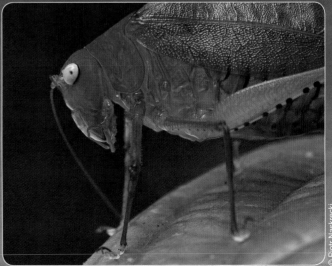

© Piotr Naskrecki

© Piotr Naskrecki

CAPACITY BUILDING

Lakekamu, Papua New Guinea

Of 20 PNG nationals trained through RAP, three have gone on to obtain PhDs, four received Masters, and two achieved Honours degrees.

© Conservation International/photo by Leeanne E. Alonso

Haute Dodo, Cote d'Ivoire

Twenty African scientists learned RAP methods from 12 RAP experts in the field. Five joined future RAP surveys, and at least three received graduate degrees.

© Piotr Naskrecki

Suriname

Over 30 students have been trained in a five year RAP program to build local capacity for biodiversity assessment. Seven students joined a recent RAP survey of southwest Suriname in August 2010.

SPATIAL PLANNING

Mantadia-Zahamena, Madagascar

RAP data collected between these two parks guided creation of a conservation corridor that now protects a critical watershed for this key rice growing region.

© Piotr Naskrecki

Coral Reefs of Mont Panié, New Caledonia

MarineRAP data helped identify priority sites for marine protected areas and fisheries management by local communities.

© Burt Jones

Pic de Fon, Guinea

RAP and other CI programs worked closely with Rio Tinto to identify key species and habitats within their iron ore concession in need of protection. Further RAP surveys of sites in southeastern Guinea provided the context for regional spatial planning.

© Piotr Naskrecki

HUMAN WELL-BEING

© Josefa C. Señaris

Venezuela

A series of six AquaRAP surveys provided key baseline data for the sustainable management of critical watersheds through actions such as community monitoring of water quality, fish, and turtle populations.

© Piotr Naskrecki

Southern Guyana

RAP results are being used by the indigenous Wai-Wai people to develop ecotourism and a management plan for their Community Owned Conservation Area (COCA).

© Piotr Naskrecki

Mountains of Southwest China

In this culturally Tibetan region, sacred sites harbor significant biodiversity. A local Conservation Stewardship Program used RAP data to support official protection of hallowed sites.

OVER 1,300 SPECIES DISCOVERED

Wattled Smoky Honeyeater
(Melipotes carolae)

This new honeyeater was discovered during the 2005 expedition to the Foja Mountains. It was found to be a common but quiet species in the upland forests, spending most of its time foraging for small fruit.

Web-footed salamander
(Bolitoglossa sp. n.)

This genus of salamanders has fully webbed feet which help them climb high into the canopy of tropical forests; they also have no lungs and breathe instead through their skin. This new species was found in the wet forests of the tepuis in southern Ecuador.

Ant (*Strumigenys* sp. n.)

Collected at nearly 2,900 m in the Muller Range – this represents the highest altitude ever recorded for an ant in New Guinea. Its amazing trap-jaw mouthparts are held open at 180 degrees and snapped closed when tiny sensory hairs detect a small, soft bodied invertebrate prey item.

Species New to Science

© Piotr Naskrecki

Big-headed Katydid
(Ingrischia macrocephala)

This new genus and species of large, seed-feeding katydids was discovered in the forests of Papua New Guinea by entomologist Piotr Naskrecki.

© Conservation International/photo by Stephen Richards

Forest frog
(Batrachylodes sp. n.)

This bizarre little frog measuring just two centimeters long belongs to a genus previously known only from the Solomon Islands. Its discovery high in the Nakanai Mountains of Papua New Guinea's New Britain island came as a complete surprise to RAP herpetologist Stephen Richards.

© Gerald Allen

Walking shark
(Hemiscyllium galei)

Don't be fooled by its name, this shark can swim! However, it prefers to walk along the shallow reef flats on its fins, preying on shrimp, crabs, snails, and small fish. The discovery of this shark during a MarineRAP survey has created a media sensation!

OVER 1,300 SPECIES DISCOVERED

Coral (*Asteropora* sp. n.)

Corals belonging to this genus build reefs that support unique marine communities. This was one of at least 20 new species of coral discovered during MarineRAP surveys in the Bird's Head Seascape in Indonesia.

Arboreal Chinchilla Rat (*Cuscomys ashaninka*)

During the RAP survey in Vilcabamba, researchers discovered this new species of large arboreal rodent which closely resembles a species known only from skulls collected at pre-Columbian burial sites in Macchu Picchu. Both species were then included in a new genus described by Louise Emmons in 1999.

Suckermouth catfish (*Pseudancistrus kwinti*)

This catfish was uncovered during a RAP in Suriname. RAP ichthyologists named the new species *Pseudancistrus kwinti* after the indigenous Kwinti people who live along the lower reaches of the Coppename River.

IUCN Red-Listed Species

Purple Marsh Crab
(*Afrithelphusa monodosus*)

Status: Endangered

The discovery of a population of these crabs on a RAP survey in Boké, Guinea confirmed the persistence of the species and helped downgrade its threat status from Critically Endangered.

Fiji Ground Frog
(*Platymantis vitianis*)

Status: Endangered

Babies of this frog hatch directly from eggs in a nest, forgoing an independent tadpole stage. These frogs are only found on the four large islands of Fiji.

Black and White Ruffed Lemur
(*Varecia variegata*)

Status: Critically Endangered

Endemic to the island of Madagascar, this loud and gregarious primate has been spotted on at least one RAP survey in Madagascar.

OVER 400 THREATENED SPECIES DOCUMENTED

Giant Otter
(Pteronura brasiliensis)

Status: Endangered

These aquatic weasel relatives form cohesive family groups. They communicate with loud vocalizations and are often heard before seen. They have been recorded on RAP surveys in Guyana, Peru, Bolivia and Brazil.

© Andre Baertschi

Gola Malimbe
(Malimbus ballmanni)

Status: Endangered

This Upper Guinea endemic was observed in mixed-species flocks in Diécké Forest, southeast Guinea, during a RAP in 2003. Previously, it was known only from eastern Sierra Leone, Liberia and western Côte d'Ivoire.

© David Monticelli/RSPB

Impressed Turtle
(Manouria impressa)

Status: Vulnerable

Asian turtles in general are severely threatened by overharvesting for the pet and food trades. Little is known about the natural history of this beautiful tortoise which has been spotted at high elevations during RAP surveys in Cambodia.

© Conservation International/photo by David Emmett

IUCN Red-Listed Species

© Conservation International/photo by David Emmett

Siamese Crocodile *(Crocodylus siamensis)*

Status: Critically Endangered

Only small populations remain of this shy and unaggressive crocodile, native to Southeast Asia. Individuals have been observed during RAP surveys in Cambodia.

© Conservation International/photo by Russ Mittermeier

West African Red Colobus *(Procolobus badius)*

Status: Endangered

These primates are highly sensitive to hunting and habitat destruction and are important prey for Chimpanzees. They have been documented on several West African RAP surveys.

© David Harasti

Humphead Wrasse *(Cheilinus undulatus)*

Status: Endangered

Heavily exploited by fishermen, these large colorful fish grow to over 2 meters in length and live to upwards of 30 years. MarineRAP scientists are always on the lookout for these and have seen them on RAP surveys in Indonesia, Madagascar and Papua New Guinea.

Exploring new places, finding new species, and bringing their rich diversity into our thinking about conservation planning, RAP is an enduring critical part of CI's scientific work.

– Andrew A Rosenberg, Senior Vice President, Science + Knowledge, Conservation International

History and Overview of Terrestrial RAP

Leeanne E. Alonso

Introduction

The lack of data on the incredibly high species diversity of tropical ecosystems has often been a barrier to effectively plan and implement conservation action in the tropics. How do you evaluate and conserve what you don't even know is there? Exploration of remote tropical wilderness had been going on for centuries, led by eminent explorers such as Charles Darwin, Alfred Russell Wallace, William Beebe, Richard Archbold and many others. But these wilderness areas are so vast and the species so numerous that each expedition discovered more and more species, without an end in sight. Exploration continues today, with the world's top scientists from universities and museums penetrating the remotest corners of the planet. However such exploration and subsequent publication of the results can take years, and the results are not often made available on a time scale needed for conservation decision making. With the acceleration of habitat and species loss around the globe, there arose a great need for the development and application of a more rapid means of collecting species data to guide conservation and development.

As Russ Mittermeier so eloquently explains in the Foreword (p. 9), the concept for Conservation International's (CI) Rapid Assessment Program (RAP) was created in 1989 by the late Ted Parker, Nobel Prize-winning physicist Murray Gell-Mann, and Spencer Beebe, one of CI's founders. The expertise of the RAP scientists was the basis of RAP's success from the very beginning. Their ability to find and detect the elusive and threatened species, and to document and rapidly identify the vast number of species in the tropical areas they explored, was unparalleled and allowed them to evaluate the conservation importance of a site based on the species they found. They knew how to use their data to make the case for conservation and the establishment of protected areas.

RAP uses an integrated approach that pulls together information on a variety of taxa to obtain a portrait of the habitat under study. The combined knowledge of the RAP scientists allows them to quickly assess the uniqueness and conservation value of an area and to make recommendations about its management. RAP methodology has never been viewed as a substitute for more in-depth inventory or monitoring but is designed to provide critical scientific information quickly. Information collected includes biological diversity, degree of endemism, special habitat types, threatened species, degree of habitat degradation, presence of introduced species, and the degree of risk of extinction on a national and global scale. See page 18 for more details on the RAP approach.

The first RAP teams focused on plants, birds, and mammals. Specialists studying reptiles and amphibians were added to the team early on, and RAP added selected groups of invertebrates in 1996 for the Kanuku Mountains, Guyana RAP survey. While the core RAP team often consists of non-local scientists, a trademark of RAP from the very beginning has been a close integration with local scientists. RAP team members work closely with host country scientists, exchanging information, methodologies and training young scientists.

The conservation capacity of tropical countries often suffers from a lack of collaborative interaction between conservation organizations, academic institutions, and government agencies. A key feature of RAP is to link scientists and academic institutions with conservation organizations and the government agencies in charge of natural resources. In-country scientists and institutions gain more prominent visibility within country when collaborating on a RAP expedition, as well as additional experience and research opportunities by participation in the fieldwork, and a greater voice in consultations with conservation planners. RAP participants are also invited to contribute to the final report of a trip, which is published in the *RAP Bulletin of Biological Assessment* series, formerly *RAP Working Papers*.

Targeting the Most Threatened Sites

After Madidi, the RAP team, working closely with CI staff and collaborators at The Field Museum, continued to explore the unknown wilderness of Central and South America, where their expertise could be applied most readily. They surveyed sites that were suspected to contain high diversity, endemic species, and/or unique species and habitats found in few other parts of the world. Their focus fell on areas most threatened and in danger of disappearing in the very near future. The Cordillera de la Costa, site of the second RAP survey, is a prime example of such a highly threatened site. Located in the highly fragmented forest of Western Ecuador, at the time of the RAP survey in 1991 this region contained just 6% of its original forest cover. The RAP team collected biodiversity data from nine sites with the hope that their data would be used to raise

© Randall Hyman

The original RAP team (left to right): Al Gentry, Ted Parker, Louise Emmons, and Robin Foster

© Piotr Naskrecki

awareness of the unique biological diversity of this area and identify key sites for protection. While this region has continued to degrade since the RAP survey, the future of some sites is hopeful (see page 193). Providing the scientific basis for such conservation efforts is the ultimate goal of RAP.

Over the next few years, from 1991 through 1994, this RAP team and local collaborators surveyed other highly threatened unique ecosystems, including the lowland dry forests of Santa Cruz and Noel Kempff Mercado National Park in Bolivia, the Columbia River Forest Reserve in Belize, the Tambopata-Candamo Reserved Zone and Pampas del Heath in Peru, and the Kanuku Mountains of Guyana. Most of these sites have received some degree of improved protection based on the RAP data or actions are underway. The process that leads to formal, legal protection of a site can take a long time, as evidenced by the conservation actions pending at many of the RAP sites. There must also be people willing to keep pushing for action. The RAP program and its scientific team members have always been highly committed to this follow-up action. One prime example is the RAP scientists' involvement in the development of a national park feasibility study leading to the creation of the Tambopata-Candamo protected area of 1.5 million hectares. Arguably the richest region on the planet, this park in northeastern Peru could hold as much as 10% of global avian diversity.

Expanding within the Andes and to Asia with USAID

From 1994 through 1998, the RAP program had a cooperative agreement with the U.S. Agency for International Development (USAID) aimed at 1) advancing the conservation of biodiversity in the Tropical Andes and 2) expanding RAP in Southeast Asia and the Pacific. RAP carried out rapid biological assessments in four tropical countries, Peru, Bolivia, Indonesia (in Irian Jaya, now Papua Province), and Papua New Guinea under this agreement, assisting decision makers and conservationists to identify conservation priorities in these countries. RAP activity was also expanded in Bolivia and Peru to include four expeditions (Chuquisaca, Bolivia; two to Vilcabamba, Peru; Madidi, Bolivia) and two training courses (Noel Kempff Mercado, Bolivia; Pampas del Heath, Peru).

The New Guinea region is globally significant both in terms of numbers of species and in terms of endemism. In 1994 RAP chose to conduct its first survey in the Asia-Pacific region on the island of New Ireland in Papua New Guinea. The RAP team experimented with methods that could measure ecological parameters and could be standardized and repeatable. From 1996-1998, RAP was very active in Papua New Guinea with a full RAP expedition to the Lakekamu Basin in 1996 and ongoing training conducted by then RAP Asia Team Leader, Andrew Mack,

Table 1. The First Decade (1990-1999) – 18 surveys		
Year	**Country**	**Site**
1990	Bolivia	Alto Madidi Region
1990-1992	Bolivia	The Lowland Dry Forests of Santa Cruz
1991	Ecuador	Cordillera de la Costa
1991-95	Bolivia	Noel Kempff Mercado National Park
1992	Belize	Columbia River Forest Reserve
1992	Peru	Tambopata-Candamo Reserved Zone
1992, 1996-1997	Peru/Bolivia	Pando and Alto Madidi, Bolivia & Pampas del Heath, Peru
1993	Guyana	Western Kanuku Mountains
1993-94	Ecuador/Peru	Cordillera del Cóndor
1994	Papua New Guinea	Southern New Ireland
1995	Bolivia	Humid Forests of Chuquisaca
1996	Papua New Guinea	Lakekamu Basin
1996	New Caledonia	Province Nord
1997	Madagascar	Reserve Naturelle Integrale d'Ankarafantsika
1997-98	Peru	Cordillera de Vilcabamba
1998	Côte d'Ivoire	Parc National de la Marahoué
1998	Indonesia	Wapoga River Area
1998-1999	Madagascar	Mantadia-Zahamena Corridor

in conjunction with the Wildlife Conservation Society. The Lakekamu Basin represents one of the largest and best tracts of lowland forest in Papua New Guinea. In just one month, 35-47 new species and several new genera (ant, damselfly) were discovered. CI formally presented the RAP report to appropriate agencies in Papua New Guinea and the international development and conservation community including the World Bank and local NGOs. Building on this first RAP expedition to the Lakekamu Basin, 1998 activities in Papua New Guinea included a mini-RAP and a more extensive training session for Papua New Guinea graduate students in the field of conservation biology and RAP methodology.

Conservation efforts in Papua New Guinea must take a different approach than in Latin America. Most of the land is owned not by the government but by individual landowners. Successful conservation will not come from national parks, reserves or centralized laws but by working with local landowners to develop sustainable practices on their land that have the least impact on local ecosystems. Results from the RAP expedition are an important contribution toward formulating conservation policies in the Lakekamu Basin. Before and after the RAP survey, CI scientists Andrew Mack and Kurt Merg spent a lot of time presenting communication and educational activities to help landowners think more about biodiversity. The RAP surveys and training courses have stimulated more local participation and discussion of management of the land in the Lakekamu Basin.

Additional RAP surveys in New Guinea were delayed for several years due to an unstable political climate and logistical challenges in Indonesia, but a RAP survey was finally successfully carried out in Indonesian New Guinea in 1998 with the help of P.T. Freeport Mining Company. The survey area was chosen because it was identified by the 1997 Irian Jaya Biodiversity Conservation Priority-Setting Workshop conducted in Biak as an area where ecological and biogeographic data are particularly inadequate. One goal of the survey was to provide data on the biota of an area that has remained virtually unexplored by biologists. The RAP survey revealed a very high diversity, with many species endemic to New Guinea and many new to science. The success of this RAP expedition was notable for three reasons. First, in the context of the political situation there, it is significant that permission was secured and that the expedition proceeded without incident. Second, this RAP filled in a significant gap in our biogeographic knowledge of this part of the island. This region of New Guinea had never before been surveyed. Third, the expedition itself set a strong precedent for successful and productive scientific collaboration in Indonesia. For participating Indonesian scientists, the survey was useful to learn the RAP methodology of scientific field assessment, as well as an important opportunity to obtain important reference materials from this under-studied and under-surveyed province of Indonesia.

Expanding RAP's Approach

During the latter half of the 1990s, RAP expanded to coral reef and freshwater ecosystems, launching MarineRAP and AquaRAP programs (see those sections of this book). RAP began conducting surveys in Africa starting in the Reserve Naturelle Integrale d'Ankarafantsika, Madagascar in 1997 and Parc National de la Marahoué, Côte d'Ivoire in 1998. RAP also surveyed Laguna del Tigre National Park, Guatemala in 1999, a site highly threatened by oil operations and an encroaching agricultural frontier. These three RAP surveys were conducted in

Table 2. The Second Decade (2000-2010) – 33 surveys		
Year	Country	Site
2000	Indonesia	Cyclops Mountains and the Southern Mamberamo Basin
2001	Guyana	Eastern Kanuku Mountains
2001	Cambodia	Central Cardamom Mountains
2002	Côte d'Ivoire	Haute Dodo and Cavally Classified Forests
2002	Guinea	Foret Classée du Pic de Fon, Simandou Range
2003	Ghana	Southwestern Forest Reserves
2003	Guinea	Déré, Diécké, and Mont Béro
2003	Botswana	Okavango Delta III - Terrestrial
2004	Dem. Rep. Congo	Lokutu
2004-2006	Brazil	Tumucumaque Mountains National Park
2005	Guinea	Boké Préfecture
2005	Suriname	Lely and Nassau Plateaus
2005	Liberia	North Lorma, Gola and Grebo National Forests
2005	Papua New Guinea	Kaijende Highlands
2005	China	Mountains of Southwest China Hotspot, Sichuan
2005	Indonesia	Foja Mountains I
2005	Nepal	Makalu-Barun National Park
2006	Ghana	Atewa Range Forest Reserve
2006	Ghana	Ajenjua Bepo and Mamang Forest Reserves
2006	Guyana	Konashen Community Owned Conservation Area
2007	Cambodia	Virachey National Park
2007	Indonesia	Northwest Mamberamo Basin
2007	Madagascar	Andrafiamena
2008	Venezuela	Ramal de Calderas
2008	Fiji	Nakauvadra Range
2008	Indonesia	Foja Mountains II
2008	Papua New Guinea	Upper Strickland Basin
2009	Ecuador	Upper Río Nangaritza Basin
2009	Papua New Guinea	Nakanai Mountains, East New Britain
2009	Papua New Guinea	Muller Range
2009	Fiji	Nakorotubu Mountains
2010	Suriname	Kwamalasamutu
2010	New Caledonia	Mont Panié

© Piotr Naskrecki

protected areas in need of biological information for management and to promote increased protection of the park. RAP finished up its first decade with a survey of unprotected forest that lay between Mantadia and Zahamena national parks in Madagascar, with the objective of identifying key sites to include in a corridor between the parks.

Expanding Roster of RAP Team Collaborators

As RAP expanded geographically during these 10 years, so did its roster of collaborating scientific team members. Most field biologists/taxonomists focus their work on a specific group of organisms (ie. small mammals or dung beetles) in a particular region of the world. Most are experts on the fauna or flora of one or a few areas of the world such as the Neotropics (Central and South America), Southeast Asia, tropical Africa, Madagascar, etc. Thus as RAP expanded to other regions of the world, new teams of RAP scientists were formed consisting of expert taxonomists and field biologists from universities, museums, governments, NGOs, etc. specializing in those new regions. Collaborating scientists from The Field Museum began their own rapid survey program, Rapid Biological Inventories (http://fm2.fmnh.org/rbi/), through which they carry out high impact field surveys in the Andes region of South America as well as other sites throughout the world.

Scientific Capacity Building

A key component of RAP activities during this decade was the training of local scientists to develop the capacity to conduct rapid biological assessments independently. Participation in RAP expeditions provides host-country scientists with experience in working on interdisciplinary teams, in rapid assessment techniques, and in the integration of data from different taxa to make preliminary conclusions regarding biological diversity. At the same time, the suggestions and input from scientific counterparts enhance and improve the RAP approach.

Under the RAP-USAID cooperative agreement from 1994-1998, RAP conducted several training courses specifically for host-country scientists and students. Training courses were held in Peru, Bolivia, and Papua New Guinea. Courses usually involved at least two or three RAP team experts as instructors and up to 20 host-country students. The philosophy and methodologies of RAP were taught over a one to two week period in the field of the host country. RAP train-

© Piotr Naskrecki

ing courses have also been very successful at developing taxonomic skills in local scientists and identifying highly motivated and knowledgeable young scientists, thus building up local capacity for biological assessment. Training courses involve field practice of biodiversity assessment techniques, thereby providing essential field experience for participants as well as collecting important biological data about the area under study.

In Noel Kempff Mercado National Park, a RAP training course in rapid ecological field techniques was organized for over 30 biologists, primarily Bolivians, in 1995. During the training course the RAP experts and trainees surveyed many poorly studied habitats and catalyzed new research programs for the park. A RAP training course was held in the Pampas del Heath National Sanctuary in Peru, near the border with Bolivia, in 1996. Ten Bolivian and 10 Peruvian students were trained in biodiversity survey techniques in order to build up local capacity for national biodiversity inventories.

From 1995-1998, Andrew Mack, RAP's Asia Team Leader, conducted several training courses for Papua New Guinea students, many of whom participated in "mini-RAP" assessments of the biodiversity of the region to practice their newly learned field techniques. The courses focused on RAP field methods but also on experimental design and on analysis of experimental data and the presentation of results.

With funds from the USAID agreement, RAP collaborators based at The Field Museum, primarily ornithologists Doug Stotz and Tom Schulenberg, and botanist/ecologist Robin Foster developed field guides to assist trainees in rapidly identifying birds and plants. These identification aids were used by RAP scientists, participants in RAP training courses, and by host-country scientists to identify species in the field. RAP collaborators John Fitzpatrick, Doug Stotz, Deborah Moskovitz and Ted Parker also created a Neotropical avian diversity database that includes information on key indicator species of birds, those with highly restricted ranges and habitat needs that indicate high habitat quality. Some of the identification aids included:

- A "Biological Inventory Methods Manual" for Bolivian trainees, October, 1995.
- A "Rapid Field Guide to the plants of Noel Kempff" for RAP trainees, October, 1995.
- A tropical lowland bird identification CD training tool for southeastern Peru, May, 1996.
- A tropical Andes bird identification CD training tool, March, 1997.
- A "Rapid Field Guide to the Birds of Madidi" for RAP trainees, April, 1997.
- A "Rapid Field Guide to the Plants of Madidi" for RAP trainees, April, 1997.
- A "Plants of Madidi" field guide.
- A "Plants of Vilcabamba" field guide from the first RAP expedition to the Vilcabamba Mountain Range, Peru, April 1997.

The Second Decade of RAP

During RAP's second decade, RAP and partners coordinated over 30 rapid biodiversity surveys. These surveys were conducted to collect biodiversity data to meet a wide variety of objectives across the globe. The choice of sites to survey came primarily from four different processes:

1. RAP continued to respond to requests from CI field programs to provide biodiversity data they need to plan and implement their conservation strategies.
2. RAP continued to train host-country scientists and students to build local scientific capacity for conservation and natural resource management.
3. RAP partnered with The Energy and Mining Program of CI's Center for Environmental Leadership in Business (CELB) to develop a means of engaging energy and mining companies in biodiversity conservation – the Initial Biodiversity Assessment and Planning approach (IBAP).
4. RAP and scientific partners continued to identify and survey the most important sites for scientific exploration. RAP has begun using gap analysis modeling to identify priority sites, starting in Papua New Guinea. This process identifies sites that are most likely to yield endemic species or species new to science based on information about the unique characteristics of the environment and lack of data about the biota of these 'environmental envelopes'.
5. CI field programs and partners carried out rapid field surveys on their own, with various levels of assistance from RAP on logistical and scientific aspects. The results from these surveys are published in the *RAP Bulletin of Biological Assessment* series with RAP editorial oversight.

Of course there are tradeoffs to each of these processes, with some RAP surveys assessing sites richer in biodiversity than others, and some that have less support for conservation follow-up than others. The common theme is that the need for biological data has been identified, and the RAP program provides scientific guidance and logistical support and brings in collaborating taxonomic experts to conduct a professional rapid biodiversity assessment.

RAP Surveys Requested from the Field

With the ultimate goal of using the RAP data to guide conservation, it is essential that CI field programs and other local partners are fully in support of and involved in the entire RAP process. Integration of RAP data into local, national and regional conservation planning is more likely to occur when the need for biological data is identified from within the region. There are many uses of the biological data, the most prominent being to identify priority areas for conservation based on high diversity or endemism, and developing management plans for protected areas. Most of the RAP surveys conducted over the last 10 years, and also within the first decade of RAP, have been by request of CI field programs. Close collaboration with local communities is facilitated by local CI staff and is essential to the successful implementation of a RAP survey. Local community members often request CI to help with conducting a biodiversity assessment so that they will have data to manage their lands; they also know the land better than anyone and provide essential local knowledge on biodiversity and the terrain.

© Piotr Naskrecki

RAP surveys are carried out in high biodiversity regions of the world, mostly in CI's Hotspots and High Biodiversity Wilderness Areas. During the second decade of RAP, RAP surveys were carried out across the globe, responding to conservation needs in areas where CI had expanded its work, including several sites in mainland Asia including Cambodia and China; into the heart of Africa in the Democratic Republic of Congo, Botswana and Liberia; and throughout the Pacific Islands.

Several RAP surveys during this second decade were conducted on indigenous lands to collect data to help them develop management and conservation plans. Data were collected on the richness and abundance of species of particular interest to the local peoples, such as large mammals and birds hunted for bushmeat, fisheries, and other products used from the forest. The 2006 RAP survey of the Wai Wai's Konashen Community Owned Conservation Concession (COCA) of Southern Guyana and the 2010 RAP survey of the lands around the indigenous Trio village of Kwamalasamutu are two examples of how RAP data were collected to inform the management of the local peoples' food sources as well as to promote ecotourism to their areas. Data from the 2005 RAP survey of southwest China continue to be used to support protection of Tibetan Sacred Lands that harbor important species such as the Panda and Red Panda.

During many RAP surveys, data on the use of natural resources by local people are often collected in addition to the biological data. Data on the socioeconomics of the region are helpful to make RAP recommendations that will benefit not only the biodiversity and habitats of the area but also the well-being of the local people. Such data have been collected on many RAP surveys but recently have become almost a mandatory part of the RAP process. During the 2009 RAP survey in the Nakorotubu Mountains of Fiji, a socioeconomic team worked with four local villages to produce a list of more than 40 non-timber forest products used for food, medicine and building supplies. These data will help demonstrate the crucial link between natural resources and the quality of life for local people. RAP is continuing to develop and expand the socioeconomic component of field surveys.

There are few places left on earth with extensive tracts of natural habitat lacking human disturbance. These are the places where CI and RAP have traditionally focused their work, in the High Biodiversity Wilderness Areas. Two of these areas are the island of New Guinea in the Asia-Pacific region, and the Guiana Shield region of northern South America, consisting of the eastern part of Venezuela, Guyana, Suriname and French Guiana. RAP has conducted many surveys in these two regions and will continue to do so, as there is so much left to explore.

Requests to Train Host-country Scientists and Students to Build Local Scientific Capacity

Continuing the legacy of training begun in RAP's first decade, scientific capacity building has grown to be a key focus of RAP surveys. The number of expert taxonomists capable of rapidly surveying and identifying species in the field, or soon after in the museum, is not large. These few people are increasingly busy working on the specimens they and others have collected. Thus the need is great to create a new cadre of taxonomic specialists available for biodiversity survey work. In addition, the scientific capacity for natural resource management and conservation within many developing countries is seriously deficient. Given the rate of habitat alteration within these countries, it is extremely important to build capacity of local scientists and students to survey the biodiversity within their country, to learn to identify the species and become taxonomic experts, and to develop skills to apply this knowledge to the management of their natural resources. Every RAP survey includes involvement of host-country scientists, most of whom are taxonomic experts already. Some are along to continue to learn from the expert RAP team members and continue to refine their field and taxonomy skills. Students are often involved to obtain more field experience and work alongside the taxonomic experts.

RAP training continued in this second decade with both RAP training courses and training surveys. The first was a 2000 training course for Indonesian students held in the Cyclops Mountains on the Irian Jaya (now Papua) coast along with a RAP survey of the southern Mamberamo Basin. A similar training activity was held for Guyanese students in 2001, followed by a second RAP survey in the Kanuku Mountains, Guyana. The West Africa Priority Setting Workshop (WAPS) in 1999 identified a great need for developing scientific capacity within West Africa. With funds from the Critical Ecosystem Partnership Fund (CEPF), RAP organized a RAP training survey in southwestern Cote d'Ivoire in 2002. A team of 12 scientific experts worked closely with 20 West African students and scientists from six African countries, who had all come to learn RAP field techniques from some of the world's top experts. This experience also served to forge collaborations among scientists from several African countries.

In 2008, RAP began a five year RAP training and survey program in Suriname. Two training courses for Surinamese students were conducted to introduce field methods and data analysis. The students most interested in field work were then invited to participate in a series of RAP surveys conducted in Suriname. The first of these was the RAP survey recently conducted around the village of Kwamalasamutu in southwest Suriname. Seven students, three government representatives and seven forest rangers from the local Trio AmerIndian community assisted the RAP scientific team, gaining new skills and field experience. RAP is currently working on developing a similar training program for Suriname's neighbor, Guyana.

Providing Data to Engage the Private Sector in Conservation

For several years, primarily from 2002-2006, RAP worked closely with CI's Center for Environmental Leadership in Business (CELB) to carry out rapid biodiversity surveys with extractive industry partners as part of an Initial Biodiversity Assessment and Planning (IBAP) process. CI's Center for Environmental Leadership in Business (CELB) works with many companies to provide information and guidance so that they can make informed decisions and address up front environmental issues they may face in their operations.

 IBAP is an approach designed to assist industry at the very earliest project stages in systematically identifying important biodiversity considerations that should be factored into project site selection and decision-making, and risk-evaluation processes as well as biodiversity offset design. The IBAP approach is designed with the understanding that highly detailed biodiversity information is not generally appropriate at the very earliest project development stages when there is a chance that the project will not proceed. However, IBAP contributes data to form a solid foundation for standard and more detailed environmental management processes (for example, ESIA) and standalone biodiversity tools required at later stages of the life cycle if the project proceeds. Based on IBAP, Birdlife International, CI and other partners developed an online tool, the Integrated Biodiversity Assessment Tool (IBAT), designed to facilitate access to accurate and up-to-date biodiversity information to support critical business decisions (www.ibatforbusiness.org). This tool is also available for use by the conservation community at www.ibat-alliance.org/ibat-conservation.

The IBAP process includes four steps. RAP was involved in all four steps since RAP data fed into the recommendations and monitoring stages:

1. Rapid Biodiversity Assessment (RAP). RAP survey of the area where the company is working or plans to work. Key areas are identified prior to the survey.
2. Threats Assessment Workshop. A workshop with scientists and local stakeholders to assess the various threats to the region and incorporate the results of the RAP and other baseline studies into a Biodiversity Action Plan.

3. Develop an Initial Biodiversity Action Plan. The product of the RAP and Threats Assessment workshop, combining the scientific and workshop results and providing conservation recommendations for the area and for the company, including consideration of biodiversity offsets.

4. Long-term Biodiversity Monitoring Plan. CI helps to develop protocols for the long-term monitoring of key biodiversity elements in the area based on the RAP results. The company and other local partners would then be responsible for implementing the monitoring protocols and utilizing the data to feedback on their operations.

The IBAP approach was implemented by RAP and CELB with several industry partners across a wide range of ecosystems. These engagements demonstrated an interest by these companies to incorporate biodiversity data into their decision making process. The first collaborative IBAP project was conducted in 2002 with Rio Tinto Mining and Exploration Limited in the Pic de Fon Classified Forest, Guinea where Rio Tinto was in the early stages of exploration for iron ore. CELB and RAP worked together to conduct IBAP projects with Alcoa World Alumina LLC (Alcoa) and Alcan Inc. in the Boké Prefecture of Guinea and in Atewa Forest Reserve, Ghana with Alcoa.

Another IBAP project was carried out in Eastern Ghana with Newmont Gold, Inc. in 2006 to identify potential offset sites for the mining project and to inform the Environmental Impact Assessment for the gold mine. In 2005 CELB and RAP also conducted an IBAP with BHP Billiton and Suralco in Suriname to assess biodiversity on two bauxite plateaus of interest for mining. Two RAP surveys were also carried out successfully in Venezuela with ConocoPhillips in the Gulf of Paria and with Gold Reserve, Inc. in the Cuyuní River Basin. See the Venezuela RAP summary (page 256) for details.

In addition to IBAP, RAP has also been a tool for engaging with business in other ways, such as the unique partnership in 2005 between RAP, CELB, the Walt Disney Company, Disney Worldwide Conservation Fund and Discovery Communications. Joe Rohde, of Disney Imagineering, had designed a new roller coaster for Disney's Animal Kingdom (Expedition Everest). Joe, an avid nature lover and conservationist, and CI President Russ Mittermeier came up with the idea of doing a real expedition in the Himalayas that would contribute to biodiversity conservation in the Himalayan region as well as promote the new roller coaster. They brought into this mix Discovery Communications who suggested that they film the RAP expedition(s) to be featured on a segment of Corwin's Quest television program. Two RAP surveys were undertaken as part of this project; the first in the Tibetan region of southwest China and the second in Makalu Barun National Park in Nepal. Despite the cool conditions of the Himalayan region, the RAP team documented many interesting species, built relationships between Chinese, Nepalese and international scientists, and catalyzed a Conservation Stewards Program in China to protect Tibetan Sacred Sites. The RAP team and methods are still on display along the queue line to ride the Expedition Everest roller coaster at Disney's Animal Kingdom in Orlando, Florida, USA.

Identification of Remote, Unexplored Sites of Interest to Science and Conservation

The most exciting surveys for the RAP scientists are those that explore the most remote, hard to reach places on earth that have the potential for new, surprising discoveries. These sites include tropical mountain areas because the species tend to have small ranges (i.e., each mountain has a different array of species). Other sites of interest include habitats that require special adaptations to survive, such as areas with low oxygen levels (e.g., swamps) and limestone caves. Sites with high rainfall, long geological history, and unique environmental conditions all have high potential for the discovery of novel and rare species. Countries and regions that contain sites such as these include: Papua New Guinea, Indonesia (especially western New Guinea, Sulawesi, Kalimantan and Sumatra), New Caledonia, Cambodia, Laos, Myanmar, India, Madagascar, the Guiana Shield (Guyana, Suriname and French Guiana), and the Andean countries, especially Peru and Bolivia. These areas can be considered to have the highest chances of revealing intriguing new biological finds.

© Piotr Naskrecki

Since the advent of RAP, the expert knowledge and opinions of the collaborating RAP scientists have played a major role in selecting sites for RAP surveys. The wish list of places they'd like to explore has led RAP to many sites with exciting results, especially in the Andes Mountains of South America and across the island of New Guinea.

© Piotr Naskrecki

In the last few years, RAP has begun using gap analysis modeling to identify sites that have not been surveyed within various environmental envelopes, starting in Papua New Guinea. These sites are most likely to yield endemic species or species new to science due to the unique characteristics of the environment.

As discussed above there are many reasons why RAP surveys are conducted, but all revolve around the need to obtain information about biodiversity to guide conservation actions. Selection of sites for surveys has often been determined by the needs of Conservation International's field programs. A number of these sites, such as the Foja Mountains, had already been identified as being of high priority for biodiversity assessment on the basis of expert opinion. This expert opinion was provided in various forms, including both personal communications from internationally recognized scientists, and through priority-setting exercises. Two examples were the Irian Jaya (now Papua and West Papua) Indonesia Biodiversity Conservation Priority-Setting Workshop, and Papua New Guinea's Conservation Needs Assessment. Both of these exercises solicited the opinions of experts on New Guinea biota about areas they considered to be both poorly known and likely to harbor high species diversity and endemism. Resulting 'consensus' documents have been used to guide survey site selection by RAP and other organizations devoted to biodiversity conservation in New Guinea.

In 2008, RAP enlisted the support of Australia's CSIRO to develop a gap modeling tool that would use biological and environmental data to identify sites in Papua New Guinea that are most poorly known biologically and most likely to contain large numbers of new and data-deficient species. This process aimed to avoid any potential biases in the 'expert opinion' approach by establishing a rational, data-based model to identify sites. The model identified 20 of the most poorly documented places in Papua New Guinea and a workshop was subsequently held to discuss the conservation benefits of a RAP survey at each of these. Three sites were selected, two of them (Nakanai and Muller Range) on the World Heritage tentative list. These two surveys were conducted during 2009 and the data collected will be presented to local, provincial and national governments to help promote the World Heritage listing of these areas. Funds are currently being sought to conduct a RAP assessment at the third site, Mt Suckling. RAP has plans to conduct gap analysis for other regions of the world to identify survey priorities.

Surveys Conducted by CI Field Programs and Partners

CI field programs and partners occasionally carry out rapid biodiversity field surveys on their own with local scientific partners, with various levels of assistance from RAP on logistical and scientific aspects. The results from these surveys are also published in the *RAP Bulletin of Biological Assessment* series with RAP editorial oversight. In particular, CI-Madagascar, CI-Venezuela, and CI-Indonesia (Bird's Head) developed strong biodiversity inventory programs within their countries. See pages 277, 256 and 272 respectively for summaries of their inventory programs. Recently, CI-Fiji has been working with the University of the South Pacific to conduct a series of rapid biodiversity surveys to guide corridor planning and CI-New Caledonia is working closely with the government of Province Nord to carry out surveys on and around Mont Panié to document native biodiversity and to control invasive species.

Media Impacts – Raising Global Awareness of Biodiversity

One of the most unexpected yet successful aspects of RAP has been the media attention that RAP expeditions and discoveries have received over the years. The discovery of species new to science continues to fascinate us all and provides a positive respite from the bad news typical of today's media. The discovery of a "Lost Eden" provides us with a glimpse of an amazing world still unexploited and full of mystery. Species discoveries resonate with people and help them to make connections with the species and habitats we are working to protect.

Some of the international media related to Terrestrial RAP discoveries have included:

- The April 1997 RAP expedition to the Vilcabamba Mountain Range in the Urubamba Region of Peru was a feature article in the March/April 1998 issue of *International Wildlife*, a publication of the National Wildlife Federation. Author Michael Tennesen accompanied the CI RAP expedition on special assignment for the magazine.
- In January 1998, the Vilcabamba I RAP expedition was featured in the CARETAS magazine.
- *National Geographic Magazine* included the May 1998 Vilcabamba II RAP expedition as a feature story in their 1999 millennium issue on biodiversity conservation. National Geographic reporter Virginia Morell and photographer Frans Lanting were in the field with the RAP team to cover the story.
- BBC Horizon's series in 1996 featured RAP for a segment entitled "Nature's Numbers".
- The 2005 RAP expedition to the Foja Mountains of Indonesian New Guinea made media history with countless internet and printed media articles across the world. It was featured in a story on the PBS Lehrer News Hour in 2006.
- Animal Planet's Jeff Corwin joined the RAP team in Nepal to film a segment on Himalayan biodiversity for his TV show, "Corwin's Quest" which aired in 2006.
- CBS' TV program 60 minutes filmed a second RAP survey to the Foja Mountains and twice aired the story, entitled "Garden of Eden," on its ever-popular Sunday program in December 2007 and then again in the spring of 2008.
- The Suriname RAP expedition in 2005 drew international attention for the discovery of several new species to science.

Most recently, RAP survey discoveries from New Guinea garnered significant media attention:

- May 2010 CI Press release on new species from 2008 RAP survey in the Foja Mountains garnered worldwide attention for new species, including a new bird species.
- The June 2010 issue of National Geographic magazine included a feature story of the 2008 Foja RAP expedition entitled "Foja Mountains Fauna". Photographer Tim Laman and writer/naturalist Mel White accompanied the RAP team in the field.
- October 2010 CI press release announcing the discovery of over 200 species new to science discovered by RAP in 2009 from two sites in Papua New Guinea. The story was featured in 672 news articles reaching 604,194,621 viewers. Key media outlets that ran the story included USA Today, CBS, ABC, Fox News, CNN, Al Jazeera, NPR, National Geographic, Yahoo!, AOL, Discovery, Guardian, Telegraph, O Globo, and the Sydney Morning Herald.

Selected Publications from Terrestrial RAP Surveys

Decher J. and J. Fahr. 2007. A conservation assessment of bats (Chiroptera) of Draw River, Boi-Tano, and Krokosua Hills Forest Reserves in the Western Region of Ghana. Myotis 43:5-30.

Decher J., R.W. Norris and J. Fahr. 2010. Small mammal survey in the upper Seli River valley, Sierra Leone. Mammalia 74:163-176.

Dijkstra K.D.B. 2008. The Systematist's Muse - two new damselfly species from 'Elisabetha' in the Congo Basin (Odonata: Chlorocyphidae, Platycnemididae). Zool. Med. Leiden 82(3): 15-27.

Ernst R., A.C. Agyei and M-O. Rödel. 2008. A new giant species of *Arthroleptis* (Amphibia: Anura: Arthroleptidae) from the Krokosua Hills Forest Reserve, south-western Ghana. Zootaxa 1697:58-68.

Howcroft N.H.S. and W. Takeuchi. 2002. New and noteworthy orchids of the Bismarck Archipelago, Papua New Guinea. SIDA 20(2): 461-486.

Luna L. and V. Pacheco. 2002. A new species of *Thomasomys* (Muridae: Sigmodontinae) from the Andes of southeastern Peru. Journal of Mammalogy 83(3):834-842.

Naskrecki P. 2008. Sylvan katydids (Orthoptera: Tettigoniidae: Pseudophyllinae) of the Guinean Forests of West Africa hotspot: an overview and descriptions of new species. Zootaxa 1712: 1-41.

Oliver P. and S.J. Richards. 2007. A new species of montane stream-dwelling *Litoria* from Papua, Indonesia (Anura: Hylidae). Hamadryad 31: 299-303.

Richards S.J. and D.T. Iskandar. 2006. A New Species of Torrent-Dwelling Frog (Hylidae, *Litoria*) from the Mountains of New Guinea. Current Herpetology 25(2): 57-63.

Robbins M.B., M.J. Braun, C.M. Milensky, B.K. Schmidt, W. Prince, N.H. Rice, D.W. Finch and B.J. O'Shea. 2007. Avifauna of the upper Essequibo River and Acary Mountains, Southern Guyana. Ornitologia Neotropical 18: 339-368.

Rödel M-O., M. Gil, A.C. Agyei, A.D. Leache, R.E. Dias, M.K. Fujita, and R. Ernst. 2005. The amphibians of the forested parts of south-western Ghana. Salamandra 42: 107-127.

Roth L.M. and P. Naskrecki. 2003. A new genus and species of cave cockroach (Blaberidae: Oxyhaloinae) from Guinea, West Africa. Journal of Orthoptera Research 12(2): 57-61.

Takeuchi W. 2007. Some notes on Ericaceae from recent expeditions to New Guinea summit environments. Harvard Papers in Botany 12(1):163-171.

Terán-Valdez A. and J.M. Guayasamin. 2010. The smallest terrestrial vertebrate of Ecuador: A new frog of the genus *Pristimantis* (Amphibia: Strabomantidae) from the Cordillera del Cóndor. Zootaxa 2447: 53-68.

Theischinger G. and S.J. Richards. 2006. Two new species of *Nososticta* Hagen in Selys from Papua New Guinea (Zygoptera: Protoneuridae). Odonatologica 35: 75-79.

When the first RAP team members gathered at CI in December 1989 to plan the program, it became clear that they were discussing a potential game-changer for conservation. What had been an interesting idea that brought Ted, Robin, Louise, and Al to the table suddenly took form as a contribution that they were uniquely suited to make to help save the planet… with the realization that they needed to race together, as a team, if they were to succeed. For two days, their discussions ranged worldwide about areas that had great potential for conservation, but which were under siege by a range of threats, and which might be lost before their real biological value was understood. Their global grasp of the planet's geography and wild places was humbling; they could envision the world's most remote places, and knew each one's unique assemblages of species.

"There are only a few dozen people in the world who do this kind of thing," Ted pointed out. "In 5 days, I can find 90% of the birds that are in a location." "I need 10 days for monkeys," Louise stated, "but six months for mammals overall." "One month for me to describe major communities," was Robin's opinion. "I'll keep going as long as I can," Al offered.

Each member emphasized the tools they would need: Tape recorders for Ted to capture bird song; transects to follow day and night for Louise; Robin's up-front assessment using satellite photos, then overflights, and ground truthing to figure out what features to examine up close; and Al's climbing equipment to scale trees for botanical collections. "I can't work without locals," Ted reminded the group, all of whom echoed the importance of local knowledge of species and terrain that would help them narrow their efforts to focus on the most important elements of a particular location.

For a group of biologists whose magnificent obsession to explore the remote corners of the planet had meant they eschewed the traditional academic and scientific paths to success, sacrificing regular salaries and predictable schedules, the notion that they could be hired to deploy the skills they'd acquired in their life's work was not just exciting, but a chance to offer what few others could to save the world's most underexplored places. "I want to do this for the rest of my life," Ted claimed.

The team was also clear about what it would not take on: RAP expeditions would not deliver thorough inventories, nor develop extensive collections. "This is not necessarily science; this is conservation," was a theme they agreed on. Certain taxonomic groups were excluded from their initial plans: Butterflies were seen as too seasonal to provide a good index of richness and diversity; frogs could best be assessed during rainy seasons, but intense rains would limit the freedom to cover large areas on foot. Economics and threats assessments would be left to others. Training of nationals, seen as a critical need, was debated as perhaps too time consuming for the team to take on. Political follow-through on RAP recommendations for creation of reserves would fall to others in conservation planning.

The latter, however, was subsequently tested when the irrepressible Ted leaped at the opportunity to meet with Bolivia's vice president after a series of RAP trips. Ted's conservation colleagues cringed as protocol and diplomacy faded as his face turned deep red, his voice rose, and his passion drove an urgent plea for the government to understand the value of the places the team had explored. His message hit its mark: "It is because of people like you that your country is great," the vice president told him. Many of those areas have indeed received protection.

A sense of urgency and RAP's potential were evident during this first planning meeting. The energy and excitement felt in the room during that 2-day session caught fire, attracted worldwide attention, and led to conservation victories around the world. RAP has evolved over time, and gone far beyond the experts-based approach that launched it. But the legacy of these four uncompromising pioneers is rich and long-term. And the game, though far from over, was changed forever.

- Brent Bailey, Director, Appalachia Program, The Mountain Institute

History and Overview of MarineRAP

Sheila A. McKenna

Introduction

Covering more than 70% of our planet, the oceans are our earth's life support system and hold an amazing amount of biodiversity including vast numbers of undescribed species. Although less explored than land and freshwater, the marine realm is known to hold more phyla and classes than land or freshwater environments. Similar to their land and freshwater counterparts, marine ecosystems suffer assaults directly and indirectly from human activities such as resource extraction, exploitation, pollution, ocean acidification (carbon dioxide released into the atmosphere is absorbed by the ocean making it more acidic), physical alterations to habitat and introduction of invasive species. Unfortunately, areas set aside in our oceans for regulated use and protection (called Marine Protected Areas) lag far behind the number and size of regulated use and protected areas on our lands.

Our overall exceedingly poor treatment of the oceans may lead some to think our oceans must not be that important or the vastness of the ocean cushions any harmful effects from human activities. Nothing could be further from the truth as our oceans are critical to life, regulating our climate and weather, providing the air we breathe and the water we drink. The oceans are a source of food and in some regions provide the sole source of protein for people. To top it off, the oceans also are aesthetically pleasing and provide an amazing playground for several activities such as surfing, swimming, scuba diving, sailing, and snorkeling. There is no doubt our behavior has a significantly negative effect on the ocean as evidenced by the Deepwater Horizon oil well blowout (2010), the increasing frequency and intensity of dead zones along our coasts (areas of the ocean where there is too little oxygen for life to live), large swirling garbage patches and the alarming worldwide dwindling population numbers of several marine species such as corals, sharks, turtles, fish and whales. In fact a study released in 2008 in the peer-reviewed journal, Science indicates that no area of the ocean is free from the impacts of humans (Halpern et al. 2008). The good news is that, as on land or in freshwater, we can take action to reverse the decline of our ocean's health and conserve biodiversity.

Connectivity between all three realms, marine, terrestrial and freshwater, renders mitigation activities on one to the benefit of the other two as well. For example, ensuring a healthy watershed with good land use practices such as keeping the native vegetation intact can prevent sediment being brought through freshwater rivers and streams to the coastal marine environment.

Effective science-based conservation requires detailed regional and place-specific descriptions and analyses of biodiversity, ecology, and socioeconomics. Recognizing the successes of terrestrial and freshwater RAP surveys with the urgent need to improve our knowledge of species and mitigate threats to the marine environment, the RAP concept was first applied to the marine realm in 1994 in Rennell Island and the Indispensable Reefs, Solomon Islands. The focus marine habitat chosen was coral reefs based on their incredible biodiversity, the ever increasing amount of threats to them, and their vital function in supporting people's survival and livelihoods. Moreover many regions of the world with coral reefs have either not been explored or have not had their reefs surveyed for biodiversity and health or state. Moreover, coral reefs have been labeled the "canary in the coal mine" – the first ecosystem humans will see the demise of due to global warming. More immediate assaults from humans such as resource extraction, poor land use practices and pollution makes this scenario even more likely. Alternatively, halting these threats makes it possible that some coral reefs can adapt and survive climate change, and be saved for future generations.

Overview

The main objectives for the MarineRAP surveys are to fill in data gaps on marine species biodiversity in coral reef areas where data is lacking or the area is under threat. The surveys provide data on select species (fish, coral and mollusks), state of the reef (e.g., incidence of disease, bleaching, and physical damage) and make recommendations to conserve the biodiversity and habitat. The RAP team members consist of international and national scientists who spend approximately two to three weeks in the field collecting and compiling the data. The surveys usually lead to the discovery of new species and range extensions of known species. The surveys also provide exchange between national and international scientists. Technical capacity building is achieved by having local scientists and students take part in the surveys. A socioeconomic component that includes education and outreach is conducted in parallel with the scientific survey to determine the concerns and perceptions of the local communities on their marine environment.

Approximately three weeks following the completion of the fieldwork, information gathered during the survey is compiled and distributed first in a preliminary report. Results from the RAP surveys are presented back to the local communities through brochures, meetings and or workshops in the local languages. A full scientific report (in the *RAP Bulletin of Biological Assessment*) of the findings is then published for wide distribution, usually in both English and at least one local language. These publications include full species lists as well as a range of conservation recommendations. The end users include scientists, managers, government officials, local and international non-governmental conservation/environmental agencies, policy makers and all local stakeholders. Many scientific peer reviewed publications also have resulted from the rapid assessment surveys. Findings from the surveys enable informed decision making, especially for the creation of Marine Protected

© Conservation International/photo by Sterling Zumbrunn

Areas and for implementation of other conservation "tools" (e.g., limitations on extraction). CI's field offices and members of the RAP survey team work together with government and local communities to implement activities to mitigate threats and conserve marine biodiversity and resources based on findings of the RAP survey in synthesis with other relevant factors such as culture.

History

In the beginning of the MarineRAP program, the main focus was on the coral reefs located in the "Coral Triangle", an area that occupies waters surrounding the countries of Australia, Japan, Indonesia, Papua New Guinea, and Philippines (Werner and Allen 1998). The first official MarineRAP survey took place in 1997 in Milne Bay, Papua New Guinea in collaboration with Milne Bay Provincial Government with the support of The Rufford Foundation and The Henry Foundation. As the diversity of coral reefs is too high to assess all species present, three focal groups were chosen as indicator taxa to be assessed by taxonomic experts. These included corals by JEN Vernon, mollusks by Fred Wells and reef and shore fishes by Gerry Allen. These three indicator focal groups were chosen for several reasons. Corals as architectural species provide the structural foundation or basis for the habitat. Fishes as a group are the most conspicuous and are important contributors to the overall biomass of the reef. Mollusks have an extremely high level of species diversity, are ecologically and commercially important, and are well studied taxonomically. In addition to documenting biodiversity for these three key indicator groups at each site, the team also made observations on the state or health of the habitat and noted the presence or absence of species targeted for local consumption or commercial sale. The fisheries and community outreach components were conducted respectively by David Tauna and Edward Kibikibi. The team was led by Tim Werner.

Prior to the next surveys, a MarineRAP priority-setting workshop was conducted in Townsville, Australia in 1998 with the taxonomic experts who participated in the 1997 Milne Bay MarineR-AP. Based on the knowledge of workshop participants, a priority list of approximately 10 areas needing surveys was produced. Four more rapid assessments followed with two in 1998 and two in 2000. Three of the four MarineRAP surveys were carried out in the Coral Triangle and included the Calamian Islands, Northern Palawan Province, Philippines (1998); Togean and Banggai Islands, Indonesia (1998) and a second survey in Milne Bay Province, Papua New Guinea (2000). Outside the Coral Triangle, a MarineRAP survey was conducted in Abrolhos Bank, Bahia, Brazil (2000). Generous support for these surveys came from the Gordon and Betty Moore Foundation, The Henry Foundation, The Rufford Foundation, and the Smart Family Foundation, as well as the Japan Bank for International Cooperation. Abrolhos Bank was chosen due to its high level of endemism for coral and reef fishes with increasing threats due to coastal deforestation and over-exploitation of marine resources. Select findings from these past surveys in Indonesia, Philippines, Papua New Guinea and Brazil comprised a special CI MarineRAP sponsored mini-symposium entitled "Coral Reef Biodiversity: Assessment and Conservation" at the Ninth International Coral Reef Symposium in Bali (McKenna and Allen 2002).

Using CI's Biodiversity Hotspot approach, an analysis of existing species distribution maps of select coral reef species (lobsters, snails, coral and reef fish) was begun in 2000 and conducted in collaboration with the main MarineRAP team consisting of Gerry Allen, Charlie Veron, Fred Wells and Tim Werner. Findings from this multi-authored study led by Callum Roberts were published in *Science* (Roberts et al. 2002). This analysis has generated much useful and continuing debate on the use of biodiversity, endemism and level of threat to set conservation priorities in the marine realm (Allen 2007).

A MarineRAP survey was conducted on the coral reefs of Raja Ampat Islands, Indonesia (2001). This area was identified as the number one survey priority in Southeast Asia at CI's MarineRAP Workshop owing to its array of habitats and location near the 'heart' of the Coral Triangle. Even before the survey, the area was surmised to be the world's richest in terms of marine biodiversity. Findings from this survey confirmed that the area supports some of the richest coral reefs in the entire Indonesian Archipelago.

Following the Raja Ampat survey, MarineRAP's methodology was slightly revised with the objectives and research focus expanded based on a review of literature in marine conservation and in consultation with colleagues in the field as well as local stakeholders. Revision of the methodology was to ensure statistical robustness and compatibility with other available global, regional and local marine data sets. The objectives were expanded to include additional data on commercially important species and to provide more data for management especially for the creation of Marine Protected Areas (MPAs). To that end, the focus and methods used for the MarineRAP surveys are tailored to meet the needs of the specific area. Further the application of the data was extended. The information obtained during the MarineRAP is analyzed, synthesized and geospatially mapped with other relevant and available data to: a) pinpoint key sites and issues within the region for imple-

Table 1. Summary of MarineRAP Rapid Assessment Surveys

Year	Country	Site
1994	Solomon Islands	Rennell Island and the Indispensable Reefs
1997	Papua New Guinea	Milne Bay Province I
1998	Philippines	Calamianes Islands, Palawan Province
1998	Indonesia	Togean and Banggai Islands
2000	Papua New Guinea	Milne Bay Province II
2000	Brazil	Abrolhos Bank, Bahia
2001	Indonesia	Raja Ampat Islands, Bird's Head Seascape
2002	Madagascar	Coral Reefs of the Northwest
2004	New Caledonia	Mont Panié Lagoon
2006	Caribbean Netherlands	Saba Bank
2006	Madagascar	Coral Reefs of the Northeast I
2006	Indonesia	Teluk Cenderawasih National Park, Bird's Head Seascape
2006	Indonesia	Fakfak-Kaimana Coastline, Bird's Head Seascape
2007	New Caledonia	Northwest lagoon (Yandé to Koumac)
2009	New Caledonia	Northeast lagoon (Touho to Ponérihouen)
2010	Madagascar	Coral Reefs of the Northeast II

menting realistic mechanisms/activities to conserve marine biodiversity (e.g., establishing locally managed marine areas) and for mitigating threats to biodiversity (e.g., curtailing blast fishing); b) identify data gaps and topics for further study (e.g., stock assessments); c) implement further surveys, activities and studies needed for identified species and regions (e.g., survey of large clam populations, contribute data to Global Marine Species Assessment and IUCN red list data) and d) address key conservation questions regarding biodiversity and the design of Marine Protected Areas.

Examples of questions for the last objective include: What is the effect of area and sampling on the documented biodiversity of coral, fish and mollusk species? How can the best MPA that captures the most diversity in the least amount of time and money given increasing threats be designed? Can surrogates or indicator species be used in conservation planning in site selections of MPAs (Beger et al 2007)?

Recognizing the global need to increase Marine Protected Areas, the geographic area of focus for MarineRAP surveys was extended to more areas outside the coral triangle. These included coral reefs off the northeast coast of Madagascar (November 2002) and off the northwest coast of New Caledonia (Mont Panié Lagoon, December 2004). In 2006, four MarineRAP surveys were conducted with two in the waters of the Coral Triangle off West Papua, Indonesia

(Teluk-Cenderawasih National Park and Fakfak-Kaimana Coastline). Outside the coral triangle, the first MarineRAP survey took place in the Caribbean on Saba Bank off the island of Saba in the Caribbean Netherlands. Results from the MarineRAP survey at Saba Bank comprised a special volume of the scientific journal, Proceedings of the Library of Science One (PLoS ONE) published in May 2010. Finally, a second survey took place in Madagascar, this time off the northeast coast from Cap d'Ambre to Baie du Loky (2006).

Following on from the successful Mont Panié Lagoon MarineRAP and the inscription of the tropical lagoons and coral reefs of New Caledonia as a UNESCO World Heritage Site, two more MarineRAP surveys took place in Province Nord of New Caledonia. These included coral reef sites along the northwest coast from Yandé to Koumac (2007) and along the northeast coast from Touho to Ponérihouen (2009).

Recognizing the importance of identifying coral reef areas for protection that appear less prone or more resilient to climate change, an additional MarineRAP survey was conducted off the northeast coast of Madagascar in 2010. This was to further assess areas such as Ambodivahibe Bay where the first survey in 2006 had discovered areas that appeared to have little or no stress and were extremely healthy with no evidence of disease or past bleaching events.

MarineRAP surveys have a high conservation impact. Surveys usually lead to discoveries of species previously unknown to science or range extensions for particular species. As of 2010, over 100 new species of coral, mollusk and fish have been documented. MarineRAP has contributed to the creation of eight new Marine Protected Areas and Locally Managed Marine Areas (e.g., Brazil, Saba Bank, New Caledonia, Indonesia and Madagascar) and to the halting of potentially destructive development and over-fishing in fragile areas. The program has trained over 55 nationals and increased technical capacity and conservation awareness in many regions. Education and awareness about the importance of marine biodiversity and resource use is also raised as a result of MarineRAP surveys. Further, national and international attention has been brought to these regions resulting in an increase in resources and activities to conserve species and their habitats.

References

Allen G.R. 2007. Conservation hotspots of biodiversity and endemism for Indo-Pacific coral reef fishes. Aquatic Conservation: Marine and Freshwater Ecosystems 18:541-556.

Beger M., S.A. McKenna and H.P. Possingham. 2007. Effectiveness of surrogate taxa in the design of coral reef reserve systems in the Indo-Pacific. Conservation Biology 21(6):1584-1593.

Halpern B. S., S. Walbridge, K.A. Selkoe, C.V. Kappel, F. Micheli, C. D'Agrosa, J.F Bruno, K.S. Casey, C. Ebert, H.E. Fox, R. Fujita, D. Heinemann, H.S. Lenihan, E.M.P. Madin, M.T. Perry, E.R. Selig, M. Spalding, R. Steneck and R.A. Watson. 2008. Global map of human impact on marine ecosystems. Science 319:.948 - 952.

McKenna S.A. and G.R. Allen. 2002. Coral Reef Biodiversity Assessment and Conservation. Pp 92-94 in Best B.A., P.S. Pomeroy and C.M. Balboa (eds). Implications for Coral Reef Management and Policy: Relevant findings from the Ninth International Coral Reef Symposium.

Roberts C.M., C.J. McClean, JEN Vernon, J.P. Hawkins, G.R. Allen, D.E. McAllister, C.G. Mittermeier, F.W. Schueler, M. Spalding, F. Wells, C. Vynne and T. Werner. 2002. Marine biodiversity hotspots and conservation priorities for tropical reefs. Science 295: 1280–1284.

Werner T.B. and G.R. Allen (eds). 1998. A rapid biodiversity assessment of the coral reefs of Milne Bay Province, Papua New Guinea. RAP Bulletin of Biological Assessment 11. Conservation International. Washington, DC, USA.

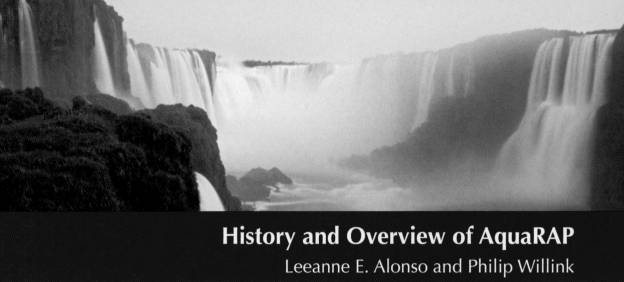

© Piotr Naskrecki

History and Overview of AquaRAP
Leeanne E. Alonso and Philip Willink

Importance of Freshwater Biodiversity Conservation

The effectiveness of RAP to provide data for conservation in terrestrial ecosystems led CI to expand the RAP approach to the freshwater realm in 1996. Again, RAP proved to be at the forefront with a novel conservation approach. For almost a decade, the AquaRAP program was the primary - and at some times the only - initiative at CI specifically addressing freshwater conservation. Freshwater conservation has fortunately become a high priority at CI and other NGOs, for many good reasons.

The streams, lakes and wetlands that comprise the world's freshwater ecosystems contain a concentration of species that is far out of proportion to their area. While the world's inland waters add up to only 0.3% of its surface area (104,590 km^2), they contain, for example, 41% of the world's fish species. Humans depend directly on clean fresh water for drinking, food, energy, industry, recreation and transportation. We also depend indirectly on fresh water for the role it plays in driving the ecological processes that support all the terrestrial systems on earth, such as forests, wetlands, grasslands, and agricultural lands, and in maintaining them resilient to change.

Unfortunately, freshwater not only constitutes the richest biome, but also the most highly threatened. More than 50% of the world's wetlands have been destroyed since 1900 and at least 20% of the world's freshwater fishes, some 2,500 species, are estimated to have become extinct or imperiled in historical time. The urgency for conservation of aquatic biodiversity and fisheries is escalating. Demands through channelization, development and damming are threatening watersheds without regard for the dynamics of aquatic ecosystems or the complexities of the life histories of aquatic organisms. Food demands also are increasing.

Another factor that complicates the conservation of freshwater systems is that they tend to be multinational resources. The great Amazon River basin, for example, borders on, or flows through, eight countries. Where not multinational, aquatic resources are usually multipolitical within a country. This multinational character challenges conservation efforts for many reasons, including: cooperation, funding, investment potential of all partners, external sources of pollution, and over-fishing. To succeed, conservation efforts for aquatic ecosystems must have a strong multinational and collaborative component, and they must adopt proper units of conservation.

Advent of AquaRAP

With funding from the W. Alton Jones Foundation in 1996, the AquaRAP program began as a joint collaboration between CI and The Field Museum with a focus on watersheds in South America. A steering committee was formed of 14 scientists from six South American countries and the US, with Dr. Barry Chernoff (The Field Museum) as the committee lead, to guide development of the AquaRAP program. The steering committee's role was one of coordination, continued program development, training and fund raising. The steering committee developed the protocol AquaRAP surveys, and the parameters for selecting priority sites for conservation action based on the AquaRAP data. The scientists represented a variety of disciplines, including ichthyology, botany, entomology, macro-invertebrate zoology, limnology and genetics. The AquaRAP protocols were tested and revised during the first AquaRAP expedition in the Río Orthon Basin of Bolivia in 1996.

In 1997, a large grant was obtained from the Rufford Foundation for an ambitious program of AquaRAP surveys in 10 South American watersheds. The AquaRAP Steering Committee identified ten basin-projects of global priority across South America to meet immediate conservation needs. In selecting these basins, the committee also focused on gathering critical information from around the continent, and from many different types of watersheds (Table 1).

Prior to the initiation of the AquaRAP program, CI had already been including freshwater biodiversity assessment as part of terrestrial RAP surveys in New Guinea, with Dr. Gerry Allen surveying freshwater fishes and Dr. Dan Polhemus surveying freshwater Odonata (damselflies and dragonflies) and other aquatic insects. Their surveys were usually in small mountain streams and did not strategically target an

Table 1. AquaRAP surveys 1990-2010		
Year	Country	Site
1996	Bolivia	Upper Río Orthon Basin, Pando
1997	Paraguay	Río Paraguay Basin, Alto Paraguay
1998	Brazil	Pantanal, Mato Grosso do Sul
1999	Ecuador/Peru	Río Pastaza Basin
1999	Guatemala	Laguna del Tigre National Park
2000	Botswana	Okavango Delta I – High Water Survey
2000	Venezuela	Río Caura Basin
2002-03	Venezuela	Orinoco Delta and the Gulf of Paria
2003	Venezuela	Río Ventuari
2003	Botswana	Okavango Delta II – Low Water Survey
2004	Suriname	Coppename River Basin
2005	Venezuela	Upper Río Paragua Basin
2008	Venezuela	Upper Río Cuyuní Basin

© Piotr Naskrecki

entire watershed as was envisioned for the AquaRAP program. The RAP program continues to conduct surveys that include both terrestrial and freshwater taxa as needed to meet the objectives of the survey.

Given the importance of watershed biodiversity and protection, the need for AquaRAP surveys in other parts of the world quickly arose. Two AquaRAP surveys were undertaken in the Okavango Delta, Botswana, bringing together a new team of aquatic biodiversity experts from across Africa to form a high impact and insightful scientific team (see page 189). CI's program in Venezuela teamed up with the Fundacion La Salle to conduct a series of successful AquaRAP surveys throughout the Guiana Shield in Venezuela (see page 256). The AquaRAP program has benefited greatly from loyal support from the Leon and Toby Cooperman Family Foundation.

AquaRAP Approach

Similar to its terrestrial counterpart, on which it is based, AquaRAP provides a first-cut assessment of the biological value, conservation priority, and opportunities of the basin surveyed. The attempt is to focus not on a comprehensive collection, or even a comprehensive inventory, but on uncovering the maximum amount of conservation-related information – e.g., biodiversity, uniqueness, unusual records – in the minimum amount of time. During an AquaRAP survey, interdisciplinary teams of expert scientists and advanced students rapidly survey the diversity of habitats in the regions of interest. AquaRAP scientists work in an integrated fashion, allowing for instant feedback and sharing of information. These daily interactions make AquaRAP highly efficient, and different from serial surveys, where information is not shared or combined into an integrated overview.

AquaRAP teams typically include scientists from international and local institutions who are experts on the taxonomy of aquatic plants, fishes, aquatic invertebrates (mollusks, crustaceans and insects), and plankton. Specialists in water quality are also a key part of the team to provide data on the relevant physical parameters (e.g., dissolved oxygen, turbidity, flow, nutrient levels) to help explain patterns in the species data.

The overarching goal of AquaRAP is to assess the biological and conservation value of a watershed based on: a) the heterogeneity of the habitats, b) a preliminary survey of the organisms that characterize each of these habitats, and c) the overall intactness of the habitats, and their capacity to support important biological resources and ecological processes. Field collections are made to identify the organisms, but the collections are minimized. Specimens are identified to the most appropriate taxonomic level (genus or species) to get at a first-cut assessment of diversity and species composition. Environmentally destructive sampling methods such as poisons are not used. Specimens are shared among museum collections throughout North and South America, as well as Africa and Australia, as relevant to the taxonomic group.

Key components of AquaRAP are to build the scientific capacity of local students and scientists in the field, to stimulate international cooperation among scientists and institutions, and to contribute to the infrastructure of participating institutions. The results of AquaRAP are published about a year after the field study and disseminated in a variety of ways, including the *RAP Bulletin of Biological Assessment*, CI web pages, RAP database (rap.conservation.org), papers in scientific journals, field guides, etc. (see references list).

The main objectives of the AquaRAP program are to:

1. Increase the priority given to conservation of freshwater systems, raising the profile of freshwater conservation to that of terrestrial conservation.
2. Serve as a catalyst for multinational, multidisciplinary, collaborative research on freshwater systems over a larger time frame.
3. Serve as a catalyst for multinational basin level conservation projects. This includes serving as a vehicle to attract other groups of scientists, conservationists and policy makers.
4. Increase the training of students in the aquatic sciences and conservation sciences in many countries.
5. Provide substantial support for the collection infrastructures of the participating institutions.
6. Highlight the role and importance of systematic research and systematics collections for conservation.

© Piotr Naskrecki

7. Generate a body of reliable data about the selected watersheds. This body of information will serve as a basis for future conservation projects, such as priority setting within basins. The data also will help AquaRAP improve on a system for surveying freshwater ecosystems in the most rapid, cost-effective manner to obtain useful, first-cut characterizations of the watersheds that will help design aquatic conservation and management strategies
8. Provide a better definition of the critical boundaries of watersheds

Watersheds as Natural Units

A distinct feature of the AquaRAP program is its focus on the entire watershed or basin. Aquatic ecosystems are dynamic, with a high diversity of geological, physical and chemical processes, and of animals and plants with complex life histories. Basins and watersheds are the units that organisms use during their life cycles. For example, some large catfishes are born in the foothills of the Andes, the young drift thousands of miles downstream to the Amazon's delta where they grow to maturity, then years later the adults migrate to the foothills of the Andes to spawn. AquaRAP includes the terrestrial environment up to the level of the 50-year flood to encompass the critical linkages between riparian forests and the aquatic environments. Flooding cycles are critical to create the nurseries for juvenile fishes, and many species of plants fruit during periods of inundation, relying on fishes not only for dispersal but also for proper seed germination (e.g., rubber tree seeds must pass through the stomachs of fishes to germinate). AquaRAP's basin concept and protocols for rapid assessments facilitate the development of management plans that allow a variety of sustainable uses for aquatic systems, while protecting the maximum biodiversity possible.

AquaRAP Criteria

The AquaRAP Steering Committee developed thirteen criteria to select a site for AquaRAP and to evaluate the site's priority for conservation (or restoration) action. These criteria were grouped into three hierarchical levels of importance. AquaRAP scientists study the biological, physical and when possible the anthropological aspects of watersheds, to categorize the level (high, medium or low) for each of the 13 criteria listed below.

Primary Criteria

Habitat heterogeneity – the number and types of habitats (e.g., lakes, riffles, rapids, vársea, etc.) found within the area. This factor is a critical predictor of species and genetic diversity that may be found in the region.

Habitat uniqueness – an estimate of the degree of uniqueness of a particular habitat within both the basin and the entire continent or world. For example, the deep channel of the Amazon River, the Chaco, or the llanos of Venezuela-Colombia are unique habitats at the global level.

Level of current threat – an estimate of the number, types and permanence of the threats that currently or potentially affect the biological or physical integrity of the basin. For example, dams, impoundments, pollution from roads, farms or refineries, impending housing development, channelization, etc. It is important to identify the nature and long term status of the threat. For example, if refinery pollution were abated, would the system cleanse itself and within what time frame?

Conservation potential and opportunity – the biological opportunities for significant conservation action in the region, within the political, social and geographic framework. For example, if the majority of endemic organisms in a region are still intact, and the surrounding human population is low, the region may offer a significant opportunity for protected reserve status, even though the current level of threat to the region may be relatively low.

Degree of fragility – the resilience or fragility of an aquatic ecosystem to human disturbance. Highly fragile systems (e.g., springs, morichales or aguajales) are of high priority for protection status; they may not be able to respond to restoration or maintenance programs depending on surrounding conditions.

Other biological significance (ecological processes) – the critical roles some habitats play in ecological processes that affect species outside the aquatic community. For example, the extremely productive low llanos are key resources for migratory birds. Areas within watersheds (e.g., floodplains) where contaminants are removed from the water play a critical cleansing role. These important processes must be considered in evaluating the region's priority for conservation action.

© Piotr Naskrecki

Secondary Criteria

Endemism – the proportion of organisms restricted to the region. Endemism often is used as the primary determinant of conservation priority. We argue, however, that percent endemism does not supersede the above criteria because the overall conservation value of aquatic ecosystems depends on the habitat, the species, and their uniqueness in relation to global or regional measures of biodiversity. Estimates of endemism also require a continental-wide perspective and standardization of nomenclature, which are currently not available for many aquatic organisms (published lists are not guaranteed to be accurate). Nonetheless, habitats with identified or estimated high degree of endemism rank highly.

Productivity – the productivity of the aquatic system for human consumption and for other wildlife (e.g., wetlands for birds).

Richness – the number of species in the aquatic region. The absolute measure of biodiversity often is considered an indicator of the importance or health of the ecosystem. However, many unique, highly important aquatic systems have relatively low biodiversity (e.g., Lake Titicaca, Lago Chapala). Although we consider richness to be an important measure, we do not rank it above uniqueness (endemism) or productivity. In this measure we also include an estimate of the actual or potential contribution to genetic diversity. For example, the potential for unique genetic composition, and eventual speciation, increases in habitats found in a series of tributaries with reduced "communication" among them.

Human significance – the economic and cultural values of the aquatic system for humans. Of particular importance are the areas and species used by indigenous peoples. Fisheries and recreational use also must be factored into management plans. This category provides both limitations and opportunities for conservation.

Degree of intactness – the extent to which the region is free of human disturbance. The conservation value of the ecosystems will vary directly with its degree of intactness. This should include, if possible, an estimate for the habitats critical for various life history stages of the aquatic organisms.

Tertiary Criteria

Ability to generalize – the ability to generalize from studies of particular habitats. This does not override the importance of unique habitats without analog.

Degree of knowledge – how unknown a particular system is.

Highlights of AquaRAP Results

During RAP's first 20 years, 13 AquaRAP surveys were conducted that focused primarily on the aquatic ecosystem and covered the entire watershed (Table 1). Several other RAP surveys were primarily terrestrial surveys but also included aquatic taxa (see Terrestrial RAP section).

The data compiled during AquaRAP surveys in Latin America (Table 2) reveal a wealth of biodiversity that, except for the plants, was unanticipated. From just the first six watersheds surveyed by AquaRAP (Pando, Paraguay, Pantanal, Pastaza, and Caura), more than 1,700 species of plants and 1,300 species of fishes were identified. The number of new records and new species encountered was impressive (Table 2). This is especially true for fishes and for decapods (given their low overall diversity). Even in a well-studied region such as the Pantanal, AquaRAP increased the known ichthyofauna by more than 30%, and collected 36 species new to science. Additional species continued to be collected every day and at each site during most AquaRAP surveys, resulting in species accumulation curves that did not plateau, which indicates that many more species remain to be found in those areas. Overall AquaRAP identified 238 new basin and country records for fishes in addition to 105 species new to science that have been identified conservatively – these data represent more than 26% of all the fishes collected. Furthermore, the number of records for

Table 2. Species Richness recorded during AquaRAP surveys in Latin America			
Taxon/Site	# Documented (species unless indicated)	New records	Species new to science
Plants			
Caura	303		
Pantanal	>600	3	
Paraguay	385	1	
Pastaza	>300		
San Pedro	130		
Phytoplankton			
Pastaza	31		
San Pedro	71		
Zooplankton			
Orthon	120		
Pastaza	20		
Benthos, incl. insects			
Caura	58 taxa		
Orthon	36 taxa		
Pantanal	70 taxa		
Paraguay	121 sp. + 10 orders		possibly many
Pastaza	12 taxa		
San Pedro	44		
Decapods			
Caura	10	2	1
Orthon	10	6	
Pantanal	10	2	2
Paraguay	13	1	1
Pastaza	10		
Fishes			
Caura	273	113	10
Orthon	313	87	14
Pantanal	193	3	36
Paraguay	173	5	2
Pastaza	312	50	43
San Pedro	41		

© Piotr Naskrecki

planktonic and benthic organisms are underestimates of the number of species, new records and new species. There just are not many taxonomists working on these groups – the specialists often identify these elements to higher taxa only (genera and above), which highlights a need to develop taxonomic expertise for these groups. AquaRAP results also highlight the urgent need for continued inventories of watersheds in Latin America and around the world.

The Structure of Biodiversity Within Watersheds

The classic literature on Neotropical aquatic communities, other than plants, indicates that watersheds are not highly structured beyond the numbers of species that may occur along elevational gradients. This generalization is particularly true for the Neotropical lowlands (< 250 meters above sea level). These notions, whether true or false, would be critical for conservation plans. With this in mind AquaRAP scientists developed a new, innovative methodology for investigating the potential structure and integration of biodiversity within watersheds among subregions and among macrohabitats. The methodology is based upon the realization that data from all rapid assessments represents point source data. That is, snapshots of the biodiversity. As such, the data are formally the same as those in paleontology, where the fossil record provides "instantaneous" snapshots and the record is largely incomplete. Thus, it becomes critical when comparing samples of taxa from different regions or different macrohabitats to test the observed similarity against the expectations of randomness (i.e., given any two collections with so many species, how much similarity should we expect just due to random movements, etc.) If we reject the null hypothesis that similarity is due to randomness then two possibilities result: 1) that the samples are biologically correlated or dependent upon one another; or 2) that a turnover or displacement of taxa is evident. The methodology includes a modified entropy analysis, rarefaction, bootstrapping, network and eigenanalysis described in detail in each of the AquaRAP volumes. These are robust and conservative procedures and are applicable to all rapid assessment data as well as for community ecology studies in general. This methodology was published in scientific journals, increasing AquaRAP's profile in the scientific community (Chernoff et al. 2004a and b).

What the AquaRAP teams determined in each of the watersheds (except for the San Pedro in Guatemala) is that the fish, invertebrate and plant communities are structured and are not random (Chernoff et al. 2004b). There are significant patterns for subregions and for macrohabitats within the basins. The patterns demonstrate well the effects of flood zones on the structure of aquatic communities. Thus, environmental alterations that would reduce or impact the natural flood cycle have a predicted impact on the loss of species. This is only one example of many that appear in the AquaRAP volumes demonstrating that conservation plans must use this type of information in order to effectively conserve biodiversity.

Furthermore, AquaRAP surveys were the first published studies in tropical ecosystems that have investigated how different groups of taxa are correlated with each other across regions and macro-habitats. For example in the Río Paraguay the AquaRAP team discovered that the pattern of species turnover among subregions of the Río Paraguay basin are almost identical for macroinvertebrates and for fishes. In the Pantanal they found that there is a strong faunal and floral transition above 200 m but that plants were less rich in the lowlands, while fishes and invertebrates were less species rich in the highlands. A similar pattern was found in the Caura River of Venezuela.

The AquaRAP teams collected scientific evidence to demonstrate how the health and diversity of riparian vegetation and forests affect fish communities: when flooded vegetation is present then the fishes are more abundant; however when riparian forest is present and healthy the number of species of fishes is significantly higher as well as their abundances. In other words, terrestrial and aquatic ecosystems are interconnected. It is unwise to examine just one or the other. We need to look at both in order to understand the big picture and conserve the biodiversity of an entire region.

Raising the Priority of Freshwater Conservation to that of Terrestrial Conservation

AquaRAP has significantly elevated the international profile of aquatic conservation and the plight of rivers with the general public, political audiences as well as conservation organizations. The large scale and scope of AquaRAP, as well as its conservation impacts, have drawn significant atten-

© Piotr Naskrecki

tion from the global conservation community. AquaRAP was identified and recognized as the premier approach to assessing freshwater biodiversity by the Secretariat of the U.N. Convention on Biological Diversity (CBD), Division for Scientific, Technical and Technological Matters (SBSTTA), a United Nations sponsored initiative addressing global biodiversity conservation issues. In 2001, the Programme on Inland Waters of the Secratariat for CBD asked the AquaRAP program to aid them in developing a protocol for the rapid assessment of inland waters. This protocol was developed along with a committee of international aquatic scientists and approved at the 8th SBSTTA meeting of the CBD in 2003.

AquaRAP is officially part of the methodologies sanctioned by the massive BIOTA Sao Paulo Program (FAPESP) in Sao Paulo State, Brasil. AquaRAP was acknowledged by the U.S. National Committee for the International Union of Biological Sciences to contribute to the International Diversitas efforts. Subsequently, Diversitas International included freshwater ecosystems as a STAR program, which thus far has led to major initiatives to study the biodiversity and conservation of ancient lakes. AquaRAP has served as a catalyst and has played a major role in bringing freshwater conservation issues to the forefront through publicity, publications, scientific and public presentations and lobbying. Despite these gains there is a long way still to go to reach parity with terrestrial conservation efforts.

Capacity Building and Strengthening International Collaborations

AquaRAP expeditions included more than 100 different scientists and students from over 30 institutions from Bolivia, Brazil, Botswana, Ecuador, Guatemala, Guyana, Mexico, Paraguay, Peru, Suriname, United States and Venezuela. Of the scientists and students who have learned the AquaRAP methodology and philosophy, a number have implemented the main ideas in separate studies in their countries, including Brazil, Guatemala and Paraguay. There has been much follow-up scientific collaboration between AquaRAP scientists and students and continued training, with several students entering graduate school. Other scientists, both students and professionals, have used specimens collected during expeditions and deposited in museums as material for numerous research projects.

Conservation Impacts of AquaRAP

Conservation results, in terms of the creation or strengthening of protected areas such as parks, usually are achieved over a longer time frame than has elapsed since AquaRAP expeditions were carried out. However, several direct conservation impacts can already be attributed directly to the data collected by AquaRAP. A few of these include:

1. Three protected areas were created in the Pantanal: The Serro Bodequena National Park (70,000 hectares); The Upper Taquaria State Park (30,000 ha); and the Pantanal do Río Negro State Park, which encompasses the Santa Sofia swamp that was highly recommended for protection by AquaRAP (78,300 ha). These are some of the first aquatic parks anywhere in South America.
2. Following the AquaRAP, CI-Brazil received a major donation which allowed them to purchase the 7,700 ha Río Negro Farm in the heart of the Pantanal. This provides a corridor of aquatic protection within the Río Negro watershed of the southern Pantanal. CI has established a field station and ecotourist lodge on the site. Teams of volunteers from Earthwatch visited the station to work on conservation projects related to water quality, limnology, fish stock assessment, and river otters.

3. The AquaRAP report on the Río Orthon Basin provided critical information to inform the decision by the state government of the Pando, Bolivia, in establishing the Tahuamanu protected area within the basin.

4. The results of the Paraguay AquaRAP are being used by NGOs in Paraguay to fight against the Hidrovía project. Furthermore, Barry Chernoff has helped form a group that is studying the economics of the entire Paraguay River Basin (Pantanal and Paraguay River) to prevent the Hidrovía. The results were presented at a United Nations Sanctioned Workshop in April, 2001.

5. Scientists are working with a Venezuelan NGO to establish a resource identification training program for the peoples of Caura Basin. Part of the final AquaRAP report is being translated into Ye'kwana, the local language, so that the indigenous Kuyijani community, who participated in the Río Caura AquaRAP, can use the results directly in their conservation planning.

6. Due to the attention and public pressure brought about by the AquaRAP team's discovery of potential DNA damage in fishes found near operating oil wells in Laguna del Tigre National Park in Guatemala, the Supreme Court of Guatemala officially declared Concession 192, a large oil concession (192,233 ha, covering almost 79% of the park) as having been granted illegally (May 2000).

7. The results from the Pantanal, Pastaza, Paraguay and Caura AquaRAP surveys are being used by CI regional and country programs and partners to design and implement broad-scale conservation corridors in these areas.

8. The AquaRAP expedition to the Okavango Delta, Botswana catalyzed a process for resolving conflicts between local fishermen and sportfishermen in the Delta. AquaRAP scientists were invited to monitor the effects on aquatic diversity of pesticide spraying for tsetse flies that took place in 2001. The AquaRAP data are currently being used to support a proposal to nominate the Okavango Delta as a World Heritage Site.

Communicating AquaRAP Adventures and Results

Online AquaRAP expedition reports including background information on the biology, threats and other issues pertaining to the area were developed and posted on the CI website for six of the AquaRAP surveys (Paraguay, Pantanal, Pastaza, Caura, Okavango, and Guyana). The Río Paraguay AquaRAP (1997) debuted the AquaRAP program on the web with daily journal reports and real time communication with scientists to help species identification in the field. The AquaRAP trip to the Pantanal (1998) was produced in Portuguese and English to access collaborators and decision-makers locally and worldwide. AquaRAP online steadily evolved into a more educationally oriented program, addressing the dire lack of awareness of freshwater biodiversity issues throughout the educational system. The 1999 expeditions to the Río Pastaza in Ecuador and Perú employed a master's student as the internet correspondent, experimenting with these interactive reports in academia. When CI launched its Investigating Biodiversity (IB) website with Intel in 2000, the dynamic, on-the-ground aspects of AquaRAP teams in the field fit hand-in-glove with IB's educational perspective. The IB site carried internet broadcasts from the field for another three AquaRAP expeditions (Okavango Delta, Botswana - 2000; Caura River, Venezuela - 2000; Rewa River/Kanuku Mountains, Guyana - 2001). These field reports and their supporting articles, interviews with scientists, species profiles, and explanation of the scientific process can still be viewed at www.conservation.org.

Major articles covering AquaRAP expeditions appeared in local newspapers and magazines from each country as well as The Chicago Tribune, the Washington Post and Veija Magazine. Bill Kurtis filmed a television program on the Paraguay AquaRAP entitled "River in Peril" for the New Explorer's Series that aired on the A&E cable network. This film was subsequently shown in Paraguay. The South African Television program 50/50 accompanied the AquaRAP team in the Okavango Delta and aired a 15 minute segment on its program. MediaVision (Suriname) just recently produced an hour long documentary on the Central Suriname Natural Reserve and the AquaRAP survey of the Coppename River Basin entitled "Pristine Treasures."

Selected Publications from AquaRAP Surveys

Buhrnheim C.M. and L.R. Malabarba. 2006. Redescription of the type species of *Odontostilbe* Cope, 1870 (Teleostei: Characidae: Cheirodontinae), and description of three new species from the Amazon basin. Neotropical Ichthyology 4(2):167-196.

Chernoff B. 1998. Biodiversity and conservation of aquatic ecosystems: rapid assessment programs, establishing priorities and ethical considerations. Pp 1-7 in Castagnoli N. (ed). Symposium on Biodiversity and Conservation, S8.2, in Proceedings of the Pan American Veterinary Congress XV, Campo Grande, Brazil.

Chernoff B., A. Machado-Allison, and N. Menezes. 1997. La Conservacion de los Ambientes Acuaticos, una Necesidad Impostergable. Acta Biol. Venez. 16(2):1-3

Chernoff B., P.W. Willink and A. Machado-Allison. 2004a. Spatial partitioning of fishes in the Río Paraguay, Paraguay. Interciencia 29(4): 183-192.

Chernoff B., A. Machado-Allison, P. Willink, J. Sarmiento, S. Barrera, N. Menezes and H. Ortega. 2000. Fishes of three Bolivian rivers: diversity, distribution and conservation. Interciencia 25(6):273-283.

Chernoff B., A. Machado-Allison, F. Preovenzano, P. Willink and P. Petry. 2002. *Bryconops imitator,* a new species from the Río Caura Basin of Venezuela (Characiformes, Teleosteii). Ichthyol. Explor. Freshw. 13(4):259-268.

Chernoff B., P.W. Willink, A. Machado-Allison, M.F. Mereles, C. Magalhães, F.A.R. Barbosa and M. Callisto. 2004b. Distributional congruence among aquatic plants, invertebrates and fishes within the Río Paraguay Basin, Paraguay. Interciencia 29(4): 199-206.

de Santana C.D. 2003. *Apteronotus caudimaculosus* n.sp. (Gymnotiformes: Apteronotidae), a sexually dimorphic black ghost knifefish from the Pantanal, western Brazil, with a note on the monophyly of the *A. albifrons* species complex. Zootaxa 252:1-11.

Lee T., S. Siripattrawan, C.E. Ituarte and D.O. Foighil. 2005. Invasion of the clonal clams: *Corbicula* lineages in the New World. American Malacological Bulletin 20:113-122.

Machado-Allison A., B. Chernoff, R. Royero-Leon, F. Mago-Leccia, J. Velazquez, C. Lasso, H. Lopez-Rojas, A. Bonilla, F. Provenzano and C. Silvera. 2000. Ictiofauna de la cuenca del Río Cuyuní en Venezuela. Interciencia 25(1):13-21.

Machado-Allison A., J. Sarmiento, P. W. Willink, B. Chernoff, N. Menezes, H. Ortega, S. Barrera and T. Bert. 1999. Diversity and abundance of fishes and habitats in the Río Tahuamanu and Río Manuripi basins (Bolivia). Acta Biologica Venezuelica 19(1):17-50.

Provenzano R.F., A. Machado-Allison, B. Chernoff, P. Willink and P. Petry. 2005. *Harttia merevari,* a new species of catfish (Siluriformes: Loricariidae) from Venezuela. Neotropical Ichthyology 3(4):519-524.

Valdez-Moreno M.E., J. Pool-Canul and S. Contreras-Balderas. 2005. A checklist of the freshwater ichthyofauna from El Peten and Alta Verapaz, Guatemala, with notes for its conservation and management. Zootaxa 1072:43-60.

Willink P.W., J.H. Mol and B. Chernoff. 2010. A new species of suckermouth armored catfish *Pseudancistrus kwinti* (Siluriformes: Loricariidae) from the Coppename River drainage, Central Suriname Nature Reserve, Suriname. Zootaxa 2332:40-48.

Willink P. W., B. Chernoff, A. Machado-Allison, F. Provenzano and P. Petry. 2003. *Aphyocharax yekwanae,* a new species of bloodfin tetra (Teleostei: Characiformes: Characidae) from the Guyana Shield of Venezuela. Ichthyological Exploration of Freshwaters 14(1):1–8.

Map 1. Location map of RAP surveys conducted during 1990 – 2010

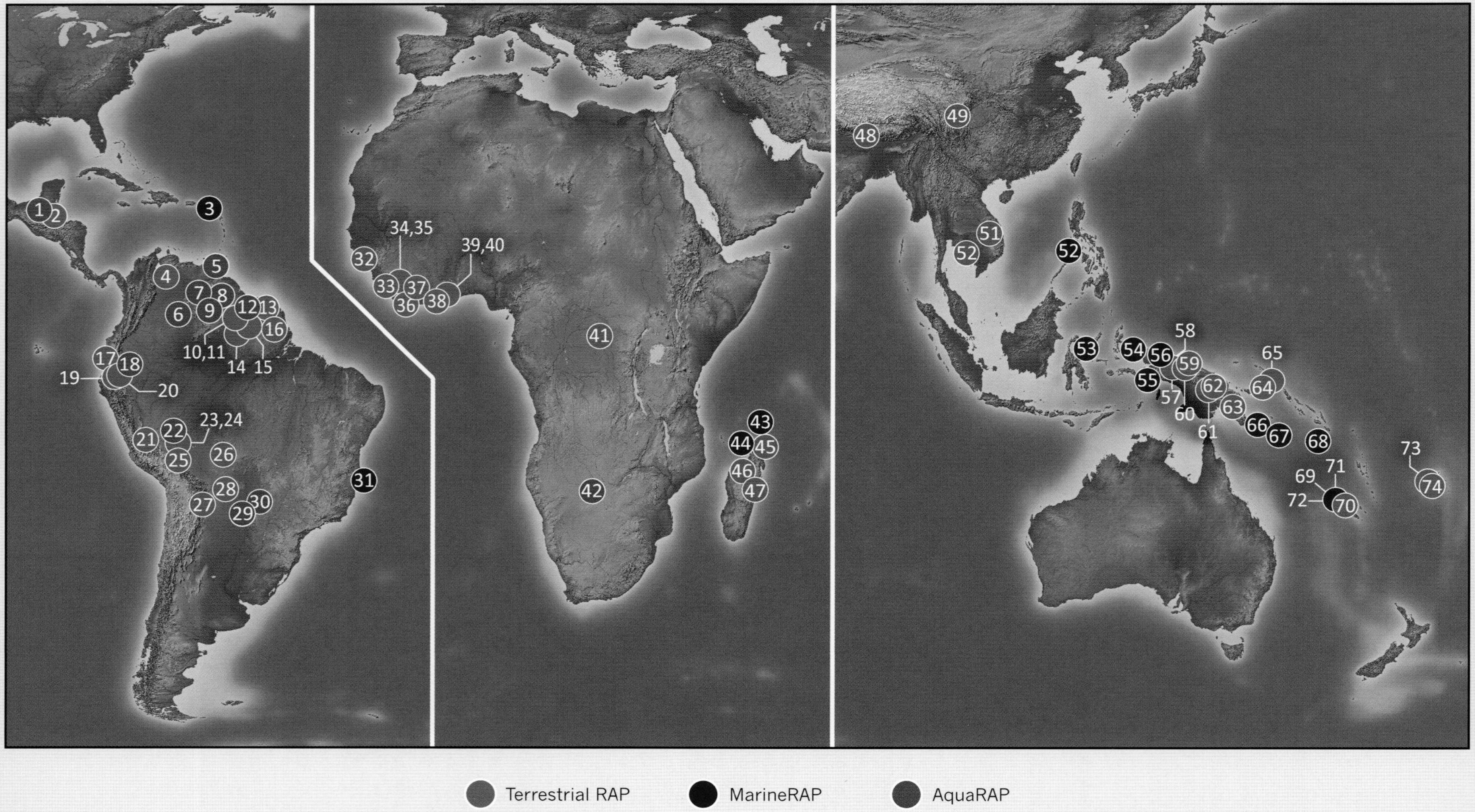

Legend:
- Terrestrial RAP
- MarineRAP
- AquaRAP

Central and South America

1. Laguna del Tigre National Park, Guatemala (1999)
2. Colombia River Forest Reserve, Belize (1992)
3. Saba Bank, Caribbean Netherlands (2006)
4. Ramal de Calderas, Venezuela (2008)
5. Orinoco Delta and the Gulf of Paria, Venezuela (2002-03)
6. Río Ventuari, Venezuela (2003)
7. Río Caura Basin, Venezuela (2000)
8. Upper Río Cuyuní, Venezuela (2008)
9. Río Paragua Basin, Venezuela (2005)
10. Western Kanuku Mountains, Guyana (1993)
11. Eastern Kanuku Mountains, Guyana (2001)
12. Coppename River Basin, Suriname (2004)
13. Lely and Nassau Plateaus, Suriname (2005)
14. Konashen Community Owned Conservation Area, Guyana (2006)
15. Kwamalasamutu, Suriname (2010)
16. Tumucumaque Mountains National Park, Brazil (2004-2006)
17. Cordillera de la Costa, Ecuador (1991)
18. Río Pastaza Basin, Ecuador and Peru (1999)
19. Upper Río Nangaritza Basin, Ecuador (2009)
20. Cordillera del Cóndor, Ecuador and Peru (1993-1994)
21. Cordillera de Vilcabamba, Peru (1997-1998)
22. Upper Río Orthon Basin, Pando, Bolivia (1996)
23. Tambopata-Candamo Reserved Zone, Peru (1992)
24. Pando and Alto Madidi, Bolivia and Pampas del Heath, Peru (1992, 1996, 1997)
25. Alto Madidi Region, Bolivia (1990)
26. Noel Kempff Mercado National Park, Bolivia (1991-1995)
27. Humid Forests of Chuquisaca, Bolivia (1995)
28. The Lowland Dry Forests of Santa Cruz, Bolivia (1990-1992)
29. Río Paraguay Basin, Alto Paraguay (1997)
30. Pantanal, Mato Grosso do Sul, Brazil (1998)
31. Abrolhos Bank, Brazil (2000)

Africa and Madagascar

32. Boké Préfecture, Guinea (2005)
33. North Lorma, Gola and Grebo National Forests, Liberia (2005)
34. Foret Classée du Pic de Fon, Simandou Range, Guinea (2002)
35. Déré, Diécké, and Mont Béro, Guinea (2003)
36. Haute Dodo and Cavally Classified Forests, Côte d'Ivoire (2002)
37. Parc National de la Marahoué, Côte d'Ivoire (1998)
38. Southwestern Forest Reserves, Ghana (2003)
39. Ajenjua Bepo and Mamang Forest Reserves, Ghana (2006)
40. Atewa Range Forest Reserve, Ghana (2006)
41. Lokutu, Democratic Republic of Congo (2004)
42. Okavango Delta I - High Water Survey, Botswana (2000), Okavango Delta II - Low Water Survey, Botswana (2003) and Okavango Delta III - Terrestrial, Botswana (2003)
43. Coral Reefs of the Northeast I (2006) and Coral Reefs of the Northeast II (2010)
44. Coral Reefs of the Northwest, Madagascar (2002)
45. Andrafiamena, Madagascar (2007)
46. Reserve Naturelle Integrale d'Ankarafantsika, Madagascar (1997)
47. Mantadia-Zahamena Corridor, Madagascar (1998-1999)

Asia-Pacific

48. Makalu-Barun National Park, Nepal (2005)
49. Mountains of Southwest China Hotspot, Sichuan, China (2005)
50. Central Cardamom Mountains, Cambodia (2001)
51. Virachey National Park, Cambodia (2007)
52. Calamianes Islands, Palawan Province, Philippines (1998)
53. Coral Reefs of the Togean and Banggai Islands, Sulawesi, Indonesia (1998)
54. Raja Ampat Islands, Bird's Head Seascape, Indonesia (2001)
55. Fakfak-Kaimana Coastline, Bird's Head Seascape, Indonesia (2006)
56. Teluk Cenderawasih National Park, Bird's Head Seascape, Indonesia (2006)
57. Wapoga River Area, Indonesia (1998)
58. Northwest Mamberamo Basin, Indonesia (2007)
59. Foja Mountains I, Indonesia (2005) and Foja Mountains II, Indonesia (2008)
60. Cyclops Mountains and the Southern Mamberamo Basin, Indonesia (2000)
61. Muller Range, (2009) and Upper Strickland Basin (2008), Papua New Guinea
62. Kaijende Highlands, Papua New Guinea (2005)
63. Lakekamu Basin, Papua New Guinea (1996)
64. Nakanai Mountains, East New Britain, Papua New Guinea (2009)
65. Southern New Ireland, Papua New Guinea (1994)
66. Milne Bay Province I, Papua New Guinea (1997)
67. Milne Bay Province II, Papua New Guinea (2000)
68. Rennell Island and Indispensable Reefs, Solomon Islands (1994)
69. Northwest Lagoon (Yandé to Koumac), New Caledonia (2007)
70. Province Nord, New Caledonia (1996) and Mont Panié terrestrial, New Caledonia (2010)
71. Mont Panié Lagoon, New Caledonia (2004)
72. Northeast Lagoon (Touho to Ponérihouen), New Caledonia (2009)
73. Nakauvadra Range, Fiji (2008)
74. Nakorotubu Mountains, Fiji (2009)

93

RAP survey profiles

The ultimate goal of all RAP surveys is to collect biodiversity data to inform conservation, although each survey over the last 20 years has had other more specific objectives and outcomes as well. Here, we present summaries of nearly 80 RAP surveys, divided into five categories of conservation impacts. It is important to remember, however, that because each survey has multiple objectives and impacts, each RAP survey meets the criteria of most, if not all, of the categories listed below.

Protected Areas

RAP data have contributed to the creation of protected areas, increased protection status for areas already designated as protected, or improved management for protected areas. In fact, RAP surveys have resulted in over 20 million hectares of new, expanded or improved protected areas for biodiversity conservation. Surveys included in this category are those which have been conducted in protected areas, or have resulted in increased protection status after dissemination of the results of the RAP survey.

Species New to Science

The primary objective of a RAP survey typically is not to find species new to science, but many of the places we visit are so isolated, so absolutely pristine and unexplored, that we have had the great fortune to discover over 1,300 new species of plants and animals in our wanderings across the globe. In this section, you will find some of our most outstanding RAP surveys in terms of the number of species new to science that were encountered during the expedition.

Capacity Building

Local knowledge of biodiversity is a priceless tool for RAP scientists. It is our privilege to work with local students, scientists, land managers, and conservationists, and to both learn from their experiences and to share our own knowledge with them to increase scientific capacity on the ground. Profiles of RAP surveys in this category include some of our most successful training courses and highlight continued successes of local stakeholders who have worked with RAP.

Spatial Planning

RAP surveys are often solicited by industry or local stakeholders who are involved in projects which necessitate the identification of priority biodiversity areas during project planning stages. Results from RAP surveys in this section have contributed to the development of wildlife corridors, industry planning, and the establishment of priority areas for global recognition such as World Heritage or Ramsar Sites, among others.

Human Well-being

At the heart of biodiversity conservation is the well-being of human communities who depend on healthy ecosystems for their survival. RAP surveys have always collected data important to human well-being, particularly information on ecosystem services such as the provision of food (through data on bushmeat and fisheries, for example) and freshwater (through data on the quality of water and watersheds). The RAP survey profiles included in this category exemplify ways in which RAP data can be used to improve the well-being of human communities living near RAP survey sites.

RAP color codes

Terrestrial RAP   AquaRAP   MarineRAP

Giant otters *(Pteronura brasiliensis)*

The very first Conservation International RAP survey was conducted in Alto Madidi and other locations in the northern part of the Department of La Paz, located in western Bolivia on the border with Peru. The topography of Madidi is extreme, as is its climate: from snow-capped mountains at over 5,700 meters above sea level to less than 200 meters elevation in the forests of the southwestern Amazon Basin; and with an annual rainfall of 700 mm in the upper areas and dry valleys to 5,000 mm per year in the Alto Madidi zone. This variability is reflected in its multiple ecoregions, from the puna in the highest zones passing through humid to perhumid evergreen montane forests and dry mesothermal valleys on the eastern slopes of the Andes down to the tropical seasonal rainforest in the lowlands and the palm savannas. Most of Madidi is inaccessible, although the southern area can be accessed from Pelechuco and Apolo, and the northern area from Rurrenabaque, San Buenaventura, Tumupasa, Ixiamas and the Heath River.

The objective of this first RAP expedition was to quickly assess the biological importance of a vast, largely unexplored wilderness area in the province of Iturralde, along the upper reaches of the Heath, Madidi and Tuichi rivers. The region encompasses nearly 5,000,000 hectares of pristine forest and grassland, none of which received any protection under Bolivian law at the time.

An in-depth assessment was made of three groups: birds, mammals and plants. Each of the sites assessed turned out to have exceptional biological diversity. In just 14 days time and in an area of 120 hectares in Alto Madidi, 403 bird species were registered, nine of which were new for Bolivia and 52 for the department of La Paz. Similar findings were reported in the savannas, or pampas, where 135 bird species were registered, and also in the Calabatea valley with 169 bird species. The diversity of mammals was more limited with 51 total species, 45 of which were present in Alto Madidi. However, important species for conservation were registered in Alto Madidi, particularly large mammals such as Jaguars (*Panthera onca*, Near Threatened) and Tapirs (*Tapirus terrestris*, Vulnerable). One significant finding was the ninth registry for science of the Bushy-tailed Opossum *(Glironia venusta)*, a very rare species that was seen coming out of its hole in the dry forest of Machariapo, near Apolo. The plant diversity in Alto Madidi was unusually high as a result of the juxtaposition of different floras and the assessment also showed a great diversity of habitats. In just one tenth of a hectare, 204 plant species were recorded, significantly more than the average of 152 species for humid forests.

The Madidi RAP team proposed nine conservation recommendations, five of which were attained within five years after the RAP survey. Today, this fantastic landscape is part of the Madidi National Park and Integrated Natural Management Area (1,880,996 hectares), one of the largest of its kind in Bolivia, which together with Apolobamba and Pilón Lajas in Bolivia and Bahuaja Sonene and

Tambopata in Peru, forms the heart of the Vilcabamba Amboró Conservation Corridor, covering a protection area of more than 4,135,039 hectares with the unique feature of harboring the most bio-diverse forest on the planet. In the RAP report, Ted Parker, RAP ornithologist, states that he believes the area has 1,000 bird species, which would represent an incredible 11% of all bird species known to exist on our planet! The now protected area of Madidi is linked to five indigenous territories, which partly overlap with the protected areas and complement the Madidi landscape: T′simane Mosetene, Leco Apolo, Leco Larecaja, Uchupiamonas and Tacana I.

To date, the Madidi protected area has been subject to 15 years of uninterrupted management, within the framework of participatory management by the National Service for Protected Areas (SERNAP), with investments of over $600,000 per year, a reasonably well-developed infrastructure and solid links with key stakeholders. Five municipalities enjoy jurisdiction in the area: Apolo, San Buenaventura, Ixiamas, Curva and Pelechuco. They all have included the Madidi in their community planning, as they recognize its value for conservation.

The RAP team recommended achieving connectivity between the Madidi area and the protected areas in the north, in the department of Pando – this action is pending, as is action regarding sustainable management of the ecosystems of the vast areas that are not yet protected, but that offer potential for sustainable development. Partial progress has been made in sustainable forest management; production forests have been certified but many efforts against illegal timber exploitation are pending. One of the greatest successes has been in the development of ecotourism: Chalalán Ecolodge, which was begun with funding from the Inter-American Development Bank and Conservation International, is now entirely managed by the indigenous Uchupiamona people, with all profits feeding back into the Uchupiamona community of San José.

Contributed by Eduardo Forno

Marsh deer (*Blastocerus dichotomus*)

Giant leaf frog (*Phyllomedusa bicolor*)

Black caiman (*Melanosuchus niger*)

Bolivia: Lowland Dry Forests of Santa Cruz (July 1990 – March 1992)

The Pantanal, the largest wetland in the world, embodies well over 10,000,000 hectares of permanent swamps and seasonally flooded grasslands interspersed among large areas of deciduous and gallery forest on higher ground. The Bolivian Pantanal, located along the most eastern part of the country, accounts for 15% of the total area of the Pantanal and is being impacted by cattle ranching and other human activities. In order to prevent repeating the pattern of forest exploitation and chaotic agricultural development that has occurred in the neighboring Brazilian Pantanal, a RAP team set out to take the first steps in the process of environmental protection: identifying biotic communities in the Bolivian Pantanal, and conducting an overview of conservation priorities and opportunities in the Department of Santa Cruz, Bolivia. During the RAP surveys, an incredible concentration of waterbirds was observed (conservative estimates cited 2,000 Snowy Egrets, 1,200 Maguarí Storks and 1,000 Jabirus, among others!). The presence of several endangered species was witnessed, among these the Marsh Deer (*Blastocerus dichotomus*, Vulnerable), the Hyacinthine Macaw (*Anodorhynchus hyacinthinus*, Endangered), the Pampas Deer (*Ozotoceros bezoarticus*, Near Threatened), and the Giant Otter (*Pteronura brasiliensis*, Endangered). Hence, this RAP survey highlighted the need for a protected area which would include the seasonally flooded grassland, permanent marshland, and deciduous forests of Santa Cruz. The region is visually spectacular and has great potential for ecotourism. Today, San Matias Natural Area of Integrated Management (3 million hectares) and Otuquis National Park and Natural Area of Integrated Management (1 million hectares), created by law on July 31, 1997, protect a great portion of the Bolivian Pantanal and associated dry forests ecosystems.

Contributed by Juan Carlos Ledezma

Aerial view of the Serrania de Santiago dry forest

© Ted Parker

For more than two decades, CI has captured the imagination of donors and the public through its commitment to field science and field assessment. This is a part of CI's institutional DNA and is an important reason that CI has such a loyal donor base. Being able to tell the world about nature's little-known wonders is critical to CI's "voice." But it is more than engaging donors – it involves having the trust of the world because of CI's demonstrated commitment to basing conservation priorities on good data and good field science. This commitment distinguishes CI from many other environmental institutions.

- Bruce Beehler, Senior Director, Biodiversity Assessment, Science & Knowledge Division, Conservation International

Guyana
Western Kanuku Mountains
February 3 – 25, 1993

Young capuchin monkey *(Cebus apella)*

Red-footed tortoise *(Geochelone carbonaria)*

The Kanuku Mountain Range, located in south-western Guyana, occupies an area of approximately 500,000 hectares (100 km east to west and 50 km north to south). The range is divided into eastern and western halves by the Rupununi River and is surrounded by the vast Rupununi Savannas. The Kanuku Mountains are considered to be one of the richest and most biological diverse areas in Guyana, and as such, this area has been earmarked by the government as one of the country's priority sites for protection. With an elevation of 150-900 meters, the mountains contain lowland evergreen, montane evergreen, and semi-deciduous forests as well as savanna. The Kanukus are known to support the world's largest identified density of the Endangered Harpy Eagle as well as other Vulnerable species such as the Lowland Tapir.

A RAP survey was conducted in the Western Kanuku Mountain Range and along the upper Rewa River in 1993 to collect data to help determine whether the Kanuku range should be designated as a protected area. Emerging threats such as a road system linking coastal Guyana to interior regions and to Brazil made this RAP survey a top priority.

A great portion of Guyana's known biological diversity was documented within the Kanuku Mountains during the RAP and previous surveys including 80% of Guyana's mammals (150 species), and 60% of the known bird fauna (349 species). High diversity of plants and bats were

also noted. Such high diversity is likely due to the wide variety of habitat types present in the area. An invertebrate group – the Scarabaeine (dung) beetles - was surveyed for the first time on a RAP survey and tested as an indicator group. Because dung beetles must have plentiful mammal dung in order to raise their young, dung beetle densities can be indicative of mammal densities. Twenty-four dung beetle species were documented, indicating a moderately diverse fauna compared to Amazonian dung beetle communities, and also indicating a healthy mammalian fauna.

A number of education and awareness tools were produced after the two Kanuku RAP surveys (a subsequent survey followed in 2001), including a booklet describing the results of the RAP surveys, a video documentary, and posters on the biological importance of the Kanuku Mountains. The information produced from the RAP surveys raised the Kanukus' potential as a tourism destination and triggered the development of a blue print for community-based tourism in the area. RAP data in combination with other socioeconomic data were used to guide the development of a Village Resources Management Plan for nearby stakeholder communities, thereby promoting sustainable use of natural resources in the Kanukus.

The RAP team recommended the development of a protected area along the Rewa River in the eastern Kanukus due to its high biodiversity and pristine state and suggested a biosphere reserve model for the western range (more heavily settled by humans) which would include promotion of ecotourism. Halting all unsustainable resource use, such as gold dredging, poaching, unmanaged hunting and farming and uncontrolled burning of forest was also highlighted.

In 2003, the government of Guyana passed a moratorium on plans for mining in the Kanukus, and currently (2010), the Kanuku Mountains are part of the proposed National Protected Areas System that will conserve 611,000 ha (46% of the Upper Essequibo Watershed; 2.8% of Guyana's land mass). Results from this and the subsequent (2001) RAP survey contributed to the development of a conservation management plan for the area and for delineating the boundaries for a proposed protected area that will include all of the Kanuku mountain range, watersheds and patches of the surrounding savannas. Additionally, this RAP survey highlighted the need for continued capacity building within communities for on-going species monitoring and enforcement to protect the biological integrity of the Kanuku Mountains. Since 2001 about 10 residents from nearby communities have been trained as rangers for community-based monitoring.

Guyana is the only country in the western hemisphere without a national protected area system. There is currently only one protected area in the country, Kaieteur National Park. In the absence of protected areas legislation, CI and other NGOs have applied innovative approaches to biodiversity conservation through community planning, development and management. Guyana's high forest cover and low rate of deforestation has been maintained largely in part by the traditional way of life of the indigenous peoples.

The proposed protected area in the Kanukus involves a co-management plan prepared using a highly participatory approach, using a structure of co-management involving some 6,500 indigenous people in 18 communities and government at the highest level of governance and implementation.

Contributed by Leeanne Alonso and Eustace Alexander

An aerial view of the Kanuku Mountains

© Conservation International/photo by Jensen Montambault

Red-tailed Catfish *(Phractocephalus hemioliopterus)*

© Piotr Naskrecki

Belize: Columbia River Forest Reserve (April 2 – 14, 1992)

The RAP team surveyed the Columbia River Forest Reserve of Southern Belize along the border with Guatemala in April 1992. This RAP survey was solicited by several agencies in Belize because of increasing concern about illegal encroachment into the reserve, including logging, hunting and agriculture. The Columbia River Forest Reserve lies at the southeastern edge of the Maya Mountains and at the time of the RAP survey included approximately 52,600 hectares of primarily old growth subtropical lower montane wet forest ranging in elevation from 300-900 meters. In 12 days, researchers found over 430 species of plants, at least 30 of which were new records for the country of Belize; 224 species of birds; 29 species of mammals, including the Baird's Tapir; and 10 species of frogs, four of which were new country records, one of these new to science. RAP team members played a key advisory role in efforts to increase the area's legal status to national park and suggested improved protection of the reserve, including control of incursions by people into the reserve, extension of the reserve's boundaries, and infrastructure to attract ecotourism and employ local villagers. Unfortunately, the area is still a Forest Reserve, not a park, and incursions, particularly from the border with Guatemala, have increased since 1992, as have logging and hunting rates. The size of the reserve has actually been decreased to allow for agriculture. A monitoring post was built at one of the park entrances but has since fallen into disrepair and the level of ecotourism is low because of unsafe conditions in the park (J. Meerman, pers. comm.). This important reserve, which is a significant spring flyway for North American migratory birds like the Cerulean Warbler, is in dire need of conservation action.

Contributed by Jessica Deichmann

Twenty years ago when it was launched, RAP was a disturbing concept to many in the scientific community. Surely it was not possible to fast-track the painstaking process of biodiversity inventory and taxonomy without unacceptable compromises in scientific rigour. But RAP has proved all its sceptics wrong. RAP recognizes the need for rapid assessments in the face of our global extinction crisis, but has done this without sacrificing the science, as testified by the numerous papers in the peer-reviewed literature arising from RAP expeditions. I hope that in the next 20 years we shall see a huge expansion in the RAP approach in all parts of the world. This is urgently needed so that our conservation actions can proceed on the basis of the best possible information.

- Simon N. Stuart, Chair, Species Survival Commission, International Union for Conservation of Nature

The Cordillera del Cóndor, a mountain range consisting of tortuous and intricate geological formations, spans the border between Ecuador and Peru and is a key element in the complex hydrological cycle linking the Andes with the Amazon. The proximity of the eastern slopes of the equatorial Andes to the vast sea of Amazonian rain forests create ecological and evolutionary conditions that generate and sustain extraordinary biological wealth. As such, the Cóndor is an area of great global conservation significance.

Indigenous communities have inhabited these majestic mountains for centuries. The Jivaroan populations living at the base of the Cóndor and along the rivers that drain the region include the Shuar and Ashuar peoples, who mainly occupy the Zamora, Nangaritza and Pastaza river basins, and Aguaruna and Huambisa peoples of the Cenepa and Santiago river basins. As one of the largest indigenous ethnic groups in Amazonia, the Jivaroan communities depend heavily on the ecosystems within the Cordillera del Cóndor and are in a position to play the leading role in land-use management.

Despite the fact that the Cordillera del Cóndor remains remote, largely roadless and completely uninhabited above 1,500 meters, this pristine area has been allocated into numerous mining concessions. It has also been the site of several cross border military conflicts and as a result has been virtually off-limits to biologists for half a century. The RAP surveys were conducted, beginning in Ecuador in 1993, and continuing in Peru in 1994 with the aim of contributing to a better understanding of the biology of one particular area of humid lower montane forest within the mountain range. The second objective was to encourage the appreciation of the importance of the Cordillera del Cóndor as a global conservation priority, contributing to a satisfactory resolution of the many competing demands on the region's resources.

The most important outcome of the two surveys of the Cordillera del Cóndor was the discovery of the remarkable plant communities found along the top ridges and on sandstone mesas at Achupallas and at Machinaza. Many of the plants found in these herbazales, or grassland meadows, appear to represent species new to science; the herbazales of the Cordillera del Cóndor probably are the largest anywhere in the Andes. Although lower elevations in the Cóndor are more accessible to human encroachment and settlement and to date have experienced the greatest amount of habitat disturbance in the cordillera, bird and mammal surveys suggest that the small mammal and avian fauna there are fairly diverse and are represented by many Amazonian species. The higher elevation areas surveyed had lower richness of birds and mammals and included more species typical of montane ecosystems.

Some of the most interesting records from these RAP surveys were found in the herbazales; for example, the presence of 40 species of orchids, as many as 26 potentially new to science; the discovery of a new species of mouse opossum; and also the record of a bird typically found at much higher elevations, the Mouse-colored Thistletail *(Schizoeaca griseomurina).* These results indicate that additional studies in these localities would undoubtedly produce further discoveries.

The Cordillera del Cóndor represents the largest and most diverse area of Sandstone Mountains in the Andes and may have the greatest richness of vascular plants in South America. The RAP team recommended that the Cordillera del Cóndor be recognized for its diversity and given protection status, so that its unique flora and habitats will be preserved.

These RAP surveys were the basis for the creation of the Santiago-Comaina Reserved Zone in 1999, after the peace agreements between Peru and Ecuador. With 1.6 million hectares, the Santiago-Comaina Reserved Zone was the foundation for the creation of Ichigkat muja-Cordillera del Cóndor National Park (88,477 ha) and Tuntanin Communal Reserve (94,968 ha) in Peru, both created in 2007. The fact that the new protected areas are smaller in comparison to the original reserved zone is because most of the Santiago-Comaina Reserved Zone covered territories of indigenous communities, who already implement conservation activities as part of their traditional use of natural resources. Since the RAP surveys, two additional biological assessments have been implemented to complement the 1993 and 1994 surveys, and to contribute to the development of management plans for both areas. There are still 398,449 ha in the Santiago-Comaina Reserved Zone that remain to be categorized.

Contributed by Carmen Noriega and Luis Espinel

Andean condor *(Vultur gryphus)*

Atelopus spumarius, a Vulnerable species of harlequin frog

The RAP team planning a field survey

Peru: Tambopata – Candamo Reserve Zone (May 15 – June 20, 1992)

Located in the Peruvian Amazon Basin, south of the Madre de Dios River in Tambopata Province's Inambari and Tambopata districts, the Tambopata-Candamo Reserve Zone is part of the largest and least disturbed remaining areas of Upper Amazonian and Lower Andean ecosystems. The Tambopata-Candamo Reserve Zone was created on January 26, 1990 to protect the forests adjacent to the Heath and Tambopata rivers.

CI has collaborated with the Peruvian government since 1990 to carry out ecological and social studies to assess potential land uses in the region. The primary goals of the RAP survey of Tambopata-Candamo in 1992 were to provide a clearer picture of biological diversity in the region, and to apply that knowledge to the zoning process. The survey focused on two main areas: a) The Río Tambopata and the Cerros del Távara and b) The Rio Heath and Pampas del Heath National Sanctuary. Both areas offer unique opportunities for long-term research projects on their biological communities. These areas are distinct in the diversity of habitats, which support diverse native flora and fauna: 165 species and 41 families of trees, 103 mammal species, 1,300 butterfly species, and 90 species of amphibians. There are large populations of species that have become rare from overhunting, especially tapirs, jaguars, peccaries, otters, and river turtles. At least

Juvenile Emerald Tree Boa (*Corallus caninus*)

seven species new to science were recorded for the area.

The RAP team recommended establishment of a national park within the Tambopata-Candamo Reserve Zone due to the biological importance of the different types of forest on the floodplains of the Río Tambopata. In 2000, these expectations were fulfilled as the National Park Bahuaja Sonene (1,091,416 ha) and the Tambopata National Reserve (274,690 ha) were created from the Reserve Zone.

Contributed by Carmen Noriega and Luis Espinel

CI's Rapid Assessment Program surveys and publications have been critical components of our work in the Center for Environmental Leadership in Business when engaging with companies in biodiversity assessment and planning in the early stages of project design. The survey results have provided detailed data about the species, habitats and ecosystems in a project area. That information coupled with socio economic assessments have informed the development of action plans that demonstrate the sustainable use of the biological resources in a project area.

- **Mahlette Betre, Center for Environmental Leadership in Business, Conservation International**

Cambodia
Virachey National Park
October 1 – 15, 2007

White-lipped Pit Viper (*Trimeresurus albolabris*)

Virachey National Park is located in the northeast corner of Cambodia, near the borders with Laos and Vietnam. It is the largest national park in Cambodia, and one of the least accessible. Virachey contains a variety of natural habitats (e.g., bamboo, pine forest, semi-evergreen rainforest, dry dipterocarp forest) depending on altitude, aspect, history, geology, and hydrology. The most abundant formation is tropical evergreen rainforest, much of which appears to be in primary condition. Virachey National Park massif contains a range of mountains that reach over 1,400 meters in altitude to the east, and over 1,500 m towards the Laos border. These high elevation sites are far from any footpaths or villages, and have never been surveyed. This remoteness has protected the area, yet it has also prevented biological assessments because it requires 5-7 days of hiking through evergreen rainforest to get deep into the survey site.

The objective of the survey was to gain a better understanding of the biological importance of Virachey and highlight its importance for biological conservation. The survey will lead to the production of a detailed report for Cambodia's Ministry of the Environment, which will help the ministry raise awareness and funds to protect and conserve the unique biodiversity of Virachey.

The surveyed areas were found to contain an interesting diversity and abundance of species. At least 15 mammal, 37 fish, 30 ant and 19 katydid species were recorded during this survey, including direct observations of several large mammal species (e.g., Sambar deer, wild dog, wild cattle) and recent tracks and signs of other mammals (bears, Clouded Leopards). Many of these mammals are considered globally threatened.

The RAP team recorded at least 26 amphibian and 35 reptile species, a number of which may be new to science. On the basis of this survey, Virachey represents an area of extremely high amphibian and reptile diversity within Cambodia, and a relatively high diversity regionally. Many of the species documented during the RAP survey have never previously been recorded elsewhere in Cambodia, making the park of significant herpetological conservation importance for the country. The Asiatic Softshell Turtle (*Amyda cartilaginea*), Asian Giant Pond Turtle (*Heosemys grandis*), and Impressed Tortoise (*Manouria impressa*), are all classified as Vulnerable by the IUCN. None of the recorded amphibians are currently classified as globally threatened; however, this is because too few data exist for these amphibian species to be properly classified at this time. The RAP survey recorded one Endangered mammal, the Dhole *(Cuon alpinus).* While fewer than 2,500 Dhole are thought to remain in the wild, the RAP team observed a total of at least 15 of these wild dogs, highlighting the crucial importance of Virachey for the conservation of this species. Five other large mammals were recorded which are classified by IUCN as globally threatened (Vulnerable): the Gaur *(Bos gaurus),* Yellow-cheeked Gibbon *(Nomascus gabriellae),* Stumptailed Macaque *(Macaca arctoides),* Asiatic Black Bear *(Ursus thibetanus)* and Malayan Sun Bear *(Helarctos malayanus).* Tracks of otters along the rivers and hill streams appear to be from the Asian Small-clawed Otter *(Aeonyx cinerea,* Near Threatened), which the IUCN Otter Specialist Group recommends reclassifying as Endangered due to hunting for the fur trade. The presence of these globally threatened species indicates a relatively undisturbed ecosystem, with little hunting pressure. Additionally, at least two shrew species are likely to represent new country records and may even be undescribed species.

The Cambodian government has plans to mine in the mountains and dam one of the rivers that flows through Virachey. The RAP team strongly recommends surveying other rivers to ensure that species living in the river to be dammed can be found elsewhere, and that at least one biologically important wild river remains undeveloped and conserved within the park. The river to the west of the proposed dams is of particular interest as it is a very large intact river system with multiple tributaries – a watershed covering over 60,000 hectares with headwaters at over 1,300 m elevation. Conservation of this watershed and river will ensure that Virachey's globally threatened and restricted range turtles, freshwater fish and amphibians are adequately protected. RAP scientists plan to conduct more surveys in collaboration with the mining company to help mitigate the effects of the proposed mining and to ensure that development within the park has minimal impact on the most vulnerable and high biodiversity ecosystems.

Contributed by Piotr Naskrecki and David Emmett

Ants tending aphids (Dolichoderinae)

Ant plant (*Myrmecodia* sp.)

Stream frog (*Limnonectes dabanus*)

My thoughts go back over the fifteen years that I have served on the Conservation International board – experiencing train wrecks in Peru, running out of food on our trip to visit the Kayapo Indians in Brazil, and our excursion to the Cardamom Mountains in Cambodia. On our journey to Cambodia, we took helicopters on a mission to locate the endangered Indochinese tigers that once inhabited the terrain. Within minutes of landing on the mountain top my feet started to itch. I looked down and noticed that leeches and blood covered my white tennis shoes. I immediately called for the helicopter to take me back to the camp. For a city boy, the experience was all too over-whelming. Later that night in camp, Leeanne Alonso told me of the next RAP expedition to spend a week in that same mountainous landscape that forced my early return. I couldn't image anyone being so adventurous and brave.

As always, my thoughts are with you in appreciation of your amazing work for Conservation International. I would like to congratulate you on your Papua New Guinea RAP, where you made the marvelous new species discoveries. I always try to keep up with your adventures through the Conservation International webpage. Thank you for all that you do for our planet.

– Mark Feldman, Vice-chairman of the Executive Committee, Conservation International Board of Directors

Peru
Cordillera de Vilcabamba
June 1997 – August 1998

© Louise Emmons

© Conservation International/photo by Haroldo Castro

© Louise Emmons

Red Howler Monkeys (*Alouatta seniculus*)

© Piotr Naskrecki

The Cordillera de Vilcabamba in south-central Peru contains such unique and abundant diversity that it took three expeditions to study just a fraction of the 3 million hectare mountain range - two by RAP in 1997 and 1998 and one by the Smithsonian Institution (SI) in 1998 - which were all published together in the *RAP Bulletin of Biological Assessment* (2001). RAP's quests to explore this remote and inaccessible range were featured in National Geographic as well as International Wildlife magazine in 1998.

The lure of the Cordillera de Vilcabamba lies in its wide variation of altitudes, from the highest peaks above 4,300 m to the lower river basins at around 400-500 m, with seven life and two transition vegetation zones. The steep slopes and isolation of Vilcabamba have created the setting for the evolution of a high number of endemic species. The Cordillera de Vilcabamba is also recognized as an area of significant conservation importance for its high diversity of indigenous peoples, including the Asháninka, Matsigenka (or Matsiguenga), Nomatsiguenga, and Yine. Vilcabamba also serves as the headwaters of many important South American rivers, which maintain a clean supply of freshwater for the communities who farm the fertile soils in the lowlands below.

RAP and Smithsonian Institution surveys of forests from 1,000 m to over 3,350 m in elevation documented exceptionally high overall species diversity and a remarkable substrate heterogeneity, which contributed to extraordinary levels of overall habitat heterogeneity, from humid canyons to high-elevation pajonales (grass- or scrub-lands). The higher elevation sites were distinct from each other and from lower altitudes. Species richness of vertebrates was high, with many endemic and geographically restricted species of mammals and birds. Most of the amphibians observed are endemic to the Cordillera de Vilcabamba. Invertebrate species were also documented and high diversities of spiders, crickets, beetles, wasps and bees were revealed. Many of the vertebrate and invertebrate species recorded were new to science or were found in unexpected habitats or in surprising abundance, further indication that this area is a special place in relation to biodiversity. Among the discoveries was even a new genus of mammal!

The RAP and SI survey results came at a critical time to provide support to a 30 year process begun by the Peruvian government in the 1960s and taken up by several non-governmental organizations in the 1980s that culminated in a proposal put forward by Conservation International-Peru, Asociación para la Conservación del Patrimonio del Cutivireni and the Centro para el Desarrollo del Indígena Amazónico to establish two communal reserves and a national park in the Apurimac Reserved Zone. Reserved Zones have only a transitory protected status. The RAP scientific data provided the scientific justification for declaring the Apurimac Reserved Zone as a region of high global biodiversity importance, deserving of conservation efforts and protection.

In January 2003, three new protected areas were officially created and designated as the Ashaninka Communal Reserve (184,468 ha), Matziguenka Communal Reserve (218,905 ha), and Otishi National Park (305,973 ha) by Supreme Decree 003-2003-AG. Of the 1,669,200 ha in the Apurimac Reserved Zone, 709,347 ha are included in these three new protected areas.

The region continues to be managed by the indigenous communities and park authorities. A gas pipeline running from the Camisea natural gas fields in the remote lower Urubamba region to the Peruvian coast runs below ground, directly under the Machiguenga Communal Reserve, reducing, but not eliminating the environmental impact of the pipeline. The Camisea project has strengthened the organizational capabilities of the local communities, but the project remains controversial due to the possible impacts on the ecosystems of the region.

Contributed by Carmen Noriega, Luis Espinel, and Leeanne Alonso

Saddleback Tamarin *(Saguinus fuscicollis)*

Yellow mushroom from the Vilcabamba-Amboro Corridor

A panoramic view of the Cordillera de Vilcabamba

Côte d'Ivoire: Parc National de la Marahoué (January 31 – February 23, 1998)

A Biological Assessment of Parc National de la Mara-houé National Park, an area of approximately 101,000 hectares in central Côte d'Ivoire, represents a unique protected area with transitions from semi-decid-uous Upper Guinea forest to savanna ecosystems. The 1998 RAP survey recorded baseline data for ecological monitoring and to aid in the development of a conser-vation management strategy for the park. During the survey, 458 plant, nine primate, 16 other mammal and 256 bird species were recorded. The savanna lacked tree species typically found in West African savannas, but herbaceous species appeared rich. Detection rates of primates were low, although interviews with local people suggested there may have been a viable popula-tion of the Diana Monkey (*Cercopithecus diana*), a highly endangered primate, within the park at the time of the survey. Eight of the 14 endemic Upper Guinea forest birds known to occur in Côte d'Ivoire were recorded, in-dicating a rich avifauna. RAP researchers reported signs of human incursions within park boundaries including scattered cocoa farms inside the forest and mammal density patterns which suggested high hunting pressure, particularly on the western side of the park. Although

Marahoué National Park at dawn

researchers made a number of recommendations for improved conservation of the park including improved surveillance within the borders and enlisting support for the park from local communities, civil unrest since 2002 has made follow-through difficult. Unfortunately, hunting and agricultural encroachment have increased and the situation of the park has largely deteriorated (S. Gonedelé Bi, pers. comm.)

Contributed by Jessica Deichmann

My first experience with the RAP program was as a guest lecturer during the second Asia-Pacific RAP project, in Papua New Guinea's Lakekamu Basin in 1996. This project had a strong focus on training young Papua New Guinean biologists, and several of the promising trainees at Lakekamu have become long-term research collaborators and good personal friends. The next RAP in the region, to the Wapoga area of Indonesian New Guinea in 1998, opened my eyes to the magnitude of the task facing scientists trying to document New Guinea's poorly-known biodiversity. At dusk on the first night of our survey a chorus of chirps, tweets and honks from a multitude of frogs ema-nated from the forest. With a thrill known only to those who have experienced discovery of a new species, I immediately knew from their calls that many of these represented species never before documented by science. Every subsequent expedition continues to evoke a sense of wonderment and excitement but more importantly RAP surveys in New Guinea have confirmed the island as a bio-logical treasure-trove, and provided invaluable information about patterns of diversity, endemism and the conservation status of many plant and animal groups.

- Stephen Richards, RAP manager for Asia-Pacific Region

Indonesia
Teluk Cenderawasih National Park, Bird's Head Seascape
February 9 – 26, 2006

© Gerald Allen

© Dan Polhemus

© Gerald Allen

Coral *(Anacropora dendracis)*

© Emre Turak

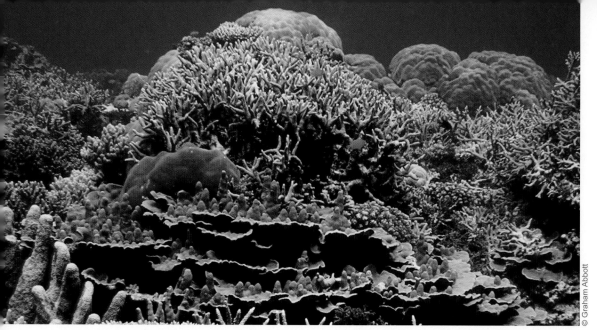

Healthy coral reefs of Cenderawasih Bay

Situated in the far eastern reaches of the Bird's Head Seascape in West Papua, Indonesia, Teluk Cenderawasih is a large bay of nearly 5,000,000 hectares which reaches depths of almost 2,000 meters in its center. The mouth of the bay is nearly blocked off by the reef-fringed islands of Yapen, Biak and Numfor, while the inner bay has a multitude of small islands, atolls and fringing reefs which are protected by nearly pristine watersheds. Teluk Cenderawasih National Park is Indonesia's largest marine national park at just over 1,500,000 hectares in size.

This MarineRAP survey had five main objectives: 1) assess the current conservation status (including reef condition and biodiversity values) of Cenderawasih National Park; 2) identify areas of outstanding conservation importance (due to the presence of endemic or globally threatened species, fish spawning aggregation sites, turtle nesting beaches, etc.) to inform the park's zonation process; 3) conduct socioeconomic and fisheries surveys of coastal villages to identify conservation threats and opportunities arising from local attitudes and practices; 4) assess the potential for the development of marine tourism in the park; and 5) estimate levels of ecological and genetic connectivity between the reefs of Cenderawasih and those in Raja Ampat and Kaimana to inform seascape-level management strategies.

The MarineRAP survey team assessed 33 sites over the course of an 850 nautical mile route covering most of Cenderawasih Bay, with over 450 man-hours recorded underwater. While the team's findings confirmed that Cenderawasih is an area of extremely high biodiversity, no one predicted the spectacular levels of endemicity that were revealed in the bay's marine populations. Of the nearly 500 hard coral species recorded, 22 are undescribed and apparently endemic to the bay! Likewise, five of the 37 stomatopod crustacean species collected were new and found nowhere else, while at least eight of the 716 reef fishes recorded were also new and endemic, including a charismatic species of *Hemiscyllium* "walking" shark. Moreover, at least a dozen species of reef fish displayed color patterns unique to populations in the bay, adding further evidence of past oceanographic isolation of the bay. Population genetic analyses of over 50 different species of marine organisms further elucidated this pattern of repeated isolation of the bay over the past 14 million years; this evidence, combined with tectonic reconstructions of the area, helped the team to hypothesize a rare case of a marine "species factory" within the bay.

Perhaps just as importantly, the survey revealed that the reefs of the national park were generally in very healthy condition (>47% average live coral cover on the reef crest), with excellent recovery from previous blast-fishing damage and rebuilding stocks of large reef fishes including groupers and sharks. Socioeconomic surveys in 18 coastal villages revealed strong conservation awareness and support for the national park – a tribute to the dedicated ranger staff working in this remote area. Incidence of blast and cyanide fishing was greatly reduced from what had been recorded a decade previous.

Based upon the striking levels of endemicity exhibited in the bay, the generally excellent condition of the reefs and the impressive community support for conservation, the team strongly recommended that Cenderawasih National Park receive much higher priority by the Indonesian government in terms of funding and community engagement programs. Two fish spawning aggregation sites were recommended for inclusion in no-take zones, while steep coastal forests were slated for inclusion in a buffer zone to protect the fragile watersheds in the bay. Finally, the team recommended that the provincial government immediately prioritize development of well-managed, sustainable marine tourism as well as pushing the University of Papua to initiate active marine biological research in the bay. A number of these recommendations have recently been put in to practice (see Indonesia Regional Summary).

Contributed by Mark Erdmann

© Gerald Allen

Cenderawasih fairy wrasse *(Cirrhilabrus cenderawasih)*

© Graham Abbott

Healthy coral reef of Cenderawasih Bay

Cenderawasih walking shark *(Hemiscyllium galei)*

© Gerald Allen

Ghana: Southwestern Forest Reserves (October 22 – November 10, 2003)

Four forest reserves (Draw River, Boi-Tano, Tano Nimiri and Krokosua Hills) classified by the Government of Ghana as Globally Significant Biodiversity Areas were surveyed to assess their faunal diversity and to secure their ecological integrity. The RAP team documented 1,309 species with one amphibian species new to science, and several new records for Ghana including two plant, one butterfly, three amphibian and one shrew species. Over 250 species of butterflies were recorded, including many endemic to West Africa. The bird fauna (170 species) included a high component of forest species. The reserves harbor 30 species of international conservation concern.

Forest rodent *(Hybomys sp.)*

These reserves have the potential to act as stepping stones for wildlife gene flow within the fragmented landscape. They need to be connected to neighboring national parks and other reserves through corridors. Draw River should receive the highest level of protection and be integrated into Ankasa/Nini Suhien National Park, with which it is contiguous. In Krokosua Hills, the greatest priority should be halting illegal clearance of forest and embarking on innovative sustainable livelihood initiatives compatible with conservation of biodiversity. Conservation will only succeed when people living close to biodiversity are aware of its value and able to enjoy the benefits from its preservation and sustainable utilization.

Contributed by Leeanne Alonso

My first RAP survey took place in the Atewa Range Forest Reserve (Ghana) from 6-24 June 2006. During this RAP, I was fascinated with the atmosphere of brotherhood that reigned between all the RAP participants. Personally, I think that this brotherhood was the key of the success of that RAP. In the Amphibian Group to which I belonged as a specialist, it was an honor for me to train Mr. Caleb Ofori Boateng, a graduate student from Ghana, in amphibian sampling and taxonomy. We recorded 32 taxa of amphibians; I was fascinated particularly in the site of Asiakwa North. I gained a valuable first impression of the originality of its topography, the steepness of its slopes, the diversity of West African frogs, and the diversity of its vegetation types. The beauty of its landscape was illustrated by a deep valley in which a succession of very huge blocks of granite constituted refuge for the critically endangered frog Conraua derooi *(Petropedetidae). I am indebted to Conservation International, Washington D.C., in general, and L.E. Alonso and J. McCullough in particular for the invitation to participate in that RAP survey. My special thinks are to Heather Wright who I affectionately call "Mommy RAP", Piotr Naskrecki, Yaw Osei-Owusu and Nana Abena-Somaa, the Accra office of Conservation International, Okyeame Ampadu-Agyei and Philip Badger for organizing the logistics!*

- N'goran Germain Kouamé, University of Abobo-Adjamé

Caribbean Netherlands
Saba Bank
January 4 – 15, 2006

© Diane Littler

© Paul Hoetjes

© Robert Thacker

Green turtle *(Chelonia mydas)*

© Piotr Naskrecki

High diversity gorgonian assemblage on the Saba Bank fore-reef

Located in the Dutch Windward islands approximately 250 km southeast of Puerto Rico, Saba Bank is a completely submerged platform (total area of 220,000 hectares) that rises 1,000 m up from the surrounding sea floor. The platform is well mapped, but largely unexplored. A large portion of the Bank lies between 7 and 20 m in depth and contains extensive coral reefs.

The hard coral, soft coral, and sponge reefs present on Saba Bank are generally healthy, but the reefs are regularly imperiled by maritime activity, especially anchoring and abrasion by tankers traveling to and from oil terminals on St. Eustatius. Traditional fisheries operating from Saba Island (about 1,300 residents) are concerned about the problem.

Sabans are directly responsible for the management of Saba Bank, so they sought to mitigate damage from passing oil tankers through a zoning plan. The Department of Environment and Nature of the Netherlands Antilles (MINA) supported the zoning process, and is seeking to designate Saba Bank a Particularly Sensitive Sea Area (PSSA) through the International Maritime Organization. The PSSA designation would ensure that fragile habitats and areas with high biodiversity are off limits to ship anchors under maritime law.

Scientific data on the biodiversity of Saba Bank were needed to justify the PSSA designation. Some key pieces of information on species and habitats were missing, so MINA sought the expertise of Conservation International's MarineRAP to fill these data gaps. In order to accomplish this, a multi-disciplinary team of RAP scientists and Saba National Marine Park managers was assembled and the team conducted biodiversity assessments at 20 sites along the Bank. The surveys focused on macro-algae (seaweeds), habitat-forming benthic invertebrates (hard corals, soft corals, and sponges) and the fishes associated with these habitats.

Species richness of all taxa was found to be as high or higher than other well-studied Caribbean sites like Puerto Rico. The species composition was similar to other Caribbean localities, thus the reef habitat is representative of the region. Over 500 species were documented, including 270 species of fish, 150 seaweeds, 81 sponges, 48 octocorals, and 43 hard corals. The number of fish species known to occur on Saba Bank rocketed from 42 to 270 over the course of the study.

Scientific findings from these studies comprised a collection in the scientific journal PLoS ONE called Biodiversity of Saba Bank (http://www.ploscollections.org). A few highlights from the volume include multiple sightings of the Critically Endangered hard coral *Acropora cervicornis*, a robust population of the Giant Barrel Sponge, *Xestospongia muta,* and exceptional species richness overall among seaweeds and octocorals. New species were discovered in shallow and deep (> 50 m) water. Octocoral colonies appeared healthy, with only a few lesions observed. Further, no signs of disease or bleaching were evident on the sponges, as reported from other Caribbean reefs.

New habitat types were described in the PLoS ONE collection, including a 50 km shallow fore-reef with high diversity and abundance of hard and soft corals and a broad plateau environment with exceptional richness of red and brown seaweeds. New high-resolution seafloor maps showed deep linear features on the southeast perimeter and deep mounds in the northeast quadrant.

However, not all the news was good. There was evidence of bleaching to hard corals at 82% of dive sites. The hard coral surveys took place in 2006, and the damage was attributed to the record bleaching event in the Caribbean in 2005. Damage to sponges and corals from anchor chains was also documented. Videotaped evidence confirmed the detrimental impacts of maritime activities on the sponge and coral communities on Saba Bank.

In the opinion of the MarineRAP science team, the majority of sites surveyed merited protective measures because of their biodiversity, and susceptibility to damage from maritime activity especially anchoring by large ships. Immediate action to protect these diverse habitats was recommended.

In October 2010, the Netherlands Antilles government declared Saba Bank the Caribbean's newest marine protected area. The declaration prohibits anchoring by large ships (i.e., tankers) on the entire Bank with a few exceptions (e.g., permitted local fishing boats). The Coast Guard of the Dutch Caribbean will be enforcing these regulations. After the constitutional changes in the Caribbean

Netherlands, the Netherlands will take on the management of Saba Bank.

An application for PSSA status was submitted by the Netherlands to the International Maritime Organization for consideration in Spring, 2011. The MarineRAP survey results highlighted the complexity and biodiversity of Saba Bank, and helped lead to its protection, but all scientists involved in the surveys agreed that more discovery and exploration awaits on this unique and expansive Caribbean atoll.

Contributed by Sheila A. McKenna, Peter J. Etnoyer, and Paul Hoetjes

© Robert Thacker

Sponge *(Aiolochroia crassa)*

© Piotr Naskrecki

Hawksbill turtle *(Eretmochelys imbricata)*

Madagascar: Coral Reefs of the Northeast II (March 27 – April 16, 2010)

The extreme northeast region of Madagascar is particularly rich in marine biodiversity; some believe it could be considered another "Coral Triangle". Spurred by results of the MarineRAP survey in 2006, additional reef surveys were conducted in Northeastern Madagascar in 2010, covering 125 km of coastline. The goals were to assess the resilience of coastal ecosystems and to produce management recommendations that would contribute to identifying Marine Protected Area priority sites for Madagascar. Moreover, this study would support the creation of "climate-smart" Marine Protected Areas as a tool to mitigate the impacts of climate change on the coastal marine environment of Madagascar. Over the course of 20 days, a multi-disciplinary team of marine scientists surveyed selected areas, namely Baie de Ambodivahibe, Baie de Loky, Nosy Ankao, Baie de Andrivana and Vohemar. The MarineRAP survey revealed 280 species of hard corals, 292 species of coral reef fishes (70% of the fish species known to occur in Madagascar waters!) and 68 species of echinoderms (starfish and the like). Moreover, 67 different species of coral associates were observed, some of which revealed unexpected diversity in color and pattern. Nine species of seagrass and over 90 species of macroalgae were recorded. Acting as nursery areas for larval forms, these provide habitat for a high diversity of fish and macro-invertebrates. These results group Northeast Madagascar with the highest marine diversity sites in Northwest Madagascar, Northern Mozambique and Southern Tanzania, lending support to the existence of a high diversity center for the Western Indian Ocean. Discussions between local indigenous communities and government agencies over the creation of Marine Protected Areas in the areas surveyed (particularly in Ambodivahibe Bay) are currently ongoing. A socioeconomic evaluation of the area was conducted in the summer of 2010 and the full MarineRAP report is predicted to be published in early 2011.

Contributed by Giuseppe DiCarlo

© Keith Ellenbogen/ILCP

In the field program, RAP remains one of the most valuable tools for engaging partnerships with officials, politicians, scientists and local communities. In many ways, it becomes the preliminary phase of potentially rewarding landscape projects in support of CI's new strategy.

- **François Martel, Conservation International – Pacific Islands program**

New Caledonia
Mont Panié Lagoon
November 24 – December 15, 2004

Mont Panié in the northeastern part of the South Pacific Island of New Caledonia is an important terrestrial reserve spanning 5,400 hectares and encompassing the highest mountain (1,629 meters), bearing the same name. In 2004, a new community-based Marine Protected Area was proposed for the coral reefs lying off the coast of this reserve and the municipalities of Hienghène and Pouebo. At the time of the survey, existing governmental management was mainly limited to regulations on the extraction of specific species such as fish, snails and crabs. Selected sites in the area are under traditional marine resource practices and conservation measures instituted by the Kanak tribes. For example some of the reefs are designated as "taboo" sites with a ban on fishing or collecting marine creatures.

This MarineRAP survey was conducted in collaboration with the government of Province Nord, Dayu Biik (a local conservation NGO supported by CI and Province Nord) and local Kanak tribes to obtain site-specific data on the ecology and socioeconomics of the area to inform effective conservation and management activities. The team consisted of two groups of local and international scientists, sociologists and local community members working in parallel. The biological group evaluated 42 coral reef sites from Grand Recif Pouma and Balade Pass in the north to Recif Doiman in the south. Sites of particular interest included the reefs adjacent to the Mont Panié reserve and culturally taboo sites. Special care was taken to ensure all sites visited were afforded the utmost respect and all tribal laws were followed. No specimens were collected as requested by the local tribes and only photographs were taken to document the species and habitats. At each site, the MarineRAP team documented the biodiversity and condition of the reefs, and assessed populations of exploited fish and macro-invertebrate stocks. The socioeconomic group conducted extensive on-site interviews with local stakeholders from 21 coastal settlements to assess their practices, needs, beliefs and concerns regarding marine resource use.

Outstanding marine biodiversity was documented with a total of 279 species of hard corals plus over 200 species of other benthic invertebrates. The number of coral reef fish species per site ranged between 109 and 229. Moreover, an incredible number of species known to be at risk of global extinction as assessed by the IUCN (referred to as "red-listed species") were observed. These included 12 fish species such as reef sharks and the Napolean Wrasses that are fished heavily throughout the world. Seeing these spectacular

animals at more than half of the sites surveyed is truly noteworthy and set a new global benchmark for such sightings during MarineRAP surveys.

Overall, the coral reefs surveyed were in excellent to good health. Bleaching was not observed at any of the sites. No evidence of large masses of the voracious coral predator, the Crown of Thorns Starfish, was noted on any of the sites. Récif Tao and Colnett, two of the proposed reefs to be protected by the anticipated Mont Panié Marine Protected Area, had the highest species richness of the survey. Findings suggest that the local traditional management scheme may work at some sites. The tribes interviewed during this survey supported increased tribal and governmental regulations regarding marine resource use and conservation.

The Mont Panié region offers an excellent opportunity to conserve terrestrial and freshwater as well as marine species and their associated habitats. The RAP team recommended that the whole area surveyed should be officially protected and managed as a network of Marine Protected Areas (MPAs). Moreover, the establishment of a proposed multiple-use MPA is politically feasible. To successfully establish and implement this network, it is imperative that all local stakeholders continue to be involved in the designation and implementation of any MPAs or other management units, and that their traditional laws and customs be incorporated into MPA plans.

This MarineRAP led to the establishment of three MPAs in the Mont Panié area, in which the government of Province Nord, the World Wildlife Fund, and CI work in partnership to complement terres-

trial conservation efforts. Each MPA is managed by their own committee which includes Province Nord. On the terrestrial side, Dayu Biik is now resourced with three full-time staff pioneering practical conservation management. This is one step in a formal process to establish a large integrated Ridge to Reef Conservation and Development Area. The value of MarineRAP was fully recognized and two more surveys have been supported by CI under Province Nord's leadership. Province Nord endorsed the MarineRAP methodology as a key baseline tool for improving information, planning and management of their UNESCO World Heritage Sites, including the Lagoons of New Caledonia Site, inscribed in 2008 following this survey.

Contributed by Sheila A. McKenna, Nathalie Baillon, and Henri Blaffart

Dedication

This MarineRAP, its success in both leveraging protection for the sites surveyed and providing a useful tool for Province Nord's further management of its marine areas is dedicated to the memory of Henri Blaffart, a dedicated and inspiring conservationist who saw only links rather than limits to land and sea conservation efforts.

I took Ted Parker and Murray Gell-Mann on a birding trip to Bolivia to discuss the RAP team idea. It was really Murray's original idea. Some of our scientific staff at the time scoffed at such an amateurish idea, but eventually saw the noble light shining through. Murray saw a handful of off scale, brilliant scientists in a variety of fields, people like Ted Parker on birds, Al Gentry, renowned "perchologist" (a term he loved to use with Peter Raven as a man who studied the things birds landed on; Murray is a bird lover), Gould the Amazon fish guy, and others with long deep field experience who, if brought together across disciplines, à la Santa Fe Institute, should be able to collectively identify the large scale tropical biodiversity hotspots. (hypothesize the quark, then test to prove it….the physicists' logic…)

We had the usual nightmare of logistics getting around in the yungas of Bolivia, unexpected road construction crews on the only highway (of mud) from the lowlands to the cloud forest, with interminable waiting between overloaded trucks with drivers fast asleep ("why are you guys always taking me to garbage dumps?" Murray asked. "Because that's where the roads end!" said Ted), a jeep from the Beni biological station with no brakes ("Stop!" Murray would shout as we rolled past a rare bird sighting.) "At least its flat ground Murray and we are not on foot!" I would retort.

At one field expedition outside of San Borja, we were suddenly surrounded overhead by what appeared to be camouflaged green DC3 DEA surveillance planes: we in our own camouflage outfits deep in the brush with binoculars and Ted's sound equipment, looking like so much drug and ammo equipment. On a multi-day side trip towards the Río Madidi-Rio Heath "hotspot" we went up a river in an Indian canoe full of smoked whole monkeys, one of which we thought might be a good welcome souvenir for Russ Mittermeier's imminent arrival to CI; but thought better of it. Murray complained constantly and bitterly; I sweated profusely; Ted Parker and I disagreed on the ID of a small forest falcon in our scope.

Looking worn and bearded but cleanly dressed, I was dragged out of the departure lounge of the Santa Cruz airport by the local drug enforcement mafia and strip searched. When I got back Murray was looking at the floor counting "one, one thousand, two, and one thousand…" But we roughed out an $750,000+ proposal to the MacArthur Foundation to launch RAP, which Russ et al. filled in with appropriate scientific rigor, and was later approved by Murray's world resources & environment committee and off we went.

About a week later Murray called to thank us for a wonderful, spectacular birding trip to Bolivia, his enthusiastic support of the RAP idea and later described the trip briefly in his book The Quark and the Jaguar *(published after Ted's untimely death, so Murray said he decided not to recount how I turned out to be right about the forest falcon ID; sadly my only claim to birding fame…)*

I was thrilled and fell asleep exhausted.

Way to go CI.

- Spencer Beebe, President, EcoTrust

An AquaRAP team of over 30 Brazilian and international scientists surveyed the wetlands of the Brazilian Pantanal in 1998. The team was exceptionally large due to the high level of interest and importance placed on the expedition by Brazilian governmental and academic institutions. The scientists were divided into two teams: one team spent the duration of the AquaRAP survey sampling the headwater regions of the Rio Taquari, Rio Aquidauana, Rio Negro, and Rio Miranda (Bodoquena region), while the other team concentrated on the Rio Negro watershed (upper, middle and lower regions), and on a stretch of the Rio Taboco. Daily reports from the field were sent via email/satellite link and posted on the CI website, allowing local stakeholders and any interested parties (including schools and university classrooms) to follow the AquaRAP team's work.

Prior to the AquaRAP survey, the fauna and flora of the headwaters of the rivers forming the southern Pantanal – between the Rio Taquari and Rio Miranda and in the Rio Bonito region – were poorly known scientifically. AquaRAP results from the headwater region revealed a tremendously interesting fauna, with 30% of the fishes collected being new to science. Close to 50% of the amphibians known for the pantanal/cerrado region were registered during the survey, even though the dry season is not ideal for amphibian sampling. Four of the amphibian species collected represent new records for the pantanal/cerrado region, and may also be new species. The flora in the region had never been documented and over 400 specimens were collected. The team's bota-

nists estimated that about 600 plant species occur in the region.

Although the fauna of the Pantanal wetlands is much better known than that of the headwaters, the AquaRAP team surveying the poorly known region of the Rio Negro watershed produced several new records for the region as well as potentially new species. Twenty-eight species of fish may be new to science, not including an interesting taxonomic puzzle regarding the local "red-bellied piranha". The expedition may also have uncovered a new species of shrimp and a new species of frog. Nine of the 12 species of crabs and shrimps known from the Pantanal were registered during this rapid assessment, as were 28 of the 35 known species of amphibians. One interesting finding was the different association of fish species with different species of aquatic plants. As an example, about 60% of the fish species found associated with purple hyacinths was different from the fish associated with white hyacinths. If floating or emergent aquatic species support different fish communities as preliminary results indicate, future fish sampling and conservation measures should take special note of the associated plant species.

In addition to scientific discoveries, the AquaRAP team documented the current environmental status of the Pantanal and put forth some critical conservation recommendations. The team found substantial deforestation throughout the headwater areas surveyed. Natural habitats are being replaced or altered for ranching, farming, and wood extraction. Deforestation of riparian forests along streams and rivers of the Pantanal destroys the condition of aquatic habitats both in the zone of deforestation and downstream. In the mid to lower Pantanal, riverside vegetation and back swamps, critical for the maintenance of the productivity of the Pantanal, are also disappearing. The *veredas* or *Mauritia* swamps, unique areas within the headwaters region, are currently in good shape but in need of protection. Although legislation exists to protect the critical vegetation along river margins, these laws need to be more strongly enforced.

Lack of effective regulation of commercial and sport fishing along the lower courses of the Pantanal has become another threat. The impact of fishing (both sport and commercial) on fish populations should be assessed, and regulations adjusted accordingly. The area and habitats required for successful reproduction of commercial, sport, and ornamental fishes must be determined and monitored constantly. The Rio Negro watershed forms a largely intact green corridor across the southern portion of the Pantanal and provides a tremendous opportunity for an integrated conservation plan that combines human-use of the land with conservation of the natural communities of the Pantanal, including its unique aquatic communities.

The AquaRAP data contributed to the creation of three protected areas in the Pantanal: The Serro Bodequena National Park (70,000 hectares); The Upper Taquaria State Park (30,000 ha); and the Pantanal do Rio Negro State Park (78,300 ha), which encompasses the Santa Sofia swamp that was highly recommended for protection by AquaRAP. These are the first aquatic parks anywhere in South America. Following the AquaRAP, CI-Brazil received a major donation which allowed them to purchase the 7,700 ha Rio Negro Farm in the heart of the Pantanal. This provides a corridor of aquatic protection within the Rio Negro watershed of the southern Pantanal. CI has established a field station and ecotourist lodge on this site. Teams of volunteers from Earthwatch come to the station to work on conservation projects related to water quality, limnology, fish stock assessment, and river otters.

Contributed by Leeanne Alonso

Leaf frog *(Phyllomedusa hypochondrialis)*

Flowers of *Eichhornia crassipes* (Family Pontederiaceae)

Floating mats of river vegetation

Papua New Guinea: Kaijende Highlands (August 19 – September 9, 2005)

In August-September 2005, a RAP expedition to the Kaijende Highlands in Enga Province, Papua New Guinea, documented plants and animals in a near-uninhabited expanse of spectacular montane grasslands and rainforest. The conservation value of this region was recognized nearly 20 years ago when Papua New Guinea's Department of Environment and Conservation recommended that it be considered a Wildlife Management Area. However at the time of this RAP survey little progress had been made towards protecting the area and information about the biodiversity of this remarkable alpine environment remained scant. To redress this lack of information, and to generate impetus towards declaration of the region as a conservation area, Conservation International and Papua New Guinea's Department of Environment and Conservation conducted a RAP biodiversity survey with support from the nearby Porgera Joint Venture mining operation. The RAP expedition surveyed sites ranging in elevation from 2,100-3,200 meters in lower montane rainforest on the shores of beautiful Lake Tawa, in stunted montane forest around Paiela Road, and in spectacular subalpine grasslands dotted with *Cyathea* treeferns behind the Porgera mine. Over a period of 22 days, researchers found nearly 500 species of plants, at least 16 of which were new to science; 102 species of birds; 30 species of mammals; and 17 species of frogs, 10 of which were new to science. The results of this survey generated a great deal of interest within Papua New Guinea, and Conservation International is currently working with local communities and the Forest Stewards Program in progressing towards the formalization of a conservation area that encompasses these important montane habitats.

Contributed by Stephen Richards

Spectacular scenery of the Kaijende Highlands

© Conservation International/photo by Stephen Richards

New Caledonia: Mont Panié (October 10 – 20 and November 1 – 30, 2010)

Cascade crayfish (*Atyopsis spinipes*)

© Province Nord / Photo by Julien Barrault

Two teams of botanists, entomologists, herpetologists, ornithologists, hydrobiologists and experts on invasive species assessed the biodiversity value and conservation status of five sites in and around the Mont Panié Wilderness Reserve in Province Nord of New Caledonia. Led by a partnership between Province Nord, Conservation International, and their local conservation partner Dayu Biik, the RAP survey involves New Caledonian and international experts, including five regional scientists, as well as local guides who will also be able to improve their taxonomic and scientific skills during the expedition. This RAP survey aims at providing a sound baseline for the development of the reserve management plan, as well as for the extension of the reserve. It currently covers 4,000 hectares of mountain forest within a forested block of 30,000 ha around Mont Panié, one of the highest peaks in the country (1,629 m). Mont Panié is already known to host many micro-endemic species, sometimes with ranges of only a few square kilometers, and many more species new to science are expected to be discovered during this RAP survey. Invasive species, wild bushfires and climate change are thought to be the most critical threats to the forest and its rivers, all lying in the buffer zone of a World Heritage Site which includes a world-class reef just north of the mainland that was assessed during a MarineRAP in 2004. Mont Panié's forests play a critical role in the traditional Kanak culture, providing wild food, construction wood, medicinal plants, and erosion control within an area of high biological value.

Contributed by François Tron and Jean-Jérôme Cassan

Guatemala
Laguna del Tigre National Park
April 8 – 30, 1999

© Conservation International/photo by Sterling Zumbrunn

© Piotr Naskrecki

© Conservation International/photo by Leeanne E. Alonso

Green iguana (*Iguana iguana*)

© Piotr Naskrecki

Laguna del Tigre National Park is located within the Maya Biosphere Reserve, a largely dry forest system that extends from southern Mexico through northern Guatemala and Belize.

The western portion of the park is characterized by flooded savanna wetlands and lagoons designated as "Wetlands of International Importance" under the Ramsar convention. A combination freshwater and terrestrial RAP survey was carried out in the park in 1999 to evaluate the biodiversity of a wide variety of habitat types with respect to phytoplankton, aquatic insects, fish, amphibians, reptiles, ants, birds, and mammals. The primary objectives of the RAP survey were to augment the park's biodiversity database, highlight the park's regional importance, evaluate the nature of the threats to animals and plants within the park, and provide this information to natural resource managers and decision makers.

Other objectives included bringing international attention to an important scientific resource, the Guacamayas Biological Station, a research station located near the southern boundary the park, and training local students in species identification and ecological monitoring techniques. The ecological work focused on documenting the biodiversity value of several aquatic and terrestrial taxa in the park, investigating the relationships between taxa and different habitats and areas of the park in order to ascertain the conservation value of those areas, and evaluating the potential effects of ongoing deforestation and petroleum development on the park's biodiversity.

The RAP team recorded 647 species, including range extensions for one mammal, three birds, and two ant species. The species list included 71 species of phytoplankton, 44 species of aquatic insects associated with Eared Watermoss (Salvinia auriculata), 130 species of plants, 41 species of fishes, 173 species of birds, 36 species of reptiles and amphibians, 40 species of mammals, and 112 species of ants. This RAP survey provided the first species lists of ants and phytoplankton for Laguna del Tigre National Park. Remarkably, the park harbors 16 vertebrate species that are of international concern and that are listed by IUCN and/or the Convention on the International Trade of Endangered Species of Wild Fauna and Flora (CITES). Also, an extremely rare freshwater reef habitat, composed of living and dead bivalve mollusks, was discovered on the Río San Pedro. This reef harbored a unique assemblage of plants and animals. Environmental heterogeneity was recognized differently by each taxon. For some taxa, marshes were important; for others, lagoons, rivers, or complex forests were important.

A great variety of both aquatic and terrestrial habitats were observed in the course of the RAP sampling, including marshes, lagoons, rivers, streams, regenerating forests, and pristine forests. The diversity of species and the representation of endemic, rare, or endangered species were also high, underscoring the park's value for conservation in Central America. An ecotoxicological assessment of two fish species revealed an impact of mutagenic contaminants within some of the park's aquatic ecosystems. Publication of this finding led to investigations into oil operations within the park that identified an illegal concession in operation, which was revoked and shut down.

Since the RAP survey, threats to Laguna del Tigre National Park have greatly escalated. Oil operations and other extractive industries have spread within the park. Human colonization along roads created for oil operation and illegal activities such as cattle ranching have increased.

Some important actions have been recently carried out to address these threats, which endanger the long term viability of the park. Networks between Civil Society and the Government have been strengthened to improve and restore the governance of Laguna del Tigre National Park. Governmental agencies responsible for territorial management and control, the National Protected Areas Council (CONAP) and Conservationist Studies Center of San Carlos de Guatemala University (CECON), have increased their capacity in strategic zones with Laguna del Tigre National Park and the Maya Biosphere Reserve over the last three years, with the following results: removal of more than 1,260 head of cattle from illegal ranches; injunctions and legal proceedings initiated against five illegally established ranches; commitment for more than 250 new soldiers to be trained as "green brigades"; and confiscation of several truckloads of illegally logged timber and trafficked wildlife.

These actions are making progress in the battle to maintain the ecological viability of this critical wetland within the Maya Biosphere Reserve, but the long term survival of Laguna del Tigre National Park is still very much in jeopardy. More resources and global efforts to stem the threats and restore habitat are needed.

Contributed by Miriam Castillo, Leeanne Alonso, Roan Balas, and Bayron Castellanos

Red Bay Snook *(Petenia splendida)* – color polymorphism

Montezuma's Oropendula *(Psarocolius montezuma)*

Acacia ant *(Pseudomyrmex flavicornis)*

133

The Glamorous Life of a RAP Scientist: A fine dining experience

All photos © Piotr Naskrecki

Spacious, comfortable seating

Elegant dining companions

Delicious smoked fish (with barely any maggots)

A typical expression of utter culinary bliss

Authentic, local cuisine, served fresh and still warm

© Conservation International/photo by Peter Hoke

© Phillip Willink

Rocks on Coppename

© Jessica Deichmann

RAP ichthyologists sampling fish

The Coppename River Basin is a large basin that originates in the heart of the Central Suriname Nature Reserve, a large protected area in the center of Suriname that has received protection and international interest in large part due to Conservation International's activities. In 1999, CI President Dr. Russell Mittermeier and the President of Suriname signed an agreement designating the 1.6 million hectare area as a national Nature Reserve. The Coppename River travels northward through pristine forests of the Reserve before reaching the Atlantic Ocean. The Coppename River is fed from black, white and clear water tributaries, which create diverse aquatic and terrestrial ecological communities. The Coppename River drains two-thirds of the reserve area, making it a vital part of the entire ecosystem.

CI-Suriname and partners were tasked with developing a management plan for the Reserve, for which data on the aquatic diversity and water quality were needed. Thus an AquaRAP survey was conducted in 2004 to assess the aquatic biodiversity of the Coppename River and its major tributaries. During the AquaRAP survey, the team surveyed all three of the upper branches of the Coppename - the Rechter Coppename, Linker Coppename, and the Midden Coppename - down to the mouth. Access to these river branches is very difficult and few people have ever ventured up them. Due to extremely low water levels at the time of the AquaRAP survey, the RAP team

traveled to the Upper Rechter Coppename River by helicopter, landing along the river bank and unloading all the scientific equipment and rubber zodiacs for the trip. The team then traveled down the Rechter Coppename River into the other branches, continuing down the main Coppename River back to the Reserve headquarters at Ralleighvallen and finally to the mouth of the river. Only the lower parts of the Coppename River outside of the reserve have human settlements along it. While all members of the RAP team and their specimens survived the trip in good condition, the zodiacs did not! Next time RAP will stick with the local dugout canoes which are better suited to the enormous boulders and rocks of Suriname's rivers.

The AquaRAP team was pleased to find the Coppename River Basin to be one of the largest, most intact and pristine watersheds they had ever encountered. Water quality was good in all sections of the river surveyed and fishes were large with brilliant colors. Overall species richness recorded was moderate for a Neotropical river with plants and aquatic animals comparable in species richness to other lowland forests and rivers of the Guiana Shield. Aquatic insect richness was higher than found in other areas due to the abundance of rock-clinging aquatic plants of the family Podostemaceae, known commonly as riverweed. Ten species of fishes were new to science, and four were new records for Suriname. No exotic or invasive species were recorded up river of Ralleighvallen. Several species indicative of pristine forest and high water quality, including Ephemeroptera (mayflies) and freshwater sponges were recorded. Many species of crabs, shrimps, and fishes demonstrated specific habitat requirements that should be considered in conservation planning. The shrimp *Macrobrachium faustinum* requires both freshwater and the coastal environment to complete its life cycle, which highlights connectedness of freshwater and marine ecosystems within the Coppename River Basin.

Given the remoteness of most of the Coppename River Basin from human settlements and its pristine nature, most of the conservation recommendations resulting from the AquaRAP survey focused on regulating and monitoring human activities such as fishing, hunting, tourism, and the export of natural resources from the reserve. The main threat to the Coppename River Basin and the Reserve comes from possible future bauxite mining in the Bakhuis Mountains to the west and the construction of roads to the north. Of particular interest and concern was the Adampada Creek, which originates in the Bakhuis Mountains and joins the Coppename inside the Reserve. The RAP team strongly recommended: 1) control and monitor future mining activities in the adjacent Bakhuis Mountains to avoid potential impacts on Adampada Creek and other areas of the Reserve, and 2) expand the boundary of the Reserve to include the entire Coppename watershed, especially to include the Adampada Creek. CI-Suriname and RAP have plans to survey the area between the Reserve and the Bakuis mining concession to delineate an area that can serve as a buffer zone between the two areas.

Contributed by Leeanne Alonso and Annette Tjon Sie Fat

In early 2008, I was very fortunate to be given the opportunity to travel to southeast Venezuela to take part in the Río Cuyuní AquaRAP. The trip lasted three weeks; my days in South America are ones that I'll remember for the rest of my life.

We arrived in Venezuela a day late as a snow storm in Atlanta delayed our departure from Washington; we did get bumped up to business class so things were already looking up! We reached the capital, Caracas, in the early hours, and after just 4 hours sleep, headed back to the airport. We then flew to Puerto Ordaz accompanied by Anabel Rial who was managing logistics. On arrival we connected with Henry Briceño (limnologist) and Bruce Holst (botanist) who were also travelling to the RAP camp. It was a 6 hour drive to the Brisas mining camp; from there we would leave the following morning by boat to the RAP camp.

Up at 5:30 am, we headed to the river in 4x4's. The short journey was plagued by the most unbelievable mud I have ever seen, and the 4x4's were sliding all over the place. We arrived unscathed, and once the boats were loaded up we began our trip to the RAP camp. We finally reached our destination and on gazing at our new home I felt like I had arrived at Allie Fox's Geronimo camp in the film "Mosquito Coast". There was an incredible wooden-tarped structure peering out of the jungle which served us well as a meeting/dining/sleeping area during our time there.

Over the next few days I filmed the scientists at work, documented camp life, and got used to spending an extended period of time in the jungle. We had 3 cooks who did an amazing job so we never went hungry. Bathing was a little different - each day I would head to the river in my swim shorts and immerse myself in the freezing river water; after a few days, it felt perfectly normal! (I tried to keep any thoughts of snakes and caimans in the back of my mind…) The climate was warm and a little muggy and it would rain on and off during the day. I was often placing the camera in a zip lock bag throughout my time in the field.

As the days wore on I was surprised how tiring life in the jungle was. We'd be up early (5:30 or 6:00 am), and after breakfast the teams would head off to conduct their surveys. By 9:00 pm most nights I would be hitting the sack (something I could never imagine doing so early at home in the US!). Halfway through our time in the field, I joined a group travelling to a higher elevation site by helicopter. In one word, WOW! I had never travelled by helicopter, let alone over the jungles of Venezuela. During the flight I was able to shoot some great video which included an amazing waterfall which was tumbling off a table-top mountain (tepui) and appeared to be pouring directly out of the clouds themselves.

I made the most of our 3 days at this camp and worked alongside ornithologist David Ascanio who I filmed conducting bird surveys and playing bird calls on his iPod, trying to draw out different species to add to his records - very cool stuff. After the weekend, we headed back by helicopter (a hairy ride as it was so misty that at one point the helicopter was having issues with visibility). During our time away, there had been lots of flooding at the first camp and the water had risen 9 ft!

My remaining days in the jungle were spent conducting on-camera interviews with team members and shooting more footage of the teams at work. One day while hiking, we arrived at a beautiful waterfall in the middle of nowhere. We took advantage of this and had a refreshing swim in the very cold water. Travelling back to camp that day was challenging and the last parts of the hike were lit by headlamps. Before I knew it we were breaking down camp and preparing for departure. On the final morning, the team spent many hours trying to recover a boat that had capsized and sank overnight! The next day, we were back in Puerto Ordaz. The team was in fine spirits as we had all made it safely out of the jungle, and everyone was looking forward to getting back to civilization and family. We all said our goodbyes at the airport and then caught our respective flights. I went to Caracas where I connected with some of the team to help get the plant samples down to the botanical gardens for analysis and pressing.

Finally it was time to leave Venezuela, an incredibly beautiful country in which I had the good fortune of spending time in the rainforest with a great team of scientists and staff. RAP surveys are an amazing tool that draws on experts around the world and following the surveys themselves, produces a powerful and tangible document that can be placed in the hands of key decision makers. My time in Venezuela taking part in an AquaRAP will not easily be forgotten and I'll treasure the experience for years to come.

- Edward Lohnes, Conservation International

Indonesia
Raja Ampat Islands, Bird's Head Seascape
March 27 – April 10, 2001

Coleman shrimp *(Periclimenes colemani)*

Located near the heart of the Coral Triangle – the richest area of coral reefs on Earth – the Raja Ampat Islands' diverse array of marine life, coupled with striking island scenery, make it one of the world's most spectacular tropical wildlife areas. The Archipelago lies west of Papua Province, Indonesia and is surrounded by approximately 4,000,000 hectares of sea. The Raja Ampat Islands are composed of four main islands (Misool, Salawati, Batanta, and Waigeo) and hundreds of smaller islands, cays, and shoals. The population consists of just under 49,000 residents, most of Papuan origin, inhabiting 89 villages, with about seven people per km². The survey area covered approximately 600,000 ha, encompassing reefs of the Dampier Strait between northern Batanta and Waigeo. The survey was implemented by Conservation International in collaboration with the University of Cenderawasih and the Research and Development Center for Oceanology, a branch of the Indonesian Institute of Sciences.

The main objectives of the survey were: 1) to document local marine biodiversity of the three selected indicator taxa of mollusks, hard corals and coral reef fishes, 2) to assess the condition of coral reefs, 3) to take an initial snapshot of the existing level of fisheries exploitation and 4) to assess the importance of marine resources to the economic livelihood and general well-being of local villagers. The purpose in collecting such data was to guide regional planning, marine conservation, and the use of sustainable marine resources. Forty-five different MarineRAP biodiversity survey sites were reached by motor boats, operating from base camps at Kri Island and Alyui Bay. For the socioeconomic component of the survey, the MarineRAP team visited 22 villages and sought input from about 7,700 people. These villages ranged in size from Arborek with just 98 people, to Fam with 785 inhabitants.

The MarineRAP survey results indicated an extraordinary marine fauna. Totals for the three major indicator groups surpassed those for all previous MarineRAP surveys at that time in Indonesia, Papua New Guinea, and the Philippines. Researchers identified 456 species of hard corals, more than half the world's total. For mollusks, a total of 699 species were recorded during the survey. Among reef fish, 828 species, including four species never before recorded by science, were documented raising the total known from the area to 972 species. Reefs were generally in very good condition compared to most areas of Indonesia, with high live coral diversity and minimal stress due to natural phenomenon such as cyclones, predation and freshwater runoff. Almost every village in the area complained about the use of explosives for fishing by outsiders (i.e., non-villagers) and explosive damage was noted at 13.3% of the survey sites. Illegal logging (in designated nature reserve areas) that can lead to heavy siltation stress and ultimately death for the delicate coral reefs was also noted.

More than 90% of the adult population of this area is engaged in sustenance-level fishing. At most villages there is relatively little commercial activity, although some people collect sea cucumbers (relatives of starfish) that are sold to merchants in Sorong, the nearest large population center on the mainland. Fishers from at least seven villages were found to be using chemicals containing cyanide to catch Napoleon Wrasse and large groupers. Many villagers expressed concern about various illegal fishing methods. There was a scarcity of large groupers, Maori or Napoleon Wrasse, and sharks observed during the survey. This represents a potential consequence of being targeted by illegal fishers, either for the lucrative live fish trade or for food.

Although much of the area is already gazetted as a wildlife reserve, there is no real enforcement of conservation laws as evidenced by the illegal logging and destructive fishing practices. There is an urgent need for marine and terrestrial conservation action. Several sites were identified as deserving of special attention and included Cape Kri, Kri Island, Gam-Waigeo Passage, Majalibit Passage and the adjacent Majalibit Bay Pam Islands, Equator Islands, Saripa Bay and Wayag Islands. Further recommendations were for more RAP surveys, both terrestrial and marine, such as those that subsequently took place in 2006 (see MarineRAP profiles of Fakfak-Kaimana and Teluk-Cenderawasih Bay). The results of the Raja Ampat survey catalyzed local communities, the government, and nongovernmental organizations to develop a strategic conservation plan for the region. Conservation work in the region grew from that point onward to form the multi-national Coral Triangle Initiative, a new multilateral partnership to safeguard the region's extraordinary marine and coastal biological resources.

Contributed by Sheila A. McKenna, Gerry Allen, and Suer Suryadi

Wayag Islands

Mayalibit Village

Lionfish (*Pterois* sp.)

It was early 2004 and José Maria Cardoso da Silva, then CI Brazil's Vice president of Science – and my director, since at that time I was CI's Amazonia Program Manager – came to my office and said:

"Enrico, as part of our work to implement the Amapá Biodiversity Corridor, we have to increase the scientific knowledge on the biodiversity there. We need such information to refine our scientific analysis about species occurrence, endemism, diversity and their conservation status. Moreover, none of the conservation units there have management plans and they also need this information. We are missing the data and we definitively need to go to the field. Get ready to coordinate such task."

That sounded like music to my ears. As a biologist working in Amazonia for more than a decade, I knew Amapá was a large data gap. In other words, it was a real chance to sample large untouched areas of Amazonian forest – a dream for any biologist. Still excited about the possibilities, I didn't realize at that moment the size and the complexity of the task José Maria just had asked me to do. Days later, when I finished putting the project on paper, I had a better idea about the dimension of the challenge: 10 million hectares. That was the size of Amapá Biodiversity Corridor. The core of the Corridor was Montanhas do Tumucumaque National Park, then the largest continuous forest protected area in the world, with 3.6 million hectares alone. Tumucumaque is huge. To be more precise, 220 km from north to south, 250 km from east to west, and 1750 km of perimeter. There were no roads; the area is accessible just by small boats due to its rocky and shallow rivers, or by air, using helicopters – what a challenge!

Fully supported by CI and our partners in Amapá (IBAMA and IEPA), the project moved on and I put together a team of young and motivated scientists to conduct the inventories. Motivation was the # 1 requirement, since we realized that a minimum of 5 expeditions would be necessary to sample Tumucumaque's large and diverse area. Motivation was also necessary because, due to the remoteness and difficulty of access, our expeditions would require around 30 days of field work each. No cold drinks, no toilet and no amenities for 30 days in the jungle. In the first expedition, we had requested support from the Brazilian Army to help us with the logistics and a sergeant was responsible for our food menu for the entire expedition. Confident in his capacity, I didn't check his food list. What a mistake! The guy was cruel: we had 30 days of rice and sausage – for breakfast, lunch and dinner. Needless to say, food lists became a priority for me in the next expeditions.

The work was also physically challenging. I still remember one expedition when we had to drag our heavy wooden boats (safer for the rocky waters) over 14 waterfalls and rapids to reach the selected sampling point. One after another, we cursed our satellite images that were not able to detect the rapids hidden by the forest. In another expedition, the goal was to reach a special area in the park, a place where the forest was dotted with inselbergs (huge rock blocks, like Rio de Janeiro's Corcovado). At this time, thanks again to the Brazilian Army, we skipped the small, slow boats, and were transported by helicopter. The pilots took the opportunity to train their skills and practice low altitude flights. Flying a Black Hawk chopper, with doors open, just two meters above the forest canopy, almost touching the tallest trees, was surreal.

But it was the scientific and biological experience that marked me most. The chance to have close encounters with animals not familiar with humans was fantastic. Spider monkeys, which always shy away in other areas of Amazonia, never avoided curious contact with us. One day while working on a trail, I was surprised by a huge female tapir and her infant coming exactly in my direction. I became completely silent and still. With a poor sense of sight and contrary wind, the female did not detect me. I decide to see how close our encounter would be. She changed direction when we were literally less than half a meter apart and I decided to move to avoid being hit by them. Another exciting experience was seeing the specimens recorded by my colleagues: so many different colors, shapes, sizes, appendages, tails, fins, nails and beaks – amazingly different life forms.

After almost two years, we successfully concluded our five expeditions to Tumucumaque, recording nearly 1,700 species, several of them new to science. We assessed the conservation status of the park and concluded that Tumucumaque is in excellent shape, providing immensurable ecosystem services, not just locally but globally as well. Today, almost 6 years after the first expedition to Tumucumaque, while I was writing this text and revisiting those experiences in my memory, I realize that I was a privileged person. In a world that is changing so fast and so intensely, I had the privilege to experience nature at its best.

- Enrico Bernard, Adjunct Professor at Universidade Federal de Pernambuco, Brazil

© Gerald Allen   © Burt Jones   © Burt Jones

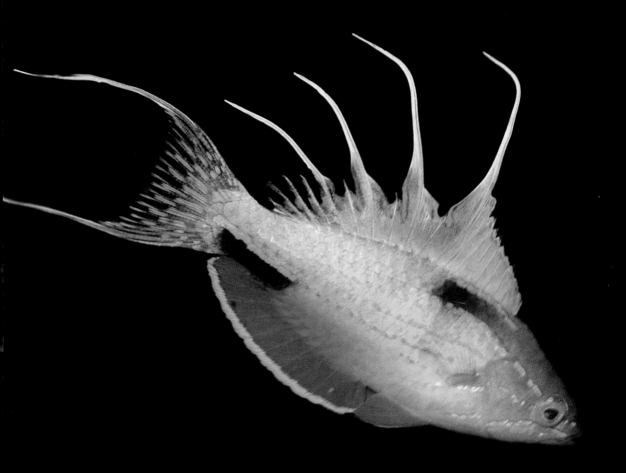

An endemic flasher wrasse *(Paracheilinus nursalim)*

© Gerald Allen

Rounding out the trio of Bird's Head Seascape MarineRAP surveys, this survey covered the topographically complex southern coastline of West Papua province from Fakfak to Kaimana regencies, including the Bomberai Peninsula and Triton Bay.

As with Cenderawasih Bay, this MarineRAP survey had five main objectives: 1) assess the reef condition, fish biomass and marine biodiversity values of the southern Bird's Head Seascape; 2) identify any areas of outstanding marine conservation importance that should be prioritized for inclusion in marine protected areas (MPAs); 3) conduct socioeconomic and fisheries surveys of coastal villages to identify conservation threats and opportunities arising from local attitudes and practices; 4) assess the potential for the development of marine tourism in the region; and 5) estimate levels of ecological and genetic connectivity between the reefs of the southern Bird's Head and those in Raja Ampat and Cenderawasih to inform seascape-level management strategies.

The MarineRAP survey visited 39 sites over an 1,300 km route, with over 550 man hours underwater recorded. The first half of the survey covered the stunning reefs of Fakfak and the Bomberai Peninsula, revealing excellent hard coral cover (particularly in Sebakor Bay) and a host of new coral species (up to 16, most of which are con-

sidered endemic). Three of these sites contained world-record coral diversity, with over 250 coral species recorded at each site.

As the survey entered the waters of Kaimana Regency and Triton Bay, the tremendous influx of freshwater from large coastal river systems led to a dramatic shift in reef communities. Hard corals became few and far between, while stunning soft coral gardens replaced them. Reef fish diversity, apparently enhanced by the presence of extensive soft bottom habitats in immediate proximity to the reefs, skyrocketed; a world record 330 fish species were recorded at a single survey site at Tanjung Papisol! The team was amazed at the diversity and abundance of normally rare fish species like tilefishes, jawfishes and garden eels. At least ten new fish species were uncovered, as well as three new stomatopod mantis shrimp species.

The reefs around Kaimana were not only diverse, they were thick with at least 232 different species of economically important reef food fish including groupers and snappers: the team recorded the highest reef fish biomasses of anywhere previously surveyed in SE Asia, averaging 228 tons/km². Perhaps taking advantage of this abundance, a unique resident population of Bryde's whales *(Balaenoptera brydei)* was also uncovered in the area, as well as a hammerhead shark *(Sphyrna lewini)* pupping ground in Triton Bay.

Unfortunately, the team also determined that local communities lacked the conservation awareness seen elsewhere in the Bird's Head, with shark-finning and turtle poaching (eggs and adults) rampant throughout the region. On the bright side, the local government was extremely enthusiastic about the MarineRAP survey findings and keen to both develop a new MPA and marine tourism in the area.

The team highlighted three areas of extreme conservation value for possible gazettement in new MPAs, including Sebakor Bay (due to its stunning and endemic coral gardens), Tanjung Papisol (outstanding reef fish biodiversity and near pristine coastal watersheds), and Triton Bay (unique soft-coral dominated reefs with extremely high fish biomass and resident Bryde's whale population). They also recommended that the local and national government immediately institute a turtle nest-guarding program on the highly endangered nesting beaches in Pulau Venu Nature Reserve. Finally, the team highlighted the strong potential for marine tourism development in the southern Bird's Head as a potential source of sustainable income for local coastal communities. For an update on the follow-through with the recommendations of this and the other two Bird's Head Seascape MarineRAP surveys, see the Indonesia Regional Summary on page 272.

Contributed by Mark Erdmann

© Gerald Allen

Mantis shrimp *(Busquilla plantae)*

© Gerald Allen

Endemic tilefish *(Hoplolatilus erdmanni)*

Kaimana fish

© Burt Jones

Bolivia
Upper Río Orthon Basin, Pando
September 4 – 20, 1996

© Barry Chernoff

© Theresa Bert

Armoured catfish *(Liposarcus disjunctivus)*

© Theresa Bert

The first survey of RAP's South American AquaRAP program focused on the watershed of the Río Orthon in northern Bolivia. This area, which encompasses the Tahuamanu and Manuripi river systems in the northern department of Pando, Bolivia, had been largely unexplored previous to the AquaRAP expedition. The upper Río Orthon basin represents an important transition zone between drier deciduous forests to the south and the wet lowland Amazonian forests to the north and east. The Río Orthon basin, a remote section of the larger upper Río Madeira basin, is typified by unique, heterogeneous riparian forest communities and floodplain vegetation. It has been said that this area has the potential to hold the richest aquatic biodiversity within Bolivia, if not within the Amazon River Basin.

The Río Orthon's natural ecosystems were being threatened by increasing human occupation and commercial activities. Large tracts of forests were being converted to pastures for cattle, with the hardwood being removed for lumber. Such habitat conversion puts great pressure on both terrestrial and aquatic ecosystems. Freshwater ecosystems were further stressed by an unregulated food fishery. Because so little was known about the ecosystems in the Río Orthon basin, especially freshwater systems, and due to the threats occurring in this area so close to the northern boundary of the Heath-Madidi conservation region (created as a result of the very first RAP expedition in 1990), immediate attention was required to support conservation activities.

Over the course of 17 days, the first AquaRAP team uncovered 120 species of zooplankton with Rotifera and Protozoa being the most diverse groups. Over 1,500 different benthic macroinvertebrates belonging to 19 orders were identified, including many bivalves, oligochaete worms, gastropods, and leeches, among others. Seventeen different genera of chironomid flies, indicators of water quality, were also found in the waters of the Tahuamanu and Manuripi rivers. Water quality was assessed at 22 different sites within the rivers. The water appeared to be of good quality and did not exhibit significant signs of contamination or eutrophication.

The AquaRAP team collected 10 species of freshwater crabs and shrimps including six new records for Bolivia. Shrimps and crabs are important players in aquatic and terrestrial food chains, acting as predators, filterers, decomposers and prey. It is anticipated that they can be conserved as long as their habitats are not significantly modified.

Over 300 fish species were collected from 85 stations, of which 87 are new records for Bolivia and 45 of these are likely new to science. This small region in northeastern Bolivia contains 63% and 49% of all the species known to inhabit the Bolivian Amazon and Bolivia, respectively. The AquaRAP team collected 500 samples for genetic tests and employed novel analyses of the fish diversity to investigate fish distribution patterns within the Río Orthon basin. They found that fish species were not distributed randomly among the rivers within the basin, but showed highest diversity in the Rio Manuripi. This is important for conservation, as 75% of the fish species were documented in the Rio Manuripi and Rio Nareuda, making them key areas for conservation. Tributaries and flooded areas are also important as over 80% of the fishes depend on flooded areas for reproduction and food. Thus maintenance of the seasonal flooding regime is critical to maintaining fish diversity.

The surveyed area was originally located within the Manuripi-Heath National Amazon Reserve, which was created in December 1973. This national reserve was assessed by the Land Use Plan of the Pando department in 1995 and the Reserve's limits were adjusted in 2000. Today, the Bolivian headwaters of the Manuripi River are included within the Manuripi Amazonian Wildlife National Reserve which comprises in total more than 700,000 hectares. Additionally, a 22,000 hectare conservation concession surrounding the Tahuamanu Biological Station located in the Tahuamanu river basin has been proposed and is the subject of on-going discussions.

Contributed by Juan Carlos Ledezma

Indonesia – Papua Province: Wapoga River Area (March 31 – May 2, 1998)

Every survey is unique and presents challenges, but the Wapoga RAP survey stood out as one of the more complex efforts in RAP's history. Fifteen scientists and several support staff surveyed five sites from near sea level to 1,900 m in an extremely remote and rugged area of western New Guinea. Sites were accessible only by helicopter and the terrain was so rough, we could barely move more than 500 m from some of our base camps. When the team arrived they found themselves deep in a part of New Guinea where no biologist had previously set foot, and during the survey they were visited by a small group of indigenous people dressed completely in traditional manner and showing no evidence of experience with the outside world. The biodiversity of the region was spectacular, and even by New Guinea standards the number of new species discovered was outstanding. These included more than 20 new species of frogs, dozens of new species of ants and aquatic insects, and several new species of freshwater fishes and plants.

Colorful weevil *(Eupholus sp.)*

© Conservation International/photo by S. Richards

The best protection for conservation of biodiversity in places like Wapoga might be the rugged mountains, heavy rainfall and frequent landslides that make road building and colonization by humans so difficult.

Contributed by Andrew Mack

© Galo Buitron

© Jessica Deichmann

© Galo Buitron

Velvet worm (Onychophora: Peripatidae)

© Jessica Deichmann

© Jessica Deichmann

The Cordillera del Cóndor in southeastern Ecuador lies within one of the most critically threatened ecoregions in the world. Owing to its isolation from the Andes mountains, its unique soil characters, and the unusual presence of both black and white water rivers, the Cordillera del Cóndor contains a unique complement of species with origins in the Andes as well as species found in the Guiana Shield, thousands of kilometers away. Unlike much of the Andes, the Cordillera del Cóndor has, up to now, escaped major deforestation and maintains much of its original forest cover and associated biodiversity.

Lying close to Ecuador's historically contested border with Peru, the Nangaritza River Basin in the Cordillera del Cóndor is geologically unique. Ranging in altitude from 950 to 1,850 meters, the higher elevation points form flat-topped mountains known as "tepuis" (pronounced te-poo-ees). Tepuis are best known from further north in South America, where they are much larger and contain a vast array of unique and endemic species. Although the tepuis of the Nangaritza are smaller, the cool wet weather and characteristic poor soils set the stage for an equally unique diversity of life in the Nangaritza tepuis.

In 2004, over 90,000 hectares of the Upper Nangaritza River Basin were declared a Protected Forest, and its protection was assigned to the indigenous Shuar Tayunts and the community of San Miguel de las Orquídeas who inhabit the area. Currently, these communities are working with the Ecuadorean Ministry of Environment toward obtaining increased protection status there. In 2009, a RAP survey was conducted to provide the Shuar and the San Miguel community with information on the biodiversity and ecosystems in the Nangaritza tepuis so that they can build a strong case for strengthening official protection for the area.

RAP botanists noted unique vegetation as an adaptation to the poor soils and wet climate: on top of the tepuis, vegetation was stunted and composed primarily of mosses, terrestrial bromeliads, dwarf shrubs and a few trees, while the forests surrounding the tepuis were mainly lower montane wet forests with trees densely covered by epiphytes. In total, the RAP team found 274 plant, 93 invertebrate, 27 amphibian, 17 reptile, 205 bird and 65 mammal species – an incredible number for such a small area of mid-elevation forest. Among these were many species recorded for the first time ever in Ecuador, including two katydids, one frog, one mouse species and the Endangered Lesser Yellow-shouldered Bat *(Sturnira nana)*. The RAP team also discovered at least 31 species new to science: three plant, 13 katydid, 10 stick insect, one salamander, one reptile and three frog species, including *Pristimantis minimus*, which is now the smallest known terrestrial vertebrate in the country.

The RAP team made another surprising discovery – a healthy population of a species of harlequin frog *(Atelopus* aff. *palmatus)*. Over 90% of *Atelopus* species are listed as Endangered, Critically Endangered or Extinct by the IUCN Red List of Endangered species, and of the 21 species known from Ecuador, the vast majority has been devastated by disease and appears to be extinct. This discovery represents just the third healthy population currently known in the country. Conservation of this frog is important not only for posterity, but frogs also provide a number of ecosystem services important to humans: adult frogs prey on mosquitoes, ticks and other pest and disease-carrying species, and tadpoles help maintain water quality by grazing on algae while at the same time providing a food source for commercially valuable fish.

The RAP team recommended that land titles be provided to the Shuar Tayunts and the San Miguel community who are currently in charge of managing the Nangaritza Protected Forest. They also recommended the establishment of zones in the conservation area for no-trespassing, scientific use only and for ecotourism, and that the communities develop clear sanctions for failure to comply with the zoning. The Upper Nangaritza River Basin is of significant conservation importance and warrants increased protection designation under Ecuadorean legislation. Creation of a National Park or Biological Reserve should include this area of the Cordillera del Cóndor and also the nearby Cutucú mountain range, which would conserve one of the most biologically and culturally diverse regions of South America.

After the RAP survey, the team designed a colorful booklet for local communities describing the findings of the survey, including drawings of species found in the conservation area. The booklet was distributed in the community of San Miguel de Las Orquídeas, and can be used for communicating the biological importance of the region as well as promoting ecotourism. Fundación Ecológica Arcoiris, a local NGO based in Loja, and Pontificia Universidad Católica del Ecuador, two of the partners in this RAP survey, have also begun "Project Atelopus", supported by CI-Ecuador and designed to protect the healthy population of harlequin frogs discovered during the survey.

Contributed by Jessica Deichmann, Juan Manuel Guayasamin, Cristina Félix, and Luis Suárez

Leaf katydid *(Typophyllum* sp. n.*)*, a new species discovered during the survey

Tepui harlequin frog *(Atelopus* aff. *palmatus)*

Camp "Los Tepuyes"

151

The Glamorous Life of a RAP Scientist: Meet new friends

"Stompy", the friendly elephant (who came to inform us that the protective fence around our camp in Botswana was not working)

"Sandy", the affable leishmaniasis-transmitting sand fly

"Sleepy", the sleeping sickness-transmitting tsetse fly

"Clingy", the affectionate tick

"Piercy", the always hungry malarial mosquito

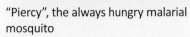

"Swarmy", the inquisitive driver ant, and hundreds and hundreds and hundreds of her sisters

All photos © Piotr Naskrecki

Golden-fronted Bowerbird (*Amblyornis flavifrons*)

High Foja summits

Until 1979 the Foja Mountains of Papua Province, Indonesia, remained a mystery to scientists documenting biodiversity on the island of New Guinea. In 1979 and 1981 Professor Jared Diamond became the first scientist/explorer to visit the Fojas where he rediscovered the "lost" Golden-fronted Bowerbird, a species previously known only from trade skins. This unusual discovery hinted that the Foja Mountains may be an important center of biological endemism and the home of additional novel species.

Rising to about 2,200 meters elevation, and entirely isolated from other mountain regions, the Foja Mountains constitute an unroaded and unpopulated forest reserve of 300,000 hectares on the northern fringe of the great Mamberamo Basin. At more than 7 million hectares, this basin contains the largest single block of humid tropical forest in the Asia-Pacific region. At higher elevations rain falls all year round, and clouds persistently cloak the highest peaks. Although their isolation and constantly warm, wet conditions make the uplands an ideal site to search for endemic biodiversity, the rough terrain characteristic of the area prevented

access by scientists until Jared Diamond reached the interior with the aid of a helicopter. To this day a helicopter is required to gain access to the interior uplands of this isolated mountain range.

After more than a decade of planning, preparation, and negotiation, the first RAP expedition to the Foja Mountains was conducted in November-December 2005. This was followed by a second RAP survey in October-November 2008. These two expeditions were conducted as a partnership between the Indonesian Institute of Science, Conservation International, and several international research institutions (Smithsonian Institution, South Australian Museum, Harvard University, and the National Geographic Society). Each trip fielded more than 20 fieldworkers, who focused their work on either the foothills or the highlands interior.

The Foja Mountains RAP surveys documented at least 75 species new to science, including more than 40 new arthropod species, over 20 new frog species, no less than 10 new plant species, five new mammal species, and two new species of bird. The announcement of these discoveries created a media sensation and put the Foja Mountains on the map as a "Lost World."

Highlights of the RAP survey research included: 1) first record for Indonesia of the Golden-mantled Tree-Kangaroo, one of the rarest mammals in the Asia-Pacific region; 2) re-discovery of the "lost" bird of paradise, Berlepsch's Parotia; 3) two new species of birds – a honeyeater and an imperial pigeon; and 4) discovery of the world's smallest kangaroo (a tiny terrestrial wallaby).

The discoveries led to an Indonesian postage-stamp series commemorating the 2005 expedition, and enhanced government attention to the importance of the Mamberamo Basin region. The Governor of Papua (Barnabas Suebu) has taken these discoveries as evidence of the global importance of Papua's forests and biodiversity, and has publicly declared his intention to develop the Province following green economic principles. Protected today as a national wildlife sanctuary, the Foja Mountains are one of the Pacific's most pristine forest environments with a rich endemic biota. Conservation International has encouraged the Government of Indonesia to upgrade the conservation status of this national reserve.

Contributed by Bruce Beehler

Rhododendron species

A microhylid frog *Albericus* sp.

Mosses on the forest floor

Ecuador and Peru: Río Pastaza Basin (July 12 – August 17, 1999)

The Pastaza River originates in the Ecuadorean Andes and flows southeastward more than 700 km to the Marañón River in Peru. In Ecuador, where most of the river is at high elevations, the Pastaza is characterized by quick flowing cascades with many rapids; while in Peru, the Pastaza flows on flatter ground and transforms into a meandering lowland river. Although remote, the Pastaza watershed is increasingly threatened by mining and oil exploration activities. An AquaRAP survey was done in 1999 to provide data to environmental authorities, conservation organizations, and to the indigenous communities controlling the central reaches of the river in order to ensure proper management of the natural resources in the Pastaza River watershed.

RAP fish team seining through aquatic vegetation

The AquaRAP team explored the Pastaza from its headwaters in Ecuador to its lower reaches in Peru. Aquatic habitats were highly disturbed by agriculture and logging in the headwaters, but less so along the transitional zone between the headwaters and the lower floodplain stretches. In the Peruvian portion of the Pastaza, aquatic habitats were healthy, showing little evidence of human impacts. As many as 44 new species of fish and four new plant species were discovered. In addition, five plant, eight shrimp and crab, and 22 fish species were recorded in the Pastaza River for the first time ever. The AquaRAP team recommended development of a green corridor or biosphere reserve to protect key areas along all reaches of the Pastaza River, from headwaters to the mouth, in order to preserve migration routes for fish, to prevent the spread of invasive species and to maintain the biological integrity of the Pastaza River watershed. Since September 2008, more than 166,000 hectares of native forests in the Ecuadorean province of Pastaza have been included in *Socio Bosque*, an innovative national forest conservation program that provides economic incentives to forest owners (individuals and communities) in exchange for their commitment to protect key biodiversity areas in their lands.

Contributed by Jessica Deichmann and Luis Suárez

During the Haute Dodo RAP, I was trained to implement standard methods for inventorying insect biodiversity. Then I received support from RAP to attend the second edition of the Ant Course in Arizona in 2002. This capacity building has been crucial in planning and conducting my PhD research on biodiversity of savanna ants in Côte d'Ivoire. When doing my PhD, I was able to lead my taxonomic group for the RAP surveys that followed and I did it during Boké RAP in Guinea (2005) and Ajenjua Bepo and Mamang River Forest Reserves RAP in Ghana (2006). In order to improve my taxonomic capacity I received another grant from the RAP (as a complement to an Ernst Mayr Award) to visit the ant collection of the Museum of Comparative Zoology at Harvard University in 2005. Since then I've become a regional expert and I did other surveys in Mount Nimba (Guinea) and Liberia with Afrique Nature International. This training I obtained from RAP has guided my research topics towards nature conservation and I'm happy with that. I can say I'm a pure child of RAP!

- Yéo Kolo, University of Abobo-Adjamé

© Piotr Naskrecki

© Piotr Naskrecki © Conservation International/photo by Stephen Richards

Stag Beetle *(Cyclommatus eximius)*

© Piotr Naskrecki

View from Tompoi camp

The Nakanai Mountains form a rugged, rain-forest-covered spine along the central-eastern interior of the large Pacific island of New Britain. Extending from sea level to 2,185 m at the highest point, the mountains are a predominantly karst (formed by the erosion of soluble carbonate rocks) landscape of exceptional natural beauty and geological interest. Some of the world's largest underground rivers flow through massive cave systems here, many emerging from the caves as beautiful waterfalls that fuel torrential white-water rivers in spectacular gorges.

The forests of East New Britain are under intense pressure from logging operations and oil palm plantations, and Conservation International has worked in the province since 1995, collaborating closely with local non-governmental organizations and communities in Pomio District to promote the establishment of a protected area covering the upland forests of the Nakanai Mountains. The ultimate goal of Conservation International's work in the region is to establish a conservation corridor over these forests that would encompass one existing and one proposed Wildlife Management Area. The spectacular cave systems and natural beauty of the Nakanai Mountains also prompted Papua New Guinea's Department of Environment and Conservation and other interested parties to prepare a nomination of the Nakanai Mountains for World Heritage status. This spectacular range

has been on the World Heritage Tentative List since 2006, along with the Muller Range and Hindenburg Wall, in a submission titled 'The Sublime Karsts of Papua New Guinea.' However, despite a long history of cave exploration in the Nakanai Mountains, the biodiversity of these remote and inaccessible rainforest habitats remains poorly documented.

To redress this lack of data, RAP scientists joined forces with the East New Britain Provincial Government's Environment and Conservation Management Committee, and the local communities of Marmar, Irena and Muru to assess the biodiversity of three sites in the proposed World Heritage Area. These sites were in lowland rainforest at 200 m, in hill forest at 850 m and in lower montane rainforest at 1,600 m altitude, near the summit of the Galowe Plateau in Pomio District. Valuable information on the local fauna was also obtained from the vicinity of Palmalmal and Pomio townships during the team's transit to the field.

The 2009 RAP survey, a collaboration between Conservation International, the Papua New Guinea Institute of Biological Research, and A Rocha International, documented a treasure-trove of previously unknown and unique biological diversity in the Nakanai Mountains that we hope will provide impetus to the World Heritage nomination process. The most significant re-

Tiny bats *(Mosia nigrescens)*

Pandan katydid *(Segestidea defoliaria)*

sults included 36 species of katydids, at least 15 of which are new species, and one that was recently described as an entirely new genus; 34 species of dragonflies, including many new records for the island of New Britain; more than 100 species of spiders, of which at least half are likely to represent new species; 39 species of herpetofauna, including four frogs new to science; and 26 species of mammals, of which four rodents are new to science, including two that appear to represent entirely new genera. Sixty-nine species of birds were observed during this expedition, including a number of species that are endemic to New Britain or the Bismarck Archipelago. The most significant bird record was an immature individual of the rare Slaty-backed Goshawk, *Accipiter luteoschistaceus*.

In addition to providing feedback to the local communities to promote interest and pride in their local biodiversity, the results of these surveys are being made available to Papua New Guinea's Department of Environment and Conservation and to the East New Britain Provincial Government to encourage their efforts in nominating this region as a World Heritage Area.

Contributed by Stephen Richards

Blue-breasted Pitta *(Pitta erythrogaster)*

Cuscus *(Phalanger orientalis)*

It was 6:30 am one cold morning in May 1990 when we crossed the narrow streets of La Paz, Bolivia to gather Ted Parker, Al Gentry and Brent Bailey from the hotel in the center of the city where the nucleus of the first RAP team spent the night without sleeping – I don't know if it was the altitude or dreaming of the trip that kept them up.

We arrived at the El Alto airport, 4,070 meters above sea level; Captain Echalar's twin-engine airplane awaited us on the runway. The airplane careened down the long runway before soaring out over the extensive plateau. After 15 minutes of flight, we crossed the mountain range and reached an altitude of 6,000 m. To our right lay two imposing mountains of the Andes, Illampu and Ancohuma, and we began to fly through a dense mat of clouds that shrouded the mountain range. Seated in the copilot seat, I listened as Captain Echalar explained the function of the flight instruments and then he said to me: "Eduardo, I have never landed on the Alto Madidi runway: I don't know it. Nevertheless, we can land in Ixiamas and formulate a flight plan there to arrive at the final destination."

I looked at the captain with surprise, but calmly told him that five years earlier, during two evaluations of forest activity in Northern La Paz, I had flown over the zone and knew the location of the Alto Madidi runway which had been used during the military dictatorships to isolate the opposition to the regime. I told him that from Ixiamas it would be very easy for me to identify the flight path to our destination. Initially, Captain Echalar had his doubts, but confronted with the team's enthusiasm to arrive as soon as possible at the final destination, he decided not to land in Ixiamas. He saw a clearing in the clouds and lowered the plane to 1,000 m. From there, in just a few minutes we could see the town of Ixiamas. I showed him the mountain chain to the west of the town, indicating that if we followed it parallel northward, then once we saw the Madidi river, the Alto Madidi runway would be at the foot of the mountains. So we followed that path and in less than 20 minutes, the airplane was descending towards a short, dirt runway, cleared two days prior of the dense green pasture that covered it by men with machetes who had arrived in a helium plane, which had the capacity to land in difficult situations and on short runways, and was piloted by Hermes Justiniano, private pilot, photographer, lover of nature and director of the Fundación Amigos de la Naturaleza.

We landed and were struck with a heat wave as we opened the airplane door. Hermes and the other members of that first RAP team were waiting for us on the edge of the runway, next to the trees. We exited the plane and after an enthusiastic welcome, the adventure of the first RAP survey in history began. Captain Echalar and I returned to La Paz later that afternoon.

- Eduardo Forno, Conservation International - Bolivia

© Conservation International/photo by Stephen Richards

© Conservation International/photo by Stephen Richards

© Piotr Naskrecki

Large Green Treefrog (*Litoria* sp.)

© Conservation International/photo by Stephen Richards

View of Camp III at high elevation

In 2008, RAP enlisted the help of Australia's Commonwealth Scientific and Industrial Research Organisation (CSIRO) to develop a modeling tool that would help to identify areas of Papua New Guinea that lack even the most basic information about local biodiversity. A site on the southern edge of the Muller Range in central-western Papua New Guinea was identified by this gap analysis as one of the three highest priorities for biodiversity documentation in the country. As early as 1992, the Muller Range had been recognized as a High Biodiversity Priority Area by the Papua New Guinea Conservation Needs Assessment, and more recently it was included in a World Heritage nomination titled 'The Sublime Karsts of Papua New Guinea', which is on the Tentative World Heritage List. However despite recognition of its global significance, the rugged topography and difficulty of accessing the remote and sparsely populated interior of the Muller Range have hindered documentation of the region's biodiversity.

In September 2009, Conservation International's RAP team joined forces with the Papua New Guinea Institute of Biological Research and A Rocha International to launch an expedition that penetrated deep into the remote foothills and high-montane peaks of the Muller Range. With helicopter support from the nearby Porgera mine, the team had an opportunity to investigate a broad elevational transect in a poorly-documented area that promised to reveal a treasure-trove of biological novelties.

The scientists spent a week at each of three camps at 500, 1,600 and 2,875 meters altitude. Camp I (500 m) was on a low ridge in lowland rainforest at the base of the Muller Range. Surprisingly, the vegetation there contained some floristic elements more typical of montane forests elsewhere in New Guinea, presumably reflecting the incredibly wet environment at this site. Camp I also had the highest overall biological diversity found at the three sites, and many new species of ants, katydids, odonates (dragonflies and damselflies) and spiders were documented.

Camp II (1,600 m) was wet, steep, and located in montane southern beech *(Nothofagus)* forest where the shrubs, trees, and even the ground were covered with dripping moss. The abundance and diversity of invertebrates was lower here than in the lowland forest, and permanent water was scarce so that odonates were absent altogether. However a number of new and interesting species of katydids, ants and spiders were found, along with several new frog species and many new plants. Camp II also had a high abundance of small mammals, many possums, and signs of long-beaked echidnas and tree kangaroos. These larger animals have been hunted to rarity or extinction in many areas of New Guinea, and our sightings of tree kangaroos and numerous possums and cuscus indicate that hunting pressure is low and fauna populations in the remote interior of the Muller Range are still healthy.

Camp III (2,875 m) was located in an unusual mosaic of sub-alpine fernland and extremely dense and mossy upper-montane forest. Many orchids and rhododendrons were present and, although animal diversity was low, many species found by the RAP team were of great interest biogeographically including new species of both plants and animals.

Overall the team discovered dozens of new species including nine new plants, two of which have already been described by the team's senior botanist Wayne Takeuchi. Other highlights included 2 new mammal and 20 frog species, and numerous new insects (damselflies, ants, and orthopterans including katydids and stick insects) and spiders. The total number of new species documented during this survey was between 100 and 140 – this will be settled once all spiders have been carefully examined. The team also observed many Birds of Paradise, and a number of bird species with plumage patterns distinctly different from populations elsewhere in New Guinea, suggesting that the Muller Range is a biogeographically significant area.

The results of this expedition are being made available to the National and Provincial Governments in the hope that these remarkable biological discoveries will add impetus to the declaration of the Muller Range Karsts as a World Heritage Area.

Contributed by Stephen Richards

Feathertail Glider *(Distoechurus sp.)*

Bizarre microhylid frog (*Asterophrys* sp.)

Pandanus spider (Lycosoidea)

RAP in the media

Ghana
Atewa Range Forest Reserve
June 6 – 24, 2006

Chameleon (*Chamaeleo gracilis*)

The Atewa mountain range, located in south-eastern Ghana, runs approximately from north to south, and is characterized by a series of plateaus, which at the highest point reach the elevation of 800 meters. One of only two reserves in Ghana still covered by upland evergreen forest, Atewa represents about 33.5% of the remaining closed forest in Ghana's Eastern Region. It contains the headwaters of the major river systems (Ayensu, Densu and Birim) that provide water for all surrounding communities, including the capital city of Accra. Historically, Atewa plateau has acted as a Pleistocene refugium of forest fauna and flora during the last glacial maximum, and is likely to play the same role in the future. The only other forest of this type in Ghana is the Tano Ofin Forest Reserve which is smaller and significantly more disturbed. Atewa is home to many endemic and rare species, including black star plant species (species considered threatened in Ghana), and several endemic butterfly species. Seasonal marshy grasslands, swamps and thickets on the Atewa plateaus are nationally unique.

RAP collaborated with CI-Ghana and Alcoa World Alumina LLC (Alcoa) to conduct a RAP survey around three sites within Atewa: Atiwiredu (795 m); Asiakwa South (690 m); and Asiakwa North (769 m). The RAP sites were chosen to coincide with areas of potentially high biodiversity and concentrated bauxite deposits that had been earmarked for exploration activities by Alcoa. The RAP survey aimed to derive a brief, but thorough overview of species diversity in Atewa, to evaluate the area's relative conservation importance, to provide management and research recommendations, and to increase awareness in local communities of the value of species and ecosystem services provided by the Atewa forest.

The results of the RAP survey showed that Atewa is an exceptionally important site for national and global biodiversity conservation, and the ecosystem services it provides are critically important for the welfare of its surrounding communities. All taxonomic groups surveyed were comprised almost exclusively of forest species, indicating a nearly intact forest ecosystem, which is a highly unusual and significant finding for West Africa where most forests are strongly fragmented and disturbed. Atewa has the highest butterfly diversity of any site in Ghana and the highest site diversity of katydids anywhere in Africa! Atewa also harbors a high diversity of dragonfly, bird and plant species.

Included among the many rare and threatened species at Atewa are six black star plant species, six bird species of global conservation concern, two primates and 10 other large mammals, and a high proportion of threatened frog species such as *Conraua derooi* (Critically Endangered), *Hyperolius bobirensis* (Endangered), and *Phrynobatrachus ghanensis* (Endangered), for which the Atewa Range is likely to hold the largest remaining populations. The unique and diverse species assemblages documented during the RAP survey, especially of amphibians, Odonata (dragonflies and damselflies) and fishes, all depend on the clean and abundant water that originates in Atewa for their survival. Ghanaians around Atewa, and as far as Accra, also depend on this water source, provided by the plateau formations, which soak up rain and mist and then hold, filter, and discharge fresh water. The RAP survey confirmed that Atewa is a site of extremely high importance for global biodiversity conservation and should be protected in its entirety.

The conservation recommendations that followed the survey included the need to establish within the Atewa Range Forest Reserve an integrally protected area with high protection status, such as a National Park, which should encompass all remaining, intact fragments of the Upland Evergreen forest, especially on the plateaus. A buffer zone covering the more disturbed slopes and valleys of the reserve should be established surrounding the core protected area. To ensure the sustainable protection of Atewa, alternative incomes for the local communities, particularly in Kibi, should be developed to reduce existing or potential dependence on extractive industries and forest products from Atewa. This should be done as a collaborative effort between government, private, non-governmental, scientific, development, and community groups.

The results of the survey and its conservation recommendations were presented to local communities during a workshop held in the town of Kibi. Additionally, hundreds of color booklets that presented the biological richness and explained the role Atewa forests play in the functioning and survival of the surrounding rural communities and the rest of Ghana were distributed in villages and towns surrounding the reserve.

Unfortunately, in the years that followed the RAP survey, little has been done to ensure full protection of this unique ecosystem. Although bauxite prospecting operations were halted in 2007, in 2008-2009 illegal logging was on the increase, and it still poses a significant risk to the survival of the Atewa Reserve. This site is in urgent need of conservation action.

Contributed by Piotr Naskrecki

Giant African snails *(Achatina sp.)* for sale near the Atewa Forest Reserve

Butterfly *(Euphaedra harpalyce)*

Giant earthworms

In the summer of 2002, I began planning my first RAP expedition to the Pic de Fon - the highest point of the Simandou Mountains in Southeastern Guinea (a small country in West Africa that curls around Sierra Leone and Liberia to the south, and borders the Ivory Coast to the east). The plan was that the team (13 scientists, 3 drivers, a field cook, a camp manager - and me) would meet in mid-October in the Ivory Coast and drive nearly a thousand kilometers to the RAP site, just over the border in Guinea. Very little was known about the site, other than that it was possibly home to chimpanzees and a rare habitat known as montane grassland, so we selected a team to study plants, invertebrates (katydids in this case), herps (amphibians and reptiles), birds and mammals (we had an expert in small mammals such as shrews and mice, another for bats, two for large mammals and two primate specialists to see if the chimp reports were true). Having never been on a RAP expedition, all I knew at the time was that I would be flying 18 hours from home to visit a continent I had never seen, speak a language I had unsuccessfully studied for one semester in college, and live in a tent in the middle of nowhere with a group of 18 biologists/strangers for almost a month while we explored the great unknown.

The first (of many) 'slight' changes in plan came in late September when, due to an attempted coup in the Ivory Coast, we instead had to begin our journey in Conakry (Guinea's capital), still nearly a thousand kilometers away, but over slower, often dirt, roads. As we had no office, and no field supplies in Guinea, this meant that I would carry 140 pounds of equipment (plus a backpack filled with binoculars, cameras, a satellite phone) in duffel bags and we would buy the other necessary items (plastic pails, black plastic sheeting, coffee) in the markets of Conakry. The team assembled as planned and, after a day hunting for pails of the right size and shape, we set out to take a trip literally across the country.

And - after driving 2 days of 12 hours each in a 4x4 with 5 adults, half on unpaved, un-level roads eating (surprisingly good) baguettes, sardines and avocados, arriving after dark to drive up (or be towed up) slick, steep mining tracks that took seemingly hours to navigate, setting up camp in the rain in the dark, learning to set up mist nets, trekking 16 km up steep hills to look for primates, accidentally stepping in my first and second (and narrowly avoiding my third) pile of driver ants and having to disrobe immediately because those little guys are fast and they hurt, staying up late to listen to the bat-man and his recording of bat sounds, falling asleep to the sounds of frogs and more frogs and learning to scan nearly every puddle for any sign of one, hoping that smell wasn't me and learning that it was rather the scent of a group of red river hogs, really, really hoping that I would not encounter any of the several snakes I knew for a fact were in the area, going for a night hike to look for katydids and learning that, even with a flashlight, night on top of a mountain in Guinea is very, very dark (and in this condition piles of driver ants become much less noticeable, and my language less lady-like upon discovery), discovering the ups (cleanliness) and downs (mountain in Guinea after sundown, surprisingly not warm) of an outdoor bucket bath, discovering the downs of an outdoor latrine (you don't want details, but have I mentioned the bees?), and on the subject of bees, having heard the tales of insects that get under your skin (sometimes from your laundry hanging on the line) and then grow into giant worms that you have to remove by rolling out and if they break off..., holding contests with rubber bands and giant biting flies, petting the goat who spent the day at our camp and, after a few bleats, was later called dinner - I learned that the greatest fear in a RAP camp is the possibility of running out of coffee and that the greatest joy is the indescribable excitement and wonder of exploration and discovery.

- Jennifer McCullough
continues on p. 172

Bolivia
Noel Kempff Mercado National Park
RAP Surveys 1991 – 1997, RAP Training 1995

© Andre Baertschi

© Andre Baertschi

© Andre Baertschi

Jaguar (*Panthera onca*)

The large sandstone Huanchaca Plateau in southeastern Bolivia has intrigued biologists, geologists and explorers for centuries. The plateau is within an unusual climatic transition zone where Amazonian forest intergrades with the dry forest and savanna habitats of the cerrado, thus creating a rich mosaic of habitats for a high diversity of species. Descriptions of the area by explorer Percy Fawcett in the early 1900s were used by author Arthur Conan Doyle as the setting for his novel "The Lost World." Renowned Bolivian biologist Noel Kempff Mercado led scientific explorations to the region in the 1970s-80s and began a campaign to establish a national park centered around the Huanchaca Plateau. Sadly, he was killed in 1986 by drug traffickers during one of his expeditions, but this incident sparked public and governmental interest and led to the creation of Noel Kempff Mercado National Park in 1988 with 750,000 hectares of forest and savanna.

The park attracted the interest of many biologists, including the RAP team, to study its unique flora and fauna. Some of the RAP scientists began studying their respective taxa within the park during the 1980s which led to a RAP survey in 1991 and subsequent visits in 1994 and 1995. Highlights include high diversity of all taxa including 2,705 species of plants, 597 species of birds, 124 species of mammals including large numbers of rare small mammal species and many new records for Bolivia, 127 reptiles and amphibians, 246 fish species (about 45% of Bolivia's fish fauna), and 97 species of dung beetles. The park is an important reserve for several threatened

Amazonian and a broad range of cerrado bird species and many large mammals, including brocket deer, peccaries, puma and jaguar. The site is of national significance because it provides protection for the flora and fauna of a biogeographic region that is unlike any of the other ecosystems in Bolivia's National System of Protected Areas. It is also of global importance due to its large size, presence of many unique and threatened ecosystems, and high diversity of species.

Data collected during the RAP surveys were used in the development of the first comprehensive management plan for the park by the Bolivian government. In addition, data derived from RAP supported a proposal by Fundación Amigos de la Naturaleza to expand the park's boundaries to include forest and savanna habitats to the west of the Huanchaca Plateau. This became a reality in 1997 when the park was expanded west to the Río Bajo Paraguá for a total of 1,523,000 hectares as part of the visionary Noel Kempff Mercado Climate Action Project (NKMCAP) to reduce emissions from deforestation and forest degradation (REDD+) under consideration by the United Nation's Framework Convention on Climate Change (UNFCCC).

The many initiatives that were intended to consolidate the park's status as a globally important protected area and strengthen its management provide many lessons to today's conservation practitioners. Science, as exemplified by RAP, continues to exert a strong role in keeping the park in the public eye, especially internationally. The establishment of long-term study plots, and their integration into an Amazon-wide research network, has contributed to our knowledge of the impacts of climate change on tropical forest ecosystems, while ongoing studies of the Maned Wolf and the Giant Otter have improved our understanding of the behavior and reproductive biology of these endangered species. In preparation for the Climate Action Project, scientists field tested forest carbon measurement protocols, remote sensing technology and GIS modeling tools that are now commonly used in dozens (or possibly hundreds) of REDD+ projects worldwide. Most importantly, this proto-REDD+ project provided Noel Kempff Mercado National Park with secure and easily recognizable borders: the park is clearly more secure than it was prior to that innovative and visionary initiative. Part of this improved security comes from the creation of the Bajo Paraguá Communal Territory, which enjoyed the support of the Climate Action Project during the formative early years and is strategically situated along the park's western frontier. The National Service of Protected Areas currently invest an amount up to $250,000 annually, satisfying the core needs of this huge protected area, which still requires more resources, equipment and facilities to fulfill all its needs.

Unfortunately, the lessons learned from the Climate Action Project and the numerous other conservation investments made since the park's founding are not all positive – but that does not make them any less important. Very large sums of money were invested in tourist infrastructure that has never operated at a profit. Fortunately, part of the endowment was invested in traditional financial instruments and continues to support basic operations today – albeit at only minimal levels. Noel Kempff Mercado National Park faces many challenges. Private and international funding for biodiversity conservation has decreased and the non-governmental organizations that depended on those resources have ended almost all of their activities in the region. Carbon revenues should be available because the Climate Action Project has so obviously succeeded in its objectives of protecting the Park and reducing emissions. Communities are disappointed but still hope that the long-promised tourist boom will someday materialize – even though the strategic infrastructure necessary to receive those tourists has deteriorated. Since the local communities are not benefitting from

tourism, they are seeking alternatives, including the non-sustainable exploitation of the timber resources within their own forest reserve. Meanwhile, colonization pressure and the advance of the agricultural frontier are increasing yearly throughout the region.

Noel Kempff Mercado National Park is still important and it is still needs and deserves the support of the conservation community.

Contributed by Tim Killeen and Leeanne Alonso

Monkey tree frog *(Phyllomedusa vaillanti)*

Noel Kempff Mercado savanna

171

continued from p. 168

Prior to our team's visit to the Pic de Fon, virtually no information existed on the plants and animals that might be found there - so virtually everything we found was something unknown from that area (including 25 species never recorded before in Guinea). It was like we knew we were looking at a work of art, but it was covered with thousands of tiny tiles, and at the end of each day of searching, we could remove a few tiles and see more of the picture. In the late afternoon (when the primate folks had just returned from a grueling day of searching for nests and were taking a break before looking for galagos, the froggers were suiting up for an evening of visiting any wet spots they had noted, the birders might be going to look for owls, the bat-man was gearing up for another long night of checking mist nets until dawn, the botanists had returned with their giant books full of samples), most of the team would gather in the 'work' tent and share what they had uncovered that day - a bird known only from three other sites in the world, a bat that was only known from sites over 4,000 km away, three species of amphibian that were likely new to science, at least five new species of invertebrate, confirmation of the presence of both chimpanzees and Diana monkeys (to name only a few).

What an initiation. For all of the latrine bees, and the biting flies, and the driver ants, and the dusty, bumpy roads, and the mystery meats, and the wet tents (and the...), witnessing this journey of exploration was an unparalleled privilege - to see the world alongside a team of people who have dedicated their lives to studying the patterns of nature, to be there as they worked as an integrated team, sharing information (a newly found water hole, a possible nest site, an encounter with an unknown bird) so that as a group they could function as greater than the sum of the parts. It is grueling work in difficult conditions, and they worked with passion, enthusiasm and dedication (and generally a healthy dose of humor). Watching the picture of a place unfold with this group was truly one of the most amazing experiences of a lifetime. Would I travel for 4 days in a crowded jeep across Guinea again if given the chance? I would (and I did, a year later, well, there was a plane full of chickens involved, but that is another story...).

- Jennifer McCullough, Director, Strategic Engagement, Center for
Conservation and Government, Conservation International

Guyana
Konashen Community Owned Conservation Area
October 6 – 28, 2006

Smooth-fronted Caiman *(Paleosuchus trigonatus)*

All photos © Piotr Naskrecki

Blue poison dart frog *(Dendrobates tinctorius)*

The Konashen Indigenous District in the Upper Takutu-Upper Essequibo Region of southern Guyana is home to one of the last, and largest, swaths of pristine rainforests in the Guiana Shield. The human population of the area is one of the lowest in the world (about 0.032 people/km²), and the biodiversity of the region has remained largely unexplored and unaffected by human activity. In 2004, the government of Guyana awarded legal guardianship to an area of 625,000 hectares of Konashen to the community of Masakenari, a 200+ group of Amerindians of Wai-Wai ancestry. This area, known henceforth as the Konashen Community Owned Conservation Area (COCA), is now the largest protected area in the country, covering 3.2% of Guyana's landmass, and harboring the headwaters of South America's third largest river, the Essequibo, and 47% of its upper watershed. The COCA is comprised primarily of tall, evergreen hill-land and lower montane forest, with large expanses of flooded forest along major rivers. It is a part of the High Biodiversity Wilderness Area of Amazonia, and a part of the Guiana Shield Corridor.

Prior to the RAP survey, Conservation International-Guyana had been working with the members of the Masakaneri community to build local capacity to assess, monitor, and manage their natural resources, and trained six members of the community to survey the species richness of fishes, mammals, and birds, especially those of economic importance to the community. These six trainees also took part in the RAP survey conducted in October 2006.

The main objectives of the RAP survey were 1) to collect baseline data on the biodiversity of the COCA for potential use in the development of a small-scale ecotourism industry managed by the Wai-Wai community, and 2) to gather information on the population levels of species used for food and trade by the community in order to establish sustainable thresholds for their utilization. In addition, the RAP team assessed the water quality of rivers and streams in the vicinity of the community.

The survey was conducted at two principal sites: the first in the foothills of the Acarai Mountains at an elevation of 270 meters (with a satellite camp near the top of the Acarai Mountains), and the second on the north bank of the Kamoa River at an elevation of 250 m. Water quality was surveyed at 18 sampling stations within five additional focal areas. The organisms documented during the survey included terrestrial insects (katydids, ants, bees and dung beetles), freshwater macroinvertebrates (decapod crustaceans, gastropods, and bivalves), fishes, amphibians, reptiles, birds, and large (non-flying) mammals. Nearly 870 species of animals were recorded, although this number is likely to increase once the analysis of the vast sampling of litter insect fauna collected during the survey is completed. The highlights of the survey include at least ten species of insects new to science, four new species of fishes (including a giant, economically important yet still unnamed wolf fish species, genus *Hoplias*, known only from the rapids of the Essequibo River), and two possible new species of reptiles. In addition, the survey increased the previously virtually unknown fauna of Guyanese katydids by 130%, added several new reptile species to the fauna of the country, and recorded the first occurrence of the Large-headed Flatbill *(Ramphotrigon megacephalum)*, a 900 km range extension of a bird species never previously recorded from the Guianas. Mammalian populations at survey sites were robust, and included several species of conservation concern, such as Brown-Bearded Saki Monkey *(Chiropotes stanas)*, the Giant River Otter *(Pteronura brasiliensis)*, and the Giant Armadillo *(Pridontes maximus.)* Water quality surveys revealed the absence of any artificial pollutants, although water turbidity and pH values at sites close to the Masakenari community were somewhat below the WHO standards for drinking water.

The RAP survey confirmed that the COCA harbors exceptionally rich, virtually undisturbed assemblages of organisms typical of the Guiana Shield, and must become the priority for conservation in Guyana. Threats to the area come primarily from illegal logging and gold mining activities. These may soon increase, following the construction of a highway across northern Brazil, which forms a porous and unmonitored border with the COCA. The RAP team recommended the development of a program within the Wai-Wai community (with some help from the government of Guyana) that preemptively addresses these threats, including the deployment of patrols along the border to detect encroachment of illegal loggers.

Although the population density of the COCA is exceptionally low, the RAP team also recommended a sustainable management plan for the animals that are frequently fished and hunted by the Wai-Wai community, which includes monitoring of the most important species, and the development of a rotation system to distribute the effect of subsistence hunting over larger areas. It also stressed the importance of the avoidance of trapping birds for the pet trade, and hunting of threatened species. The results of the survey are being used now to develop a management plan for the area, including a possible implementation of a small-scale "sustainable ecotourism", which will allow visitors to experience one of the last, virtually untouched fragments of the South American rainforest. The species check-lists and a biodiversity booklet produced by the RAP team will also allow the Wai-Wai community to promote organisms of particular conservation or biological interest, including the spectacular, but unknown to general naturalists, Peacock Katydids *(Pterochroza ocellata)* and Suriname Toads *(Pipa pipa.)*

Contributed by Piotr Naskrecki

Entomologist Dr. Chris Marshall collecting symbiotic insects from a Three-toed Sloth *(Bradypus tridactylus)*

Peacock Katydid *(Pterochroza ocellata)*

Guyana: Eastern Kanuku Mountains (September 20 – 29, 2001)

Spurred by the results of a RAP survey in the western part of the mountain range in 1993, the flooded and upland evergreen forests in the eastern Kanuku Mountains in the Rupununi region of southwestern Guyana were surveyed in September 2001. Prior to the RAP survey, a training session was held for 17 Guyanese and Surinamese participants. Five of these trainees participated in the RAP survey, which focused on an area along the lower Kwitaro and Rewa Rivers that forms part of the Essequibo watershed, the largest source of freshwater in the country of Guyana. The 2001 RAP survey collected biodiversity data for policy makers considering the creation of a protected area within the Kanuku Mountain range. Over just 10 days, plant surveys revealed 40 species not previously recorded in the Kanuku Mountains and minimal evidence of human disturbance in the forest. Bird diversity was exceptional: 264 species including 17 of the 25 Guyana Shield endemics and 39 species considered uncommon in the Neotropics, like the Harpy Eagle and the Orange-breasted Falcon. RAP initiated the use of camera trapping which photographed 14 non-volant mammal species including Ocelot, Margay, and Red Brocket Deer. Other species such as Jaguar and the endangered Giant River Otter were observed or heard. Of the 52 mammal species recorded, 27 were bats, thereby bringing the total bat diversity of the area to 89 species. Aquatic surveys revealed 113 freshwater fish species, 45 of economic value, including the Arapaima. A protected area system which incorporates all the variety of habitats within the Kanuku Mountain range will provide respite for a high proportion of Guyana's floral and faunal diversity, including many threatened and endemic species. Discussions between local indigenous communities and government agencies over the creation of such an area in the Kanuku Mountains are currently ongoing and very promising.

Contributed by Jessica Deichmann and Eustace Alexander

I started working for RAP back in late August 2000. I departed in October 2006 to raise my daughter. I never realized what a gift this program had given to my life. I can honestly say to this day that those six years were some of the best years of my life. Not only did I absorb and learn about conservation and species preservation, but I also felt like the people I worked with were my second family. What a joy it is to have had a job that had given me these things.

I probably learned more in the six years I worked for this program than the 4 years I spent in college. I learned about the importance of conservation, biodiversity, various cultures in many different countries, and protecting endangered species. My boss, Leeanne, gave me amazing opportunities to flourish and learn each day. I will be forever grateful to RAP for providing me such amazing fulfillment and professional growth. I will never forget the people I worked with and the mission that we all worked to accomplish.

- Leslie Kasmir

Papua New Guinea
Lakekamu Basin
RAP Survey Oct. 15 – Nov. 15, RAP Training Nov. 16 – Dec. 12, 1996

© Bruce Beehler

© Bruce Beehler

© Bruce Beehler

View of Lakekamu Basin

After successful fieldwork on New Ireland in 1994, the RAP survey program in Papua New Guinea continued in 1996 in the Lakekamu Basin with two priorities – the first was to undertake a traditional intensive biological survey that could help guide conservation practices. The second was innovative in that it set out to train national biologists and build the capacity of New Guinea's conservationists. While RAP priorities elsewhere were guided by urgent needs in the field, the survey location in Lakekamu was not facing imminent deforestation. One advantage to building conservation in Papua New Guinea in the 1990's was that RAP scientists could develop robust conservation programs ahead of loggers or miners. In 1995, RAP scientists had selected a large pristine lowland forest basin as an ideal spot to build a conservation program: the Lakekamu Basin. Located in Gulf Province of southcentral Papua New Guinea, this basin was sparsely inhabited and thick with cassowaries, giant *Goura* pigeons and other large game animals that disappear under heavy hunting pressure. Dr. Bruce Beehler had scouted out the area years before and conducted several successful field seasons studying the birds of the Lakekamu forests.

A major reason that RAP surveys need to be rapid is that team members have time constraints. We circumvented this problem for the large team at Lakekamu by developing a flexible schedule, where some scientists visited the site for only a couple weeks, like Gerry Allen (fish), Dan Pol-hemus (aquatic insects), Allen Allison (herpetofauna), and Wayne Takeuchi (plants). Other team members stayed longer to teach a month-long field course for the University of Papua New Guinea students – Andy Mack on birds, Debra Wright on mammals, David Bickford, Geordie Torr, and Steve Richards on herpetofauna, Roy Snelling on ants, and Alexandra Reich on botany; Kurt Merg helped coordinate logistics. This was a large team and was supplemented by 20 University of Papua New Guinea students in training. The goal in setting up for a couple months at one site was to generate better data and to offer a truly meaningful training experience.

The Lakekamu project demonstrated the power of RAP to teach and inspire young conservationists. The course was enthusiastically received by students who had never done field work. It led to similar annual courses for the next ten years, reaching hundreds of students. Each year the course helped develop a new, young generation of well-trained conservation biologists that are playing a growing role in Papua New Guinea's conservation scene. That first course is a fine example: of the 20 trainees on the course, 11 are in work as biologists in conservation-related programs. Two have completed doctorate degrees and one is currently working on a PhD, four have completed Master's degrees and another two have Honours Degrees in Biology. These nine also participated in the following year's RAP course and other training provided by Debra Wright and Andrew Mack. These are remarkable achievements for a small nation like Papua New Guinea and for a group of just 20 young students on their first field experience. The RAP field experience can be transformative and an inspiration – this is one of the most important, yet least appreciated values of the RAP program.

The *RAP Bulletin of Biological Assessment* and training materials produced by the Lakekamu RAP have found many uses in Papua New Guinea, but the contributions of the students inspired to become conservationists by RAP are much more significant and continue to grow. Several of that first cohort still plan to pursue PhDs in order to build their impact as conservationists. That initial investment back in 1996 is continuing to yield dividends. In a nation where so little is known scientifically and the logistics are so difficult, foreign researchers on short RAP-style research visits can only do so much. The next era in New Guinea's scientific history will leave behind the Archbold-to-RAP tradition of short intense surveys by foreign biologists. A new generation of national biologists, borne from programs like the RAP training at Lakekamu, will help bring Papua New Guinea to a higher level of sophisticated understanding of their tropical nation. Young biology students will get to go in the field with native mentors, not just the expatriate visitors like us on the Lakekamu RAP in 1996.

Contributed by Andrew Mack

Millipede (Diplopoda)

Blue-tongued skink *(Tiliqua gigas)*

Buttress roots

Nepal: Makalu-Barun National Park (October 27 – November 12, 2005)

Saisima, Makalu Barun National Park

To the east of Mount Everest in the Nepalese Himalayas lies Makalu-Barun National Park. A RAP team of Nepalese and international scientists visited the park in 2005 to document the species diversity of plants, birds, mammals, reptiles, amphibians, and ants with the objective to enhance scientific capacity in the Himalayan region by developing collaborations between international and local scientists. The three sites visited by the RAP team, ranging from 2,200 to 3,550 meters elevation, were all in good condition with few imminent threats. A few areas had been cleared by the local communities for agriculture and for pasture, and summer grazing sites (kharkas) were quite common, with heavy grazing and man-made fires in some areas. However, the mountain brooks, streams and marshes were in excellent condition. The presence of large mammals like Wild Boar (*Sus scrofa*) close to local villages indicated that hunting pressure by the local communities may be low. The area is difficult to access, which makes trade of wildlife and cash crops extremely difficult, and the use of natural resources seemed to be sustainable and mostly for local use. A species of *Paa* frog, though harvested for food and medicine by local Sherpas, appeared to have very healthy populations in the mountain brooks and streams. This frog is considered to be a valuable frog species in Nepal due to its large size and great medicinal value (used to treat a variety of ailments). The RAP team recommended that medicines be provided to the local communities to reduce their use of this frog species. The high abundance of small mammals form a great prey base for a variety of other animals in the area, such as birds of prey, snakes, and small carnivores. Communities of small mammals are therefore extremely important to conserving healthy ecosystems in the area.

Contributed by Leeanne Alonso

The Conservation International RAP 55 effort (Río Cuyuní, Venezuela), in conjunction with our mining project in Southeastern Venezuela was a valuable experience and tremendous success, resulting in important discoveries pertaining to the great biodiversity of the Guyana Shield of South America. The gathering of such a wide range of expertise and great personalities – all working in concert and with sincere dedication was one of the highlights of our business venture in Venezuela and a testimony to the value of cooperation between conservation and business. Definitely a win-win experience!

- Don Proebstel, former Vice President of Environmental Affairs and Sustainability, Gold Reserve Inc.

Indonesia
Cyclops Mountains and Southern Mamberamo Basin
August 19 – September 15, 2000

Crocodile skink (*Tribolonotis gracilis*)

Frog (*Oreophryne furu*) brooding eggs on the underside of a leaf

Building the capacity of local scientists and students to undertake biodiversity assessments in their home countries has been a primary focus of Conservation International's (CI) RAP program. Following the success of the 1998 Wapoga RAP survey, which involved a number of senior Indonesian scientists, the RAP program helped CI-Papua and CI-Indonesia design and implement a combined training and survey project aimed directly at young lecturers and students based in Indonesia's Papua Province.

On August 19th 2000, participants from the University of Cenderawasih, from provincial government institutions, and from the Indonesian Institute of Sciences gathered on an idyllic sandy beach in the vicinity of Yongsu Dosoyo on the northern edge of the Cyclops Nature Reserve. For the next 12 days, Indonesian and foreign scientists presented a series of lectures and practical demonstrations to an enthusiastic audience of young biologists in rustic wooden huts transformed into makeshift classrooms, and led participants on forays into the surrounding rainforest to demonstrate field techniques.

Lectures often evolved into lively discussions, which were interrupted on one occasion when the beach exploded into a frenzy of tiny flailing flippers as two Hawksbill and Green Turtle nests hatched simultaneously in the middle of camp, and on another occasion when the team's butterfly expert Henk van Mastrigt leapt onto a table in front of 20 startled students waving his net frantically in an attempt to catch a rare moth attracted to the lights in our open-air lecture hall.

During this training program team leaders identified the most enthusiastic and promising young Papuan biologists to participate in a follow-up RAP survey at the southern edge of Papua's vast and sparsely populated Mamberamo Basin. Based at two camps in dense rainforest near the village of Dabra, the RAP team surveyed plants and animals in this poorly-known wilderness area from September 1-15. The survey was supported by The Papua Environment Foundation (YALI-Papua) and the Great Mamberamo Adat Council, two local environmental and community-based groups committed to protecting ecological systems and to sustainable development for the benefit of local communities.

At the time of the RAP survey, the extensive lowland rainforests of the Mamberamo Basin were facing severe threats from a proposed 'Mega-Project' including a hydro-electric dam and extensive agro-industry. Although these projects did not proceed, the basin continues to face severe pressure from planned large-scale development projects.

Working in partnership with Indonesian and foreign scientists, the Papuan participants documented several hundred plant species along line transects, in plots and during general surveys. They also found 143 bird species, 129 butterflies, and 21 frogs, of which up to seven species were new to science. The RAP team concluded that the aquatic ecosystems of the Dabra area were in excellent condition, reflected by a diverse assemblage of 56 aquatic insect species including at least 17 water bugs that were new to science. Despite the generally healthy state of the Mamberamo drainage system, many exotic fish species were documented during the RAP survey and it remains a matter of serious concern that the Mamberamo has the highest proportion of exotic fish found in any drainage system in New Guinea. Many of these species have had serious deleterious effects on aquatic habitats and on native species in other parts of the world, but their long-term impacts on endemic fish species in the Mamberamo Basin have not yet been assessed.

Beach camp at Yongsu, Cyclops Mountains

Conservation International has continued to work with local communities in the Mamberamo Basin to promote conservation of their forest resources and to develop local community-led management plans for key forest resources in the region (especially in the verges of the Foja Mountains). One reason for optimism is the environmental leadership exhibited by Papua Governor, Bas Suebu, who has sought to create a "green economy" for Papua Province. Conservation International is currently working with the Governor to foster the development of this green economic pathway for Papua, as an alternative to the resource-extractive economy that has dominated the province for the last two decades.

Contributed by Stephen Richards

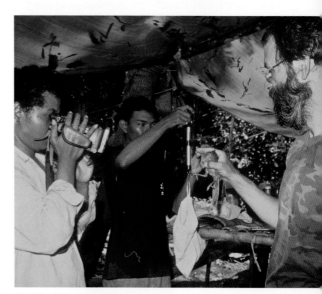

The bird team at work

Juvenile monitor lizard *(Varanus jobiensis)*

Suriname: Kwamalasamutu (August 15 – September 10, 2010)

A team of 16 international and Surinamese scientists and seven Surinamese students surveyed the diversity of plants, mammals, birds, reptiles and amphibians, and several insect groups including water beetles, dung beetles, katydids, dragonflies and ants. The team was assisted by three representatives from the Suriname government's Nature Conservation Division, seven forest rangers from the Amazon Conservation Team, and 18 people from the local Trio village of Kwamalasamutu. Preliminary results include high diversity of all taxonomic groups, especially small mammals (41 species), birds (324 species, fishes (100 species), frogs (43 species), and dragonflies (72 species). New records for Suriname were reported for birds, snakes, and many of the insect groups. At least 40 species likely new to science were discovered (pending verification), including five fishes, one frog, five katydids, and about 25 water beetles. Results from camera traps revealed a high diversity of large mammals and birds, including 24 species of mammals. Jaguar, ocelot and puma were photographed at the third site, potentially indicating less human disturbance. Water quality was good. The RAP results will be used to help the local Trio people develop ecotourism around their village and to promote the establishment of a Jaguar Sanctuary to provide refuge for wildlife.

Contributed by Leeanne Alonso

Giant armadillo *(Priodontes maximus)* photographed by a camera trap

For me, the various RAP surveys in West Africa I have participated in have permitted me to visit sites for which, up to then, no ornithological data were available. Also, working with international multidisciplinary teams has been a particularly enriching as well as a highly pleasant experience. Although we did not discover new bird species – not surprising considering the region – we did collect numerous data on species distribution and biology, and mapped many, sometimes substantial, range extensions. In Guinea, RAP reports are now routinely taken as the main reference by private consultancies producing environmental impact studies. Our discovery of Sierra Leone Prinia (Schistolais leontica) – a Red List restricted-range species – on Pic de Fon, SE Guinea, during the 2002 RAP there led Rio Tinto subsequently to commission 1) more detailed studies of the species at that site, to enable an accurate population size estimate to be produced, and 2) additional surveys at other unsurveyed sites in Guinea, in the (eventually justified) hope of finding as yet undiscovered populations that could be protected as compensation for the habitat loss on Pic de Fon. RAPs surely made a difference!

- Ron Demey, RAP Scientist, Belgium

Variegated grasshopper *(Zonocerus variegatus)*

Tree frog *(Chiromantis rufescens)*

The dense lowland forests of Haute Dodo and Cavally Classified Forests in southwestern Côte d'Ivoire have very high plant endemism and contain some of the last remaining lowland forests of the Upper Guinea forest ecosystem. Along with many partners, CI's West Africa program has been working to create a conservation corridor in this region that will maintain natural connections between Taï National Park in Côte d'Ivoire and Sapo National Park in Liberia. Conservation corridors are large-scale landscapes that link parks, reserves and other protected areas by identifying places between them that can be protected or managed in an ecologically sustainable manner. Southwestern Côte d'Ivoire and Liberia have the largest tracts of rainforest remaining in the Upper Guinea forest ecosystem. It is therefore of high priority to protect these forests and their species before they become fragmented like the rest of the region. In addition, a West Africa Priority Setting Workshop held in 1999 identified the need for further collection of biological information and for scientific capacity building in this region.

A RAP survey of these two classified forests was undertaken to determine their importance for inclusion in the corridor and to make recommendations for their management. During the RAP survey, 20 scientists from five West African countries (Côte d'Ivoire, Guinea, Liberia, Sierra Leone, and Ghana) and Botswana were trained in methods of rapid biodiversity assessment by international and regional experts. The goal was to train a group of interested and skilled regional biologists in standard methods of rapid biodiversity assessment for key terrestrial taxa. These scientists, from governmental and scientific institutions in these six countries, are now better prepared to carry out further biological assessments in their own regions. Five of the trained regional scientists continue to work with the RAP survey teams and participated in other RAP surveys in Guinea and Ghana. In addition, three of the trainees went on to do graduate work in collaboration with RAP expert scientists.

Despite the appearance of a greatly disturbed habitat, the Haute Dodo and Cavally Classified Forests were found to contain a high number of species of great importance to West African biodiversity conservation. These areas contain high endemism: 23% of the plants recorded from Haute Dodo and 13% from Cavally are endemic to West Africa. Many of these are regionally endemic species called "sassandriennes," found only between the Sassandra and Cavally rivers in Côte d'Ivoire. This highlights the uniqueness of the vegetation of the two areas surveyed in comparison to other areas in West Africa that do not have such high endemism. Similarly, 47% of the amphibians recorded are endemic to Upper Guinea forests. The RAP team documented the presence of 10 primate species, many of which are threatened with extinction. Twelve bird species documented are of conservation concern and several are restricted-range species. The high diversity of amphibians documented during the survey in both forests clearly demonstrates that these areas still have high conservation potential. However, the established presence of breeding populations of several invasive amphibian species not normally found in forested areas indicated that the amphibian communities are already impacted. Ant and termite diversity was high but also indicated impacts from timber exploitation. Only one typical forest edge bird species was recorded at each site which indicates that the forests are still of good quality for forest birds.

Based on their high levels of diversity and endemism and the presence of many threatened and restricted range species, both the Haute Dodo and Cavally Classified Forests merit increased protection and inclusion in a regional biodiversity corridor. At the time of the RAP survey, both forests had been somewhat impacted by logging and agricultural encroachment, but many areas were still well preserved.

In August 2006, local RAP team member, Yéo Kolo, returned to Haute Dodo to search for more ants of *Mystrium silvestrii*, a species which is represented by few specimens in museums. Unfortunately, he found that plantation areas had greatly increased within the forest. The site where he had collected *Mystrium* is now a cocoa plantation. The conservation status of the site has deteriorated due to the conflict between the rebels and the governmental army from September 19, 2002 to 2004 and the anarchic post conflict period. The current status of these two sites needs to be evaluated and areas of biological importance should be urgently set aside for strict protection in order to conserve the rare and endangered species that hopefully still survive in these two classified forests, which are key sites for biodiversity conservation in West Africa.

Contributed by Leeanne Alonso and Yéo Kolo

RAP ornithologists at work

Common agama *(Agama agama)*

A RAP scientist taking plaster casts of mammal tracks

Liberia: North Lorma, Gola & Grebo National Forests (November 13 – December 11, 2005)

© Conservation International/photo by Peter Hoke

Veldkamp's Fruit Bat *(Nanonycteris veldkampi)*

As part of the Liberia Forest Initiative, an initiative aimed at rehabilitating and reforming the forest sector in Liberia, a RAP survey was conducted in three national forests in 2005. The RAP survey worked to build scientific capacity within Liberia's Forestry Development Authority, the University of Liberia and local NGOs. North Lorma, Gola and Grebo National Forests all contain a wealth of biodiversity and a significant number of species of conservation concern. Over 40% of the remaining Upper Guinea forest lies within Liberia and it includes several large tracts of contiguous forest making these the last refuges for many species. A high diversity of species was documented in these forests, including 548 plants, at least 40 amphibians, 93 dragonflies and damselflies, 17 reptiles, 211 birds, nine small terrestrial mammals, and 29 large mammals. At least 12 species new to science, 36 new occurrence records for Liberia, and many species restricted to Upper Guinea forests were recorded. These three forests are particularly important for protecting many threatened and endangered species, including the Diana Monkey, Pygmy Hippopotamus, West African Chimpanzee, West African Red Colobus, two species of African puddle frogs, the Ivory Coast Frog, and the Gola Malimbe (bird) that were listed as Endangered by IUCN at the time of the RAP survey. The RAP team recommended that all three forests be granted increased protection as national parks so that they can form the core of a biological corridor from Cote d'Ivoire through Liberia to Guinea.

Contributed by Leeanne Alonso

After being involved as a small mammal expert in the wonderful CI "From the Forest to the Sea" Conference in Ghana in 1999, I participated in three RAPs in West Africa: Cote d'Ivoire (Haute Dodo and Cavally Forest) in 2002; Pic de Fon (Simandou), Guinea, in 2002; and Southwestern Ghana (Draw River, Boi Tano and Krokosua Forest Reserves) in 2003. Due to a timing conflict, Ryan Norris - then a graduate student in our department - replaced me on the second Guinea RAP (Three Classified Forests) in late 2003. The RAP experience, standards, and reports, and the network of experts that it has generated so far led to two more in-depth small mammal surveys I organized: for the Bumbuna Hydroelectric Project in Sierra Leone in 2006 (with Ryan Norris) and a more in-depth baseline study for the Simandou Project in Guinea in 2008. I am currently in the process of negotiating further survey projects in Liberia and Sierra Leone, all prompted by the increased mining exploration activities in the region.

- Jan Decher, University of Vermont

Botswana
Okavango Delta I – The High Water Survey
June 5 – 22, 2000

Situated in the semi-arid Kalahari of northwestern Botswana, where about 500 mm of rain falls seasonally, the inland Okavango Delta is one of southern Africa's largest wetlands. Given large differences in water supply and demand, the Okavango wetland fluctuates in area from 600,000-800,000 hectares during the non-flood season to over 1,500,000 ha during the flood season. The Okavango River arises from a series of headwater streams on the southern slopes of the Angolan highlands, forms the boundary between Angola and Namibia for hundreds of kilometers, and then crosses the Caprivi Strip in Namibia before entering Botswana as a single broad river. As such the drainage basin of the Okavango River is shared by three countries.

While most of the large terrestrial mammals of the Okavango Delta are well-known and well-studied, the aquatic members of the community have received much less attention. The aquatic ecosystems of the Okavango are very complex and can change yearly depending upon annual flood levels. Scientific data on the aquatic organisms and system are needed to make informed management plans for the Delta, which faces many threats including: pollution, introduced species, low flood levels, fishing, a growing tourism industry, increasing local human populations, and widespread insecticide spraying, proposed water extraction, and hydroelectric power generation in Namibia.

An AquaRAP survey was conducted during high water levels in 2000 by an impressive team of 20 expert aquatic scientists and students from Botswana, South Africa, United States, Namibia and Norway. Four focal areas of the Okavango Delta in Botswana were surveyed: the Upper Panhandle, the Lower Panhandle, Northwestern Moremi Game Reserve, and southeast of Chief's Island along the Boro River.

Water quality variables were measured, and all results reflected benign and healthy conditions, with the exception of the dissolved oxygen levels, which were low, especially in the upper permanent swamps and the Lower Panhandle. A high proportion (about 1/4) of the approximately 1,250 plant species known from the Delta were recorded. The vegetation varied greatly between the four focal areas: species richness (number of species encountered) increased from the Upper Panhandle to the lower reaches of the Delta, with landscape level heterogeneity showing a similar trend. The invertebrates displayed both moderate diversity and abundance (likely due to difficulty sampling in high water levels), and maintained surprisingly uniform populations throughout the open system. The AquaRAP fish team found measurable differences in the fish community diversity between the four focal areas, indicating that the entire delta must remain intact to preserve the overall biodiversity. A breeding colony harboring 14 species of birds was also documented and could represent the most important breeding site in southern Africa for two rare species, the Yellow-billed Stork *(Mycteria ibis)* and the Slaty Egret *(Egretta vinaceigula*, Vulnerable).

The AquaRAP team provided specific recommendations to local decision makers to facilitate conservation of the wide variety of habitats and species within the Delta, as well as the enormous array of ecological functions that these species provide to local and regional human communities. Their recommendations included 1) protect the Panhandle and Upper Delta as key areas for biodiversity and function, 2) limit water extraction from the Delta as well as from the Okavango River in Botswana and the neighboring countries that share the watershed and ensure that flow patterns are not modified, 3) maintain processes that promote the dynamic channel changes of the Delta, especially by promoting the integrity of papyrus swamp that fringes the upper channels and by promoting hippo populations that maintain channels and water flow, 4) protect riparian forest vegetation that promotes localized disposal of salts that would otherwise poison surface waters in the Okavango Delta, and 5) develop and enforce regulations for commercial fisheries and consider dividing fishing areas between commercial and tourist operations either locally or regionally.

The AquaRAP report is a thorough compilation of the aquatic biology data available for the Okavango Delta through 2002, with in-depth discussions of the ecological processes that keep the Okavango Delta functioning. This report will serve as a key reference for those studying and managing the Delta such as our colleagues from the Harry Oppenheimer Okavango Research Center (HOORC), who conducted a follow-up aquatic survey in the low water season. Soon after the AquaRAP survey, the results catalyzed a process for resolving conflicts between local fishermen and sport fishermen in the Delta, and AquaRAP scientists were invited to monitor the effects of pesticide spraying for tsetse flies on aquatic diversity that took place in 2001. The data from the AquaRAP survey are currently being used to develop a nomination for the Okavango Delta as a World Heritage Site.

Contributed by Leeanne Alonso

Reed frog *(Hyperolius marmoratus)*

Giraffe *(Giraffa camelopardalis)*

Local fishermen sorting their catch

The Glamorous Life of a RAP Scientist: Traveling in style

Zooming in luxurious, dependable cars along well-maintained highways

Smooth sailing in roomy boats with attentive, always actively engaged crew

Luxury jets (there is often enough room for one or two persons to squat comfortably among barrels of pickled fish and bags of rice)

Personalized carrier services

All photos © Piotr Naskrecki

© Conservation International/photo by Haroldo Castro

© Joe E. Meisel/Ceiba Foundation

© Joe E. Meisel/Ceiba Foundation

Lantern bug, or Machaca *(Fulgora laternaria)*

© Piotr Naskrecki

Green iguana (Iguana iguana)

The Cordillera de la Costa in western Ecuador has traditionally harbored high biological richness and many endemic plants and animals with restricted ranges which make them highly susceptible to extinction. As a result of a 255% increase in human population in the region within just two decades, more than 90% of the area was deforested and replaced with agriculture by 1990. With only small, but extremely valuable forest remnants remaining, the Cordillera de la Costa was in dire need of biological assessment at the time of the RAP survey in 1991. The goals of the survey were to determine the conservation status of endemic species with an emphasis on species of economic importance, to identify the relative conservation importance of remaining fragments of forest, and to increase awareness of the losses, both biological and economic, that Ecuador would suffer if remaining forest were not protected.

A 13-person RAP team spent six weeks assessing the state of dry (deciduous) and wet (evergreen) forests and their associated plant, bird, mammal, reptile and amphibian species in low mountains and coastal foothills of the Cordillera de la Costa between the Ecuadorean cities of Esmeraldas in the north and Arenillas in the south. At most sites visited, 20% of the plant species documented were endemic. The discovery of several new plant species, and even new genera of plants illustrated how little was known about the biodiversity of the Cordillera de la Costa prior to the RAP survey.

Like plants, the bird fauna also exhibited high endemicity, with 10% of species endemic in wet forest and 40% in dry forest sites. One of the most interesting ornithological discoveries was the presence of 17 bird species that had previously only been known to occur in the Andes Mountains. Many range extensions were documented for species across all taxa – an indication that many of the sampled forest remnants were once connected. Despite heavy disturbance and fragmentation, RAP researchers found evidence of survival of most large mammal species known from the area. For example, populations of Mantled Howler Monkeys (*Alouatta palliata*) and White-fronted Capuchins (*Cebus albifrons*) still persisted, albeit in low numbers. Perhaps the most exciting finding of the RAP survey was the sighting of the harlequin frog *Atelopus balios* which had not been recorded by scientists in nearly 70 years!

The results of the RAP survey indicated that all nine sites assessed still had high value for conservation and in fact were critical reservoirs for protecting the unique biodiversity of western lowland forests in Ecuador. As such, the RAP team recommended that priority be given to the protection and maintenance of these sites, some of the last known habitats for a number of endangered and endemic species, and that additional land connecting these fragments be allowed to regenerate to create corridors for wildlife.

Tagua palm *(Phytelephas aequatorialis)*

Spectacled owl *(Pulsatrix perspicillata)*

The results of the RAP survey were used as the basis for several conservation initiatives that have been developed in the last two decades, including the promotion of the Chocó-Manabí Conservation Corridor, a regional planning framework designed to address urgent conservation issues while also improving the livelihood and quality of life of the communities in the region. Since 1991, some RAP sites have been declared protected forests and/or private reserves. In 1996, one of the surveyed sites (Mache-Chindul) was declared an Ecological Reserve by the national environmental authority, thereby protecting 70,000 hectares. The protection of the western forests was also included as a top priority in the Ecuadorean National Biodiversity Strategy (2001) and in the National Gap Assessment (2007). The Ecuadorean Ministry of the Environment, CI-Ecuador and many local non-governmental organizations – such as Fundación Natura, Fundación Jatun Sacha, Fundación ProBosque, and Fundación Ceiba – have since also promoted the protection and effective management of several of the RAP survey sites. Additionally, since September 2008, more than 5,000 ha of dry and wet forests of the Cordillera de la Costa have been included in the Socio Bosque Program, an innovative national forest conservation initiative that provides economic incentives to forest owners in exchange for their commitment to protect key biodiversity areas.

Contributed by Jessica Deichmann and Luis Suárez

White-tailed deer *(Odocoileus virginianus)*

Cane toad *(Bufo marinus)* in its native habitat

Bolivia: Humid Forests of Chuquisaca (May 5 – 31, 1995)

The eastern slopes of the Andes from Venezuela in the north to Bolivia and Argentina in the south are covered principally by humid forest. The Andes make a spectacular bend to the east then south in Bolivia with the most dramatic shift in vegetation occurring in the Departments of Chuquisaca and Tarija. A RAP survey explored three principal areas in this region: the forest west of the town of El Palmar, the slopes of the Cerro Bufete and the Cerro Tigrecillos, and the valley of the Santa Marta River - an area encompassing the largest tracts of untouched Tucuman-Bolivian forest. Together, these areas form an ecosystem that is a recognized center of endemism. The RAP survey showed that the flora in the region comprises an excellent assemblage of species characteristic of the Tucuman–Bolivian forest, many of them endemic. Over 110 species of birds were recorded using binoculars, tape-recorders and directional microphones, including all endemic species known from the Tucuman-Bolivian Forest. There were many new registries for Chuquisaca and also a northern range extension for the endemic and Vulnerable Rufous-throated Dipper (*Cinclus schultzi*). Thirty-two of the 66 mammal species known from the Tucuman-Bolivian Forest were recorded during the survey. Large mammals were present, highlighted by evidence of the Spectacled Bear (*Tremarctos ornatus*, Vulnerable) in the area. Human pressure in the valleys and accessible areas have heavily fragmented the Tucuman-Bolivian forest ecosystem from central Santa Cruz to northern Argentina, giving special importance to conservation of this area, which has so far not been incorporated under any category of protection.

Contributed by Eduardo Forno

Voltaire said that "No revolutions are ever made by anybody with common sense." Our recent trip with CI's Mark Erdmann to explore the Arguni region of Papua, Indonesia is quintessential of this phrase in that it embodies CI's field revolutionary spirit to strive for goals which often defy all odds.

Mark led our small team that included ichthyologist Gerry Allen, explorer Max Ammer, several LIPI scientists, Fabian Oberfeld and myself to seek out isolated remote lakes unconnected from other water bodies which would likely house endemic species new to science, awaiting discovery. In spite of our efforts and a local tribal ceremony procession to protect us from crocodiles, the lakes proved to be inaccessible during our short time period. They are not only far inland, but surrounded by Karsts and ominous topography which defeated us, humbling the team by dehydration and exhaustion. However, sampling in streams along the way uncovered over 20 species new to science, which rendered the RAP survey more than worthwhile.

We had a true taste of the kind of resolve needed to carry out research in the area as it involved delicate cultural sensitivity towards the local tribes and the politics; diplomatic ability and relationship with the various Indonesian authorities; daring recognizance flying, land, water and air navigation with non existent and precarious and aged maps; obstacle river negotiation, major physical and mental endurance, and willingness for capsizing boats, after dark water landings, improvised medicine, tolerance for pain, humor and optimism; ironically, a passion for life at times so committed, that it demands the very risking of it: Voltaire would have been very proud of CI's field missions! Whether he would actually join a CI RAP to the far corners of the world, doubtful.

- Dr. Richard Sneider, One World / Weavers Apparel LLC, RAP Supporter

© Piotr Naskrecki

© Conservation International/photo by Russ Mittermeier

© Conservation International/photo by H. Randrianasolo

Leaf-tailed gecko (*Uroplatus sikorae*)

The Mantadia-Zahamena Corridor is located in the center of Madagascar's eastern rainforests and links the Réserve Naturelle Intégrale of Zahamena in the north and the Parc National de Mantadia in the south. These two protected areas are managed by Madagascar National Parks and were established to protect part of the flora and fauna in the eastern biome which are representative of dense humid evergreen forests. The corridor connecting these two protected areas, covering an area of 539,225 hectares, lies on an altitudinal band from 200 to 1,500 meters and is composed mostly of mid-elevation humid forest. A few remnants of lowland forest (<550 m) can be found on the eastern side of the corridor amidst a landscape of increasing agricultural lands. The corridor is characterized by a rugged topography with deep valleys. Many small streams originate from this corridor to feed four major rivers, the Onibe, Ivondro, Rianila, and Sahatandra, which supply people downstream with crop irrigation, hydroelectric power and water for household use.

The Mantadia-Zahamena Corridor is isolated and local people living within follow traditional practices. Threats to natural forests and biodiversity come from local economic needs and socio-cultural behavior. Forests in lower elevations are heavily fragmented due to slash and burn agriculture. The topography of the eastern region (steep and narrow valleys) limits the possibility of irrigated rice cultivation. This fragile situation is exacerbated by the rapid population increase. Pressures come also from hunting and intensive collection of forest products. In addition, natural disasters such as cyclones play a major role in the degradation of the environment. The erosion of the watershed causes silting and often reduces fertility of rice fields. Soils may become poorer and the water cycle can be disrupted. The deterioration of the natural ecosystem could aggravate the decline in production for the surrounding population.

The Mantadia-Zahamena Corridor contains some of the last remaining low and mid elevation rainforest in Madagascar. At the time of this RAP survey, many priority sites for biodiversity were outside of the existing network of protected areas. Therefore, the main objectives of the RAP survey in the corridor were to prioritize areas for conservation activities and to check the feasibility of including sites within the corridor into a protected area representing the eastern rainforest ecosystem.

A RAP survey was conducted in 1999 at five sites: Iofa (835 m), Didy (960 m.), Mantadia (895 m), Andriantantely (530 m) and Sandranantitra (450 m), selected because of their remoteness, some taking 2-3 day hikes to reach.

Floristic composition varied with the altitude and the degree of degradation of surveyed sites. RAP researchers identified 460 species of plants belonging to 72 families, four of which are endemic. Thirty species of small mammals including 18 insectivores, six rodents and six bats were observed.

Lemurs were abundant and diverse at sites with low human presence and the 12 recorded species included the Near Threatened Aye-aye *(Daubentonia madagascariensis)*, the Critically Endangered Black and White Ruffed Lemur *(Varecia variegata)* and the Endangered Indri *(Indri indri)*, the largest living lemur. Many species of rare and endangered birds were recorded, with 89 species identified in total, 79% being Madagascar endemics. The species diversity of herpetofauna was exceptional with 51 species of reptiles, including six species of the famous Leaf-tailed Gekkos (genus *Uroplatus*) and 78 species of amphibians, the majority of which belonged to the colorful family Mantellidae. Insect species richness was high, with 71 butterfly and 66 tiger beetle species, as well as 29 genera of leaf litter ants. Unfortunately, introduced rodents and ant species were also found at several sites. A number of species considered new to science were discovered such as *Plethodontohyla mihanika* (frog), *Amphiglossus* sp. (lizard) and 16 species of *Strumigenys* (ant).

Following the RAP survey, Conservation International and its partners have worked to conserve the corridor's forests and in 2005, 381,000 ha in the Mantadia-Zahamena Corridor acquired temporary protection status and became part of the new protected area system in Madagascar. This protected area now links the parks to the north and south, allowing species to pass freely between them. This corridor contains an Alliance for Zero Extinction site, shelters several critically endangered and locally endemic species, including one of the top most endangered primates, the Greater Bamboo Lemur, and four species of unique Ground-roller birds. The corridor plays an important role in regulating ecosystem functions, such as water filtration, and nutrient cycling. Maintaining forest cover also contributes to climate change mitigation by serving as a carbon sink. In these ways, the protected Mantadia-Zahamena Corridor contributes to the well-being of both biodiversity and human beings.

Contributed by Harison Randrianasolo, Michèle Andrianarisata, Hanta Ravololonanahary, James MacKinnon, Nirhy Rabibisoa, and Léon Rajaobelina

© Piotr Naskrecki

Conehead katydid (*Odontolakis* sp.)

© Conservation International/photo by Russ Mittermeier

Golden frog (*Mantella aurantiaca*)

© Conservation International/photo by Harison Randrianasolo

Malagasy villagers

Papua New Guinea: Southern New Ireland (January – February 1994)

Lying northeast of mainland Papua New Guinea, New Ireland is the third largest island in the tropical Pacific. Supporting two of the highest mountain ranges in the western Pacific, it constituted a large biodiversity "blank" on the map until CI conducted a RAP survey in southern New Ireland during January-February 1994. In partnership with Papua New Guinea's Department of Environment and Conservation and the Bernice P. Bishop Museum in Hawaii, the 1994 survey aimed to provide data that would support development of an Integrated Conservation and Development (ICAD) Project in the Weitin Valley. The survey covered a range of elevations and documented several new species of plants, butterflies, and a new frog. The major conclusions of the expedition were that a) the native avifauna and non-flying mammal fauna were strikingly impoverished, but that levels of endemism in several animal groups was high, and b) exotic invasive species (especially cats, pigs, and dogs) were abundant in disturbed areas, and having a negative impact on the forest and its biota. Although the RAP scientists recommended that

Bismarck Boobook Owl (*Ninox variegata*)

© Bruce Beehler

all of the forested uplands and representative samples of the lowland rainforest of southern New Ireland be conserved in a protected area, conservation activities in the project area were halted soon after the survey as a result of intense pressure from an existing logging company.

Contributed by Bruce Beehler

"Three levels [of biodiversity documentation] *can be envisioned. The first is the RAP approach, from the prototypic Rapid Assessment Program created by Conservation International, a Washington-based group devoted to the preservation of biological diversity. The purpose is to investigate quickly, within several years, poorly known areas that might be local hotspots, in order to make emergency recommendations for further study and action. The area targeted is limited in extent, such as a single valley or isolated mountain. Because so little is known of classification of most organisms and so few specialists are available to conduct further studies, it is nearly impossible to catalog the entire fauna and flora of even a small endangered habitat. Instead a RAP team is formed of experts on what can be called the elite focal groups --- organisms, such as flowering plants, reptiles, mammals, birds, fishes, and butterflies, that are well enough known to be inventoried immediately and can thereby serve as proxies for the whole biota around them."*

- Edward O. Wilson (1992) *The Diversity of Life*

Giant African mantis (*Polyspilota aeruginosa*)

Tree frog *(Leptopelis hyloides)*

The Simandou Mountain Range is located in southeastern Guinea, and extends for 100 km from Komodou in the north to Kouankan in the south. At the southern end of the Simandou Range lies the Pic de Fon forest reserve, approximately 25,600 hectares of which was given limited protection. The Simandou Range acts as a natural barrier against savanna fires and regulates the flow of water that originates from within the range (including the rivers Diani, Loffa, and Milo). The location of this reserve in the transitional zone between forest and savanna offers habitat types ranging from a rainforest to a humid Guinea savanna to montane gallery and ravine forests. The Pic de Fon forest reserve covers an altitudinal range from about 600 to more than 1,600 m (including the Pic de Fon, the highest point on the range at 1,656 m and second highest point in Guinea), and harbors at its highest elevation montane grasslands, rare and threatened habitats in West Africa. Surrounding the Pic de Fon forest reserve are 24 villages whose residents currently rely on the forest as a source of food, water, wood fuel, and medicine.

Two sites were surveyed during the RAP expedition: one close to the summit of the Pic de Fon, and the other at lower elevation near the village of Banko. Prior to the RAP survey there was little published information on the composition of the ecosystems of the Simandou Range, and Pic de Fon in particular. Based on its unique habitat mosaic, Pic de Fon was expected to contain high biotic diversity. In ad-

dition to its unique assemblages of ecosystems, the Simandou Range harbors potential mineral wealth, including extensive iron ore deposits. At the time of the survey, Rio Tinto was conducting exploration activities on four contiguous exploration plots within the Simandou Range. The RAP survey was initiated by Rio Tinto as a contribution to their initial environmental and social assessment studies.

The survey was conducted in a variety of terrestrial habitats, including montane grasslands, montane forests (both gallery and ravine forests), a semi-evergreen lowland forest (both primary and secondary), savannas, mountain streams, shrubby edge habitats, perennial plantations (coffee, cocoa, banana), and farmbush. Organisms sampled during the survey included vascular plants (both woody and herbaceous), insects (katydids and cockroaches), amphibians, reptiles, birds, and small (including bats) and large mammals (with special attention given to primates). The RAP team documented the presence of at least 797 species. Several of these were new to science including six new species of katydids and three new species of frogs. The team also recorded range extensions for a number of species, and added as new records for Guinea: 11 invertebrates, three amphibians, seven birds, three bats and one shrew. The Pic de Fon forest reserve harbors a number of species of international conservation concern, including the tree, *Neolemonniera clitandrifolia* (Endangered) as well as 15 other tree species listed by the IUCN Red List as Vulnerable and Near Threatened; one amphibian and four reptile species that are protected by the international CITES law; two primate species listed by IUCN as Endangered: West African Chimpanzee *(Pan troglodytes verus)* and Diana Monkey *(Cercopithecus diana)*, and two listed as Near Threatened; eight birds of global conservation concern including three Vulnerable species; and seven bat species listed as either Vulnerable or Near Threatened. Local hunters and guides also confirmed the presence of the Endangered, rarely seen Nimba Otter Shrew *(Micropotamogale lamottei)*.

The results of this RAP survey showed that the Pic de Fon forest reserve contained unique species in one of the last remaining, intact montane habitats within Guinea and the Upper Guinea Highlands. Threats to the biodiversity of the area include bushmeat hunting, conversion of forest to agricultural land, and bushfires. Others include logging, artisanal mining, road development, and unsustainable collection of non-timber forest products. Based on the results of the survey, the RAP team strongly recommended that the Pic de Fon forest reserve receive increased protection status, and that current regulations with regards to its classified status be monitored, enforced and strengthened. The limits of the protected area should be defined and enforced in collaboration with local communities and should be accompanied by education and outreach programs, as well as additional scientific and socioeconomic studies. If the Pic de Fon forest reserve is incorporated into an effectively managed protected area system that includes both forests and grasslands, and representatives of the many microhabitat variations, with special attention paid to critical habitats and endemic and threatened species, a high proportion of plant and animal species of this region would be protected.

The RAP team found few invasive species during this survey, and steps should be taken to prevent the introduction of such species. The survey results pointed to the fact that any potential exploitation of mineral resources in the Pic de Fon area, if undertaken, would require further investigation into potential hydrological impacts and possible impacts on species relying on high altitude habitats. In addition, 24 surrounding villages rely on this forest for a number of ecosystem services, and every effort should be made to ensure that the forest continues to provide these services.

Currently, the most serious threat to the survival of the Pic de Fon Classified Forest comes from the large scale iron ore mining operations. The RAP data have been incorporated into Rio Tinto's ESIA and planning for biodiversity offsets. Rio Tinto is using the RAP and other environmental data to ensure their compliance with the International Finance Corporation's Performance Standards 6 which requires companies to make efforts to protect and conserve biodiversity, including critical habitat. However, recent political instability in Guinea, and its overall poor record of enforcing conservation measures, contributes to the uncertainty of the survival of this rare and valuable West African ecosystem.

Contributed by Piotr Naskrecki

Bat *(Myotis welwitschii)* recorded for the first time in West Africa during this RAP survey

Ornithologist Hugo Rainey identifying birds (which were later released)

Savanna grasshopper (*Heteracris* sp.)

Democratic Republic of Congo: Lokutu (October 26 – November 8, 2004)

In 2004, a RAP team headed to the territory of Basoko, DRC, near an active oil palm plantation known as the Unilever concession to evaluate potential sites for long-term investment of conservation efforts as part of CI's Congo Basin High Biodiversity Wilderness Area program. Disappointingly, RAP scientists concluded that the site was highly degraded and of low conservation value. Many of the vertebrate taxa that RAP researchers expected to find at Lokutu were absent from survey samples. Mammal communities appeared to be highly depleted with only six primate and eight large mammal species recorded; other large mammals of conservation concern expected to occur there, such as elephants, were not observed. Twenty-one species of amphibians and 16 reptiles were found, most of which were highly-adaptable, generalist species. Bird species richness (184 resident species and 20 migrants) was lower than expected and contained no threatened or endangered species. However, a high number of dragonfly species were found, indicating a relatively healthy watershed in the Lokutu region. The RAP team recommended

De Brazza's Monkey (*Cercopithecus neglectus*)

against investing further in conservation practices in the Unilever concession at Lokutu and suggested that resources would instead be better spent by focusing preservation efforts on other areas of intact equatorial African forest.

Contributed by Jessica Deichmann

Madagascar: Coral Reefs of the Northeast I (March 10 – 24, 2006)

Twenty-three previously unstudied sites on the northeast coast of Madagascar between Pointe du Phoque and Loky Bay were surveyed. These sites were chosen for several criteria, including their isolation. For reef fish, 420 species belonging to 175 genera and 57 families were recorded. For commercially important reef fish, 70 species belonging to 40 genera and 18 families were identified. Serranidae, Scaridae, Mullidae and Lutjanidae families are the most important. For Scleractinia corals, 156 species belonging to 47 genera and 13 families were identified including 26 unidentified species. An average of 44 species was recorded per site.

The beach seine seems to be the fishing method most used by local fishermen. The seine, a manual trawl net, can be as long as 500 meters and is deployed along the coast and pulled to the beach, scraping the seabed. The small mesh netting and the presence of tile in the bottom screen (the catchment chamber) ensure that

everything, including juveniles and larvae, is caught in the net. This can present a major threat to some marine species. The sea cucumber is the most valuable resource because of its high price. A medium-sized sea cucumber costs between US $5 to $7, depending on the species. However, stocks of sea cucumbers seem very low in the area now. Shrimp and crabs are also harvested but the fishing is localized. Mangroves are somewhat threatened because of harvesting for charcoal. Catch per unit effort is greatly reduced and access is difficult due to navigational problems generated by the local wind "Varataraza". Among the 23 areas explored, some sites have good potential for conservation through the establishment of a Marine Protected Area (MPA).

Contributed by Jean Maharavo and Harison Randrianasolo

Guinea
Déré, Diécké, and Mont Béro
November 17 – December 6, 2003

Goliath beetle *(Goliathus regius)*

Sierra Leone reed frog *(Hyperolius chlorosteus)*

Guineé Forestière, the forested southeastern part of Guinea, forms part of the Upper Guinean Biodiversity Hotspot, and it is one of the most threatened biodiversity areas in Africa, with only an estimated 7,655 km², or 4.1% of its original extent still surviving. The forests of Guineé Forestière are home to a large number of endemic and globally threatened species, and yet this relatively very small area is increasingly under pressure from large- and small-scale logging, shifting agriculture, current and future mining projects, and encroachment by refugees.

The flora and fauna of Guinea are poorly known overall and large areas of the country have yet to be surveyed. Within Guinea, only the Mont Nimba region is relatively well studied. To increase the knowledge of the biodiversity of Guineé Forestière, CI's Rapid Assessment Program conducted a biodiversity survey in three forest reserves ("Forêt Classée") in southeastern Guinea to build upon previous work in the region (Pic de Fon RAP, 2002). This survey was conducted in a partnership with Rio Tinto.

The primary objectives of the survey were to compile a thorough overview of species diversity and status within the largest remaining forest reserves and evaluate their relative conservation importance, identify potential threats to the area's bio-

diversity, and provide management and research recommendations for its conservation. Additionally, the survey's scientists provided "on-site" training for Guinean biologists and conservationists.

The RAP survey took place in three forest reserves in Guineé Forestière: Déré, Diécké, and Mont Béro. Déré forest reserve covers approximately 8,920 ha and extends to the eastern border of Guinea with Côte d'Ivoire and lies close to the base of Mont Nimba. Déré consists of low-lying floodplains, dry lowlands, and hillsides and has its highest point at 750 m. Diécké forest reserve covers about 59,143 ha in the prefectures of N'Zérékoré and Yomou close to the Côte d'Ivoire border. It is composed of lowland humid, closed canopy forest and dense evergreen rainforest, and has an elevation range of 400 to 595 m. Mont Béro includes natural and derived wooded and grassland savanna, gallery forest along permanent watercourses, some semi-deciduous forest, and wetlands. The elevation ranges from 600-1,210 m and the reserve covers approximately 26,850 ha. The RAP team surveyed vascular plants, insects (katydids), amphibians, reptiles, birds, small mammals including bats, and large mammals. A variety of terrestrial habitats and taxa were surveyed, including low-mid elevation humid forests, afro-montane savanna, farmbush, wetlands, lowlands, and hillsides.

The results of the survey confirmed that all three forest fragments are biologically rich, with at least 1,000 documented species (in the 10 taxonomic groups sampled). Eighty-two species of conservation concern were documented at the three RAP sites, including six species listed by IUCN as Endangered e.g., the West African Chimpanzee *(Pan troglodytes verus)*, Diana monkey *(Cercopithecus diana)*, and the bird Gola Malimbe *(Malimbus ballmanni)*. In addition, the survey discovered 10 species of katydids new to science as well as one snake, 10 birds, and nine bats never before recorded in Guinea. At the same time, the survey revealed a strong negative effect of the surrounding human populations on the biodiversity of the reserves. Of the three surveyed sites, Déré was the most affected by human activity, such as logging and slash-and-burn-agriculture, while Diécké appeared to be the least impacted, and had the highest species richness. At all three sites the RAP team found evidence of intensive hunting pressure in the form of snares, hunting trails, and shotgun cartridges.

The key conservation recommendations outlined by the RAP team based on the results of the survey were: 1) the mechanism for conservation of all three sites should be collaborative, and must involve local communities to address the most pressing threats, such as hunting, logging, and clearing for agriculture; 2) Diécké, the richest and least impacted site, should receive the highest priority for conservation; 3) conservation of all three sites should be done concurrently with increased conservation of other remaining forested sites in southeastern Guinea (especially Pic de Fon and Ziama); 4) the partnership between Rio Tinto and CI should be expanded to include other national and regional stakeholders; and 5) hunting should be immediately banned for all threatened species, and timber extraction should be reduced, particularly at Diécké.

Contributed by Piotr Naskrecki

Mont Béro

Serrated hinge-back tortoise *(Kinixys erosa)*

Guinean botanists processing plant specimens collected during the RAP survey

Fiji: Nakauvadra Range (November 17 – 28, 2009)

The Nakauvadra Range runs parallel to and 7 km inland from the northern coast of Viti Levu, the largest island in the Republic of Fiji. A proposed forest reserve (11,387 hectares) in the Nakauvadra Range was the site of a combined Terrestrial and AquaRAP expedition in November 2008. The RAP team set out to collect data that would contribute to development of a conservation corridor in Viti Levu, protecting the Nakauvadra watershed in cooperation with local communities, the Fiji Water Foundation, and government entities. RAP botanists identified four distinct vegetation types in the range. Beetle and gastropod diversity was relatively high and researchers discovered two endemic and very rare stick insects. Among the terrestrial vertebrates recorded was the endangered Fiji Ground Frog thought to have been extirpated from Viti Levu; globally threatened bird species like the Long-legged Warbler and the Friendly Ground-dove; and three native bat species, two of which are threatened. Many introduced species, a common problem on inhabited islands, were also recorded. AquaRAP scientists noted that streams in Nakauvadra were healthy, as indicated by a high abundance of mayfly and caddisfly larvae. There was no evidence of invasive macroinvertebrates in sampled water catchments, although fish diversity was low and did include two introduced species. The RAP team also constructed

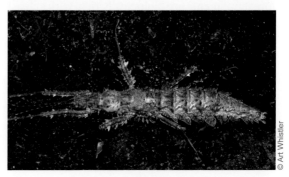

Endemic Fijian stick insect (*Nisyrus spinulosus*)

a field map of culturally significant sites such as stopover spots, fortified settlements, and land boundaries. Because of high endemicity and the fact that it still harbors stable populations of threatened and endangered species, the Nakauvadra Range is an area of high conservation value. Forests surrounding headwaters of rivers in the Nakauvadra Range should be protected in order to ensure freshwater security for local people. In order to achieve this, solutions should be offered to communities to offset impacts from human activities that contribute to the deterioration of the environment within the Nakauvadra Range.

Contributed by Jessica Deichmann

At that time, we were a group of young scientists - coming from every corner of the country - thirsty for knowledge and hungry for field experience. Thrown into a sack, we were taken to the most incredible settings with the most amazing dedicated and sapient tutors, and promised the glory of learning how to do real scientific rigorous field work. Did it end up well? Did we learn much? I believe it went way beyond what any one of us could imagine! We learned the tools of the trade, we learnt to collect data and analyze it, to discuss the context and our findings. But most importantly we learned to work together, to pursue academic goals in a community of healthy competition and support. We are now professors, professionals, conservationists and scientists and we work in the field, in universities, in projects, in NGOs. And I can assure you, we are replicating what we learned: the fundamentals of how to carry out solid scientific research in the wild and support our fellow scientists in their work.

- Armando Valdés, Smithsonian Institution – Biodiversity Monitoring and Assessment Plan Country Director, Peru

A group of puddling butterflies

A series of RAP surveys were conducted in Tumucumaque Mountains National Park, located in the northwest part of Amapá State in Brazil, between September 2004 and March 2006. Tumucumaque Mountains National Park is fully incorporated in the Amapá Biodiversity Corridor, which includes two other large protected areas in Amapá State. It is also surrounded by several indigenous lands: Juminá, Galibi, Uaçá, Waijãpi, and the Tumucumaque Indigenous Park. Together they act as buffer zones, protecting each other. The Amapá Corridor and nearby conservation units in the Calha Norte Paraense (22 million hectares) and the Parc Amazonique in French Guiana (3.3 million ha), among others, form a large block of protected areas in the Guiana Shield.

With over 3,800,000 ha, Tumucumaque is one of the world's largest tracts of continuous tropical forest within a national park. Elevation within the park is minimal, between 100 and 400 meters above sea level, although in the northern part of the park there are numerous inselbergs (small isolated mountains) that rise above the forest to approximately 700 m. The landscape of Tumucumaque lacks roads and access is only available by air or river, making it a logistically difficult place to explore.

As one of the main conservation units within the Amapá Biodiversity Corridor, a lack of biodiversity inventories within Tumucumaque has impeded the development of a comprehensive management plan for the corridor. The purpose of these RAP surveys was to document ecologically important species in the park in order to produce the information necessary to complete the conservation management plan.

Over 1,600 species of plants and animals were recorded over the five expeditions. There were 355 species of birds; many bird species nearly hunted to extinction outside the park, including Black Curassows, Great Tinamous and Grey-winged Trumpeters, were found in large numbers during the surveys. Among the 156 species of amphibians and reptiles found were seven that are potentially new to science. The park held viable populations of many mammals considered threatened both globally and in Brazil like the Black-bearded Saki and the Giant River Otter, making this a potentially valuable study site for future work on the ecology and systematics of several poorly known mammal species. The fish fauna of the park is extremely diverse with over 200 species from varied trophic levels. Of these, nine are likely new species, at least 23 are new records for the state and one is a new record for the country. Although plant identification has not yet been completed, researchers are confident that they collected over 800 species belonging to 653 genera across 147 different families in Tumucumaque Mountains National Park.

The biodiversity data produced during the RAP surveys were incorporated in the development of Tumucumaque's Management Plan (finally concluded in March 2010). The plan established a zoning system, considering the occurrence of species of special concern. Tumucumaque's excellent conservation status can guarantee the maintenance and persistence of large populations of top predators and primary producers.

These RAP surveys served to increase scientific capacity in Amapá state. In order to perform the RAP surveys we conducted in Amapá, a team of biologists was established at the Institute for Scientific Research and Technology of Amapá (IEPA). Two mammalogists, one ornithologist and one herpetologist joined one ichthyologist, one botanist and one carcinologist that were already working at IEPA. The new researchers were incorporated by the Institute and currently three of them are still working in Amapá. They have already trained nearly a dozen students (BSc. and MSc.), multiplying IEPA's capacity to study and describe Amapá's biodiversity.

Royal Flycatcher (*Onychorhynchus coronatus*)

There were also infrastructure improvements after the RAP surveys in Tumucumaque. The first park office was donated by Conservation International and opened in November 2006. It is comprised of buildings, an administrative office, one guest house and a boat house. According to the Executive Manager of the Brazilian Institute of Environment and Renewable Natural Resources (IBAMA), this office contributes to the park's management plan, making work easier for the park's management team, facilitating the integration of surveillance, scientific research and environmental education activities, and reducing the physical distance between IBAMA's headquarters in Macapá and the Park. Serra do Navio's City Hall and the Government of Amapá donated the area for the construction of the office.

Forest toad (*Rhinella* sp.)

Additionally, Tumucumaque's pristine state, size, remoteness, and excellent conservation status are able to guarantee the perpetuation of several ecological and ecosystem services, such as fixation of carbon and maintenance of the stability of water resources. In fact, most of Amapá's main rivers have their headwaters inside or very close to Tumucumaque, making this a valuable site for freshwater conservation.

Contributed by Enrico Bernard

RAP team crossing rapids at the Anotaie River

Paraguay: Río Paraguay Basin, Alto Paraguay (September 4 – 18, 1997)

In 1997, a RAP team of 26 scientists traveled to Paraguay to conduct the second AquaRAP survey of RAP's South American AquaRAP program. The team surveyed a 350 km stretch of the Río Paraguay Basin as well as the Río Apa and the tributary Riacho La Paz in eastern Paraguay. This area had remained undisturbed because of its isolation, but human settlements were on the rise and the watershed was facing an impending threat from the Hidrovía Paraguay-Paraná Project, a plan to expand the waterway to allow passage of larger barges between the ports of inland Cáceres, Brazil and Nueva Palmira, Uruguay on the Atlantic coast. This expansion would greatly alter the water flow and flooding cycles of the Río Paraguay watershed due to the channeling and dredging of large portions of the river. The AquaRAP survey found that the aquatic ecosystem was in good health, with high levels of habitat heterogeneity and high diversity of fishes and aquatic invertebrates. The existence of all these depend on the seasonal flooding cycle of the Río Paraguay. The AquaRAP team recommended the conservation of portions of all available microhabitats in the Paraguay and Apa Rivers, prevention of disruptions of seasonal flooding, continued study of environmental impacts of agriculture and ranching, and determination of sustainable fish harvest levels. Although few of the recommendations have been implemented, both the Paraguay and Apa Rivers have remained relatively unchanged since the time of the RAP survey (M. F. Mereles, pers. comm.). Progress on the Hidrovía project has been quiet; there has been virtually no progress on dredging because of much opposition to the project.

Contributed by Jessica Deichmann

My initial training was mostly on ornithology, but later on I had opportunities as a research assistant working with several foreign researchers from different universities. The Rapid Assessment Program (RAP) has allowed me to have an exchange of experiences with other biologists working on flora and other fauna. This made me further consider more the existing correlation and interdependence between the members of the forest community. Whether marine or terrestrial, the RAP permits training or retraining Malagasy biologists. Participating in a RAP survey let me live in the wild – to be in contact with nature, appreciate Vanga's and Turdidae's (birds) song, hear different calls of Boophis (frog) and listen to the Sifaka. Visiting several sites throughout the island helped to detect differences between ecosystems in Madagascar; also to make comparison of ecosystems with other African countries such as between Tsimanampetsotsa and Naivasha Lake (Kenya); the rainforest in the east of Madagascar and other sites like Kakum National Park (Ghana), and Amani Nature Reserve (Tanzania); and to understand the distinctiveness of the Renosterveld (South Africa). My participation in different RAP surveys conducted in Madagascar gave me an overview of the Malagasy biodiversity which helps partially in the preparation or the updating of the IUCN's global assessment for amphibians, mammals, fishes, turtles and tortoises and other reptiles.

If we consider that a protected area is a refuge, or a tool for biodiversity conservation, then the RAP can be considered as an ideal scientific tool to identify sites of biological significance in the world. The first RAP was conducted in 1990; now it is good to see that other researchers and CI's Partners use the same approach to assess the wealth and the biological uniqueness of a site.

- Harison Randrianasolo, Conservation International-Madagascar

Nile monitor (*Varanus niloticus*)

Purple Marsh Crab (*Afrithelphusa monodosus*), an Endangered species

The flora and fauna of Guinea are poorly known and large areas of the country, with the notable exception of Mont Nimba, have yet to be surveyed. The coast of Guinea is estimated to hold, at times, over half a million waterbirds, principally migrant waders. Chimpanzees are found throughout Guinea, except in the far east of the country from which they are believed to have only recently disappeared. In addition to the unique assemblages of species and range of habitats, Guinea's coastal area also harbors potential mineral wealth.

RAP partnered with Alcoa World Alumina LLC (Alcoa) and Alcan Inc., to collect scientific data on the diversity and status of species at a number of sites within an area that is likely to encompass Alcoa/Alcan's operations and infrastructure in Guinea, including the existing mining operations near Sangaredi, the port facilities at Kamsar, and the connecting infrastructure corridor. This partnership was formed in the spirit of providing gains for biodiversity conservation and the region's communities that rely on these resources. The information collected during the RAP expedition was to be used to guide conservation activities in the region and to provide input into the biodiversity aspects of an Environmental and Social Impact Assessment study for an Alcoa/Alcan alumina refinery in Guinea. The RAP survey was carried out at several sites in Boké Préfecture along the coast of northwestern Guinea (Guinée Maritime): Sarabaya (Rio Kapatchez), Kamsar, and Boulléré. Because the overall area of study has been highly disturbed by human activity, the RAP survey focused on remaining forest patches and wetland areas.

The first survey site at Sarabaya was located in an estuary at the mouth of Rio Kapatchez and in the surrounding area. This site has a wide variety of wetland habitats, including extensive mudflats, well-developed mangrove forest along Kaliki River, a freshwater marsh, a tidal creek and rice fields. Rio Kapatchez has been identified as one of 12 Ramsar sites and one of 18 Important Bird Areas within Guinea. The second survey site was located within the Kamsar sub-prefecture, and five individual subsites were surveyed here. Parts of Kamsar and its surrounding area were considered to be of high importance for conservation based on the high priority given to coastal marine ecosystems, mammals and freshwater biodiversity, medium priority to birds, and potential priority areas for plants. The third survey site, Boulléré, was located in the Sangaredi sub-préfecture, and consisted of a mosaic of vegetation ranging from gallery forest to open grassland to rocky outcrops of bauxite. The vegetation was highly disturbed by agriculture. The gallery forest here was inconsistent in quality.

The RAP survey evaluated species richness of vascular plants (both woody and herbaceous), insects (katydids and ants), crustaceans, amphibians, reptiles, birds, mammals, and primates. The results of the survey confirmed that all three sites were highly disturbed by human activity. Nonetheless, the team documented 709 species, including one amphibian and one katydid species new to science. The RAP team recorded significant range extensions for a number of species (including approximately 50 bird species), and added as new records for Guinea three katydids, one crustacean, one amphibian, and two bird species. An important finding from this survey was the Endangered freshwater crab species, *Afrithelphusa monodosus*. This crab was recorded for the first time since its original collection in 1947, and was previously known only from a single specimen. Other species of conservation concern recorded during the survey included the West African Chimpanzee (*Pan troglodytes versus*, Endangered), West African Red Colobus (*Procolobus badius*, Endangered), three plant species listed by the IUCN as Vulnerable, and three species of mammals, and one frog species listed as Near Threatened. Four species of reptiles recorded during the survey are protected by the international CITES treaty.

The RAP data were used by Alcoa and Alcan, Inc. to inform determination of the location of their refinery. RAP recommended conservation of the gallery forest areas, particularly those in the Boulléré area that are most at risk from slash-and-burn agricultural practices. This has the effect of conserving the sites with the highest biodiversity, while at the same time preserving the watershed areas. The area also needs a sustainable management plan that adequately protects the coastal mangrove ecosystems in the Boké Préfecture, one that takes into account the function of the mangrove ecosystems and the ecosystem services they provide, such as nursery grounds for commercially important species of crustaceans and fish. This also includes the need to rehabilitate the severely impacted mangrove plant communities of the region. It is also important to protect the region's threatened species, and thus hunting of these species. should be banned. The RAP team recommended that areas containing the recorded populations of threatened species be removed from consideration as areas for any resource extraction.

Contributed by Piotr Naskrecki

A member of the RAP team looking for frogs at the bottom of a village well

Chameleon *(Chamaeleo gracilis)* catching an insect

A young fisherman and his bait

Botswana: Okavango Delta II & III (Jan. 20 – Feb. 16 & Sept. 19 – 30, 2003)

There are few places on earth as spectacular and full of wildlife as the Okavango Delta. The Delta serves as a critical source of water, food, and habitat to thousands of animal and plant species as well as people. However, the Okavango Delta might not be this way for long. Pollution, introduced species, low flood levels, fishing, a growing tourism industry, increasing local human populations, and widespread insecticide spraying have been increasingly impacting the Okavango Delta. Long-term research on most of the large mammals of the Okavango and studies by the local Henry Oppenheimer Okavango Research Center provide a solid baseline of information. The 2000 AquaRAP survey provided data on the aquatic ecosystems (see page 189 for details). In 2003, CI-Botswana and partners conducted a second AquaRAP survey at low water levels and a terrestrial survey to fill in data gaps for small mammals, reptiles, amphibians, and many insect groups. The data have contributed to developing a central source of biodiversity information for the

© Conservation International/photo by Lani Asato

Lion lounging in the grass

Okavango Delta to be used by the Botswana government, local non-governmental organizations, and international agencies managing the Delta and to promote listing of the Okavango Delta as a World Heritage Site.

Contributed by Leeanne Alonso

Participating in the RAP expedition was one of the most wonderful field experiences that I have had in my professional career. In 1997, as a co-lead of the RAP expedition in the Corridor Mantadia- Zahamena, I really enjoyed the exploration phase of choosing sites for the RAP expedition: Identifying sites from aerial photography of the corridor, conducting an over flight of all potential sites and exploring in the field the best sites for the expedition. The biggest challenge for us was to find sites within a lowland rainforest to conduct the RAP survey. On the satellite images, the lowland forest looks intact. However, some parts of them are very damaged. After five hours hiking over hills with difficult access, we realized that we couldn't conduct a RAP survey in such a disturbed site. The canopy of this rainforest was thick on the aerial photos but inside, the forest was very disturbed. Then we had to go to other sites that took half a day more hiking. Finally, we found two sites in a beautiful, intact lowland rainforest and both lowland sites are now parts of the corridor Zahamena –Ankeniheny, one of the biggest protected areas created under the Malagasy Government Vision in tripling the surface of existing protected areas from 1.7 million hectares to 6 million hectares. During the conservation planning process in Madagascar for protected areas creation, I was very proud to know that almost all data from RAP expeditions from different sites were useful to identify new protected areas.

- Zo Lalaina Rakotobe, Conservation International-Madagascar

Fruit bat *(Myonycteris torquata)*

Ants (*Pyramica* sp.)

In the 1920s and 1930s, foresters in Ghana demarcated and placed under management 280 forests for the purpose of ensuring a sustainable use of Ghana's forest resources, and the preservation of forests with important roles as watersheds and windbreaks. Due to expanding agriculture and mining activities, combined with the rapidly growing population, Ghana has already lost roughly 80% of its original forest habitat, and the remaining forests are highly fragmented and often isolated by large stretches of farmlands. Fortunately, the reserves designated under the supervision of the Forest Services Division of the Forestry Commission have generally retained a significant integrity, in the sense that the boundary lines laid down seventy years ago are still respected, and their boundary lines are regularly maintained. These forest fragments often act as the last refuges of the highly threatened West African fauna and flora.

The Ajenjua Bepo Forest Reserve and the Mamang River Forest Reserve are located in the Birim North District of the Eastern Region of Ghana. The two reserves consist of moist semideciduous forest, and were established in 1930 (Ajenjua Bepo) and 1938 (Mamang River). Ajenjua Bepo is a relatively small reserve covering an area of hilly topography of 5.69 km². Only small patches of the original forest remain intact with the remainder of the reserve covered mostly by degraded secondary forest or agricultural plantations. Mamang River is relatively larger and flatter, covering an area of 53 km². The forest is uniform with dense tangles of lianas and a thick leaf litter layer.

The objective of the Ajenua-Mamang RAP survey was to conduct a preliminary assessment of species diversity in both reserves, evaluate the relative conservation importance and threats to the biodiversity within each area, provide management and research recommendations together with conservation priorities, and to make this information publicly available to increase awareness of this region and promote its conservation. The survey was done in collaboration with Newmont Ghana Gold, Inc. as a part of their partnership with CI-Ghana, where they worked to promote biodiversity conservation in southeastern Ghana and to help inform Newmont's Environmental Impact Assessment and biodiversity offsets commitment. The survey took place around two camp sites: Ajenjua Bepo (150-300 m) and Mamang River (130 m). Vascular plants, ants, butterflies, katydids, freshwater macroinvertebrates (leeches, insects, crustaceans, and mollusks), fishes, amphibians, reptiles, birds and mammals were surveyed by the team.

Although both Ajenjua Bepo and Mamang River reserves have been heavily impacted by human influences, such as slash-and-burn agriculture, hunting and development activities, the survey revealed that they both contained pockets of quality forest and significant biodiversity. And while neither is considered to be of the highest level of conservation priority for Ghana, because of the country's paucity of original forested areas they both deserve increased protection. In the combined reserves, scientists recorded six Black Star plant species (the highest level of conservation requirement in Ghana), twelve diurnal butterfly species of conservation concern, twelve katydid species new to science, one Near Threatened amphibian species, one Vulnerable and one Near Threatened bird species, and three Near Threatened mammal species.

Of the two reserves, Mamang River appears to be a better candidate for conservation, despite the overall greater number of species recorded in Ajenjua Bepo. The higher species diversity recorded during the survey in the latter is likely attributable to its greater habitat fragmentation, and the sun and wind's affects on the edge of the forest. Mamang River is nearly ten timems larger than Ajenjua Bepo, providing more area of continuous habitat for flora and fauna. Its larger size also has a stronger buffering effect to any negative changes caused by the activity of the surrounding populations. Furthermore, Mamang River is a part of a larger series of forest reserves, making it a candidate for part of a wildlife corridor. This series of forest reserves represents some of the last remaining, continuously forested sites in southeastern Ghana, and therefore should be preserved and protected as much as possible. However, Mamang River does not contain as varied topography as does Ajenjua Bepo. Upland areas are restricted in West Africa, and different species are associated with higher elevations in Ghana. Several notable species observed during our survey were recorded only from Ajenjua Bepo.

The RAP survey results were used to inform and guide further detailed biological surveys and the design of Newmont Gold, Inc.'s biodiversity offsets in Ghana. The RAP program also recommended increased education of local communities on hunting regulations and why they are needed, increasing sanitation in surrounding villages to decrease the impact of pollution on aquatic habitats of the reserves, a better control of deforestation and habitat degradation, and a reduction in the size of the network of roads, plantations, and paths adjacent to and within the forest reserves.

Contributed by Piotr Naskrecki

Katydid *(Tetraconcha sp.)*

Tree frog *(Leptopelis occidentalis)*

RAP scientists measuring collected mammal specimens

The tepuis in southeastern Ecuador may not be quite as grand as those of the Guianas, but they are impressive in and of themselves. Table-top mountains rising above the other peaks on the border with Peru, these tepuis, with their dwarf vegetation and potentially unique species, were little wonderlands to me that I couldn't wait to explore. This was the site of my first RAP survey. Before the trip, I thought I would see some really cool things and that we might even find new species – I mean, after all, we were going to an area that few scientists had ever visited – but I really had no idea just how exciting this trip would be for me.

One afternoon, my colleague Elicio and I were searching for frogs and lizards along the margins of a small stream near our first camp. An hour or so passed with no luck – frogs in particular are typically more active and easier to find at night. My eyes were getting a little fuzzy (we had been out late searching for herps the night before) as I approached a rock wall that bordered the stream. I ran my eyes across the wall and suddenly did a double take – staring back at me, blending in perfectly with the orange and green moss, was a small harlequin frog, about the size of my thumb! For a herpetologist in the mountains of South America, this is like finding a diamond in a coal mine. Harlequin frogs (which are actually toads) of the genus Atelopus, among many other amphibian species, have been largely wiped out in the Andes of South America by a nasty fungus which kills frogs by preventing regulation of electrolytes. That night, I went to sleep excited to have found an Atelopus, but a little sad because I assumed that she was simply an unlikely individual that had temporarily survived in the wake of the fungus...

Trudging miles back to base camp down the mountain in the dark after searching all night for herps at the top of the tepui was absolutely exhausting. To avoid the back and forth, we decided to make a satellite camp closer to the top and stay there for the next few days. After a muddy trek to the base of the tepui, and a treacherous climb up to a flatter area where camp was to be set up, we decided to rinse off in the mountain stream flowing next to our new camp. I slowly stepped down into the cold water and glanced at my feet. Once again, I couldn't believe my eyes – the rocks at the bottom of the stream were teeming with tiny, shiny black and gold critters – Atelopus tadpoles! Over the next few days, we found other healthy adult frogs; these combined with lots of healthy tadpoles indicated to us that we hadn't just found an unlikely individual survivor, but rather an entire healthy population of harlequin frogs!

Without this RAP survey, we may never have found this Atelopus population. Local communities are now working to give this population the protection it deserves, and who knows, maybe these frogs might even teach us something about how they have managed to survive a global epidemic to which so many other amphibian species have succumbed.

- Jessica Deichmann, Research Associate, Rapid Assessment Program,
Conservation International

Suriname
Lely and Nassau Plateaus
October 25 – November 26, 2005

© Jan Wirjosentono

© Jan Wirjosentono

© Miguel Pinto

An endemic rain frog (*Pristimantis zeuctoctylus*)

© Jessica Deichmann

Amazonian snail-eating snake (*Dipsas indica*)

Located within the Guaiana Shield of northern South America, Suriname has extensive tracts of pristine rainforest, within which are ancient plateaus formed over 26-38 million years ago and topped with bauxite and ferrite. The presence of extensive bauxite deposits makes these plateaus very attractive to mining interests for aluminum production. Thus, a RAP survey was conducted in 2005 to collect biodiversity data to be fed into the early stages of decision-making by BHP-Billiton Maatschappij Suriname and the Suriname Aluminum Company LLC (Suralco). Two plateaus in Eastern Suriname were the focus of the RAP survey: the Lely Plateau, a series of plateaus with a maximum altitude of 700 m and the Nassau Plateau, comprised of four plateaus ranging from 500-570 m. The RAP survey covered a variety of habitats on both plateaus above 500 m including mountain savanna forest, high dryland rainforest, palm swamp, and secondary forest. These plateaus provide essential ecosystem services for local and coastal communities, as well as key sources of employment (small-scale gold mining), food, medicine and building materials for local communities. Both plateaus were still relatively intact at the time of the RAP survey in 2005, presenting unique opportunities for conservation over a large landscape while addressing the threats of logging, hunting/poaching, and small-scale (gold) and large-scale (bauxite and gold) mining.

The RAP survey revealed that both the Lely and Nassau Plateaus contain high diversity of animals and plants, with 27 species endemic to the Guaiana Shield region and at least 24 species new to science. Eleven species listed by IUCN as threatened with extinction live on the plateaus, including many large bird (e.g., parrots, guans) and mammal species, indicating that these plateaus may be a refuge for these species. Due possibly to its larger size, greater elevational range, and pristine habitats, higher species richness was documented on the Lely Plateau compared to Nassau. The Nassau Plateau is more heavily disturbed by human activities but still contains some good populations of mammals, birds and other taxa. Only 31% of the amphibian species were found in common between the plateaus.

The plateaus harbor a high number of species endemic to the Guiana Shield: eight mammal species including the Guianan Red Howler monkey and the Red-backed Bearded Saki; 19 bird species such as the spectacular Guianan Cock-of-the-Rock and the White-throated Pewee, which has a very restricted range; five amphibian and two reptile species.

The Nassau plateau was found to harbor a unique fish fauna, including two catfish species *Hartiella crassicauda* and *Guyanancistrus* sp., that are likely endemic to the plateau. *Hartiella crassicauda* had not been seen in the wild since its initial discovery 56 years ago. The presence of species potentially endemic to the Nassau plateau prompted Suralco to support additional studies of the fish fauna of the plateau and surrounding areas to document the range of the species. However, the species have so far not been found outside of the head-waters of a single mountain stream, Paramaka Creek, on the Nassau plateau (J. Mol, pers. com). There is concern among the scientific community that mining of the Nassau bauxite deposits will affect water quality in the stream and also impact the aquifer that provides water for the Paramaka Creek in the dry season; therefore threatening these unique species with extinction. The Association for Tropical Biology and Conservation issued a resolution in 2008 calling for the halt of mining activities on Nassau plateau.

RAP and CI-Suriname continue to support the recommendations made in the 2007 *RAP Bulletin of Biological Assessment* #43, which advocate that the Lely and Nassau plateaus receive increased levels of biodiversity protection through a collaborative approach between public and private institutions, including local communities, to address and halt the threats currently and potentially facing these sites. Both plateaus contain a high proportion of Suriname's biodiversity and contain great habitat diversity that is not widely found in the region. Global amphibian declines have resulted in the loss of many higher elevation species; therefore the presence of abundant, diverse, stream associated amphibian assemblages at Nassau and Lely is of significant conservation value. These sites provide refuge for many threatened species and species endemic to the Guiana Shield. We continue to support the RAP team's principal recommendations including 1) the creation of a Nature Park on the Nassau Plateau to protect the unique Paramaka Creek watershed and 2) empowerment of the Nature Conservation Division of the Suriname government to increase monitoring in both areas, especially for hunting and illegal mining. The Nassau plateau is currently (2010) still of interest to Suralco for possible bauxite extraction.

Contributed by Leeanne Alonso and Annette Tjon Sie Fat

© Miguel Pinto

Palm forest

© Jessica Deichmann

Rufous-throated Antbird *(Gymnopitlys rufigula)*

© James Watling

Marbled Tree Frog *(Dendropsophus marmoratus)*

223

Philippines: Calamianes Islands, Palawan Province (February 6 – 21, 1998)

Lying between the South China and Sulu Seas, the Calamianes are an island group made of small satellite islands dominated by the three larger islands of Busuanga, Culion and Coron. These islands form an important part of the "Coral Triangle," an area of the world's richest coastal marine biodiversity. A team of MarineRAP scientists collaborated to assess 38 diverse sites over a 16-day period. The primary goal of the survey was to indentify sites with high biodiversity and low exposure to threats (healthy sites), and to make recommendations for areas to be included in the Palawan Council for Sustainable Development's Environmentally Critical Areas Network. At each site the number of species of hard corals, mollusks and reef fishes was determined by visual underwater census by the MarineRAP team. High biodiversity for the three groups (300 species of corals, 648 species of mollusks and 736 fish) was documented. Populations of targeted species such as octopus and various ornamental seashells were observed to be extremely low. Based on the results, several areas were recommended for inclusion in the Environmentally Critical Areas Network such as the northwest coast of Coron Island; Halsey Harbour on Culion Island; and northwestern Kalampisauan Island including Gutob Peninsula of Busuanga. As a result of the MarineRAP survey, the Calamianes were one of the first few sites with biological data to be considered in the zoning of the Environmentally Critical Areas Network and the Palawan Council for Sustainable Development and their partners are also using this information in their efforts to establish a network of Marine Protected Areas.

Contributed by Sheila A. McKenna and Jeanne G. Tabangay

During the RAP in southern Suriname, in the indigenous village of Kwamalasamutu, I came to realize that climate change can also affect scientists while on a mission to discover biodiversity. I had the privilege to work alongside a professor who is specialized in aquatic beetles and with whom I visited almost every puddle, small stream, and swamp to collect these amazing creatures. We also did some collecting on an Inselberg on which temperatures can get sky high in the afternoon. Here we made an amazing discovery of aquatic beetle species that are new to science. The excitement made us soon forget about the heat of the sun and the fact that we were actually a ray away from dehydration. All of a sudden it struck me that this could become the impediment scientists will be facing in the near future. With about half our bodyweight but still very satisfied, we sought cover underneath some trees, where I concluded that contributing to RAP is one step towards fighting climate change.

- Vanessa Kadosoe, student, Anton de Kom University of Suriname

RAPs are unique opportunities to explore the remotest regions of the planet, and then use what is found to make a difference. There are not many pristine landscapes remaining, but RAPs have been there and are working to conserve them before they are lost. To be part of such an expedition is a special experience. I have many memories from these adventures, including unanticipated discoveries, life-long friends made, and colleagues lost. It is wonderful to be part of a top-notch scientific team that uses what we discover to conserve and manage the world around us.

- Phil Willink, The Field Museum

Hermit crab

Fairy Tern *(Sterna nereis exsul)*

Three years following the Mont Panié MarineRAP in New Caledonia, a second survey was conducted off the northwest coast from Yandé Island in the north to Koumac Pass in the south. The survey covered reef sites within the Zone Côtière Nord–Est, one of six marine clusters included in the Lagoons of New Caledonia World Heritage Site, inscribed in 2008. The corresponding municipalities along this coast are Poum and Koumac with populations of 1,390 and 3,003 respectively.

Using scuba- and snorkeling-based survey methods, a team of scientists inventoried the biodiversity of hard corals and reef fish, assessed exploited macro-invertebrates (e.g., clams and sea cucumbers), and targeted fish stocks and the condition of the coral reefs at each site. Additionally breeding birds of conservation interest were evaluated as the area includes two Important Bird Areas which were identified after a survey by the Société Calédonienne d'Ornithologie (SCO) mandated by Province Nord. Additional data collected on birds during the RAP survey supplemented the May 2006 work of SCO.

In total, 322 hard coral species and 526 reef fish species were observed at 62 sites. Range extensions (additional places where species are known to live) were documented for 43 hard coral and two reef fish species. Among fish targeted by fishermen, 127 species were documented at 52 sites. In the southern portion of the survey area, the 28 sites assessed for large exploited invertebrates indicated that densities for all species were low and in need of further study. Sediment stress was the most severe impact on the reefs examined, with the inshore fringing reef sites in close proximity to nickel mining operations exhibiting the most damage. Most hard coral species require relatively clear water to survive, and under high sediment stress corals suffocate and die. Not surprisingly, the number of hard coral species tended to increase significantly away from the mainland corresponding to a decrease in sediment stress and other human impacts. The same was true for reef fish and targeted macro-invertebrates and fish.

Despite sediment stress, numerous red listed species were still spotted on 66% of the reef sites. These included several species of sharks, fishes, and sea turtles. This frequency of observation was less than that of the previous MarineRAP survey on the east coast in Mont Panié. For birds, highlights from the SCO study and RAP survey included the discovery of a new breeding species for the area, the Beach Thick-knee *(Esacus magnirostris)*. Two lagoon marine Important Bird Areas were identified that included the main breeding area in New Caledonia (about a hundred pairs) for a highly endangered subspecies of Fairy Tern *(Sterna nereis exsul)*. Previously, only about 20 pairs had been recorded in New Caledonia.

Given the severe sedimentation stress, it was recommended that sedimentation be monitored and every effort be made to restore the watershed and maintain those that are still intact. Mitigation techniques (e.g., re-vegetating denuded areas, preferably with native species) should be aggressively pursued. Reducing the effects from mining is a particularly challenging issue as there is a long history of mining in New Caledonia (since 1870's). Mines that have ceased activity are still contributing to the problem in adjacent coastal areas as the bare un-vegetated landscape still erodes. Two locales of specific concern included the reef sites adjacent to the Tiébaghi mine and the Poum mine. At the Poum mine center, activity has resumed and has been projected to increase. A potential consequence is that sedimentation loading on the reefal areas will increase, even further compromising reef health. Overall an integrated coastal zone management plan needs to be instituted that would restore, maintain and monitor the watersheds of Poum and Koumac municipalities.

Grouper among corals

This MarineRAP survey provided data for informed decision making in the next steps for development of an effective management and conservation plan for the Lagoons of New Caledonia World Heritage Site. Exhibiting outstanding biodiversity value, reefs surrounding Yandé Island and the Yandé Pass should be given full protection. This area is relatively remote from large human populations and is part of the World Heritage inscribed marine cluster, Zone Côtière Nord-Est. Outside this marine cluster, the Koumac Pass was observed to have high diversity of fish species and as such is recommended for full protection.

As an Important Bird Area, Yandé Island could form an integrated conservation project including control and/or eradication of introduced predators, and monitoring of populations of Island Thrushes and Tahiti Petrels. Likewise, islets in the Koumac area should be placed under concerted management including regulation of human visitation and eradication of introduced predators. Creation of a network of small natural reserves protecting the richest islets is recommended.

Contributed by Sheila A. McKenna, Jérôme Spaggiari, and François Martel

Oriental Flying Gurnard *(Dactyloptena orientalis)*

Indonesia: Coral Reefs of the Togean and Banggai Islands (Oct. 27 – Nov. 9, 1998)

Off of northern Sulawesi, the Togean Islands stretch for a distance of 90 km across the center of Tomini Bay. Approximately 115 km to the south, the Banggai Islands lie in the northern section of Tolo Bay. Prior to this MarineRAP no comprehensive faunal surveys that included corals, mollusks, and fishes had been undertaken in the combined Togean-Banggai area. The goal of this survey was to provide crucial baseline data for informed decision making for management and conservation of coral reefs. Moreover, information from this survey was intended to provide a guide for further study, monitoring and conservation management activities. Over a 17 day period, 47 reef sites were assessed by MarineRAP scientists through underwater visual census techniques. At each site the biodiversity of hard corals, mollusks (clams and snails) and fish were determined. Additionally, presence and abundance of targeted fish (for personal consumption or commer-

cial purposes) and observations on the environmental condition of each site were made. Rich marine biodiversity was documented with over 314 species of hard corals and 819 species of reef fish. For mollusks, 514 species were recorded for the Togean Islands alone as the Banggai Islands were not sampled. Coral bleaching was observed at nearly all sites in the Togean Islands, but only one site exhibited bleaching in the Banggai Islands. A total of 147 targeted fish species were observed. Alarmingly, illegal fishing practices including the use of dynamite and cyanide were observed at over 80% of the reef sites surveyed. Based on the findings, the MarineRAP scientists recommended that more environmental awareness is needed with stronger enforcement of the existing fishing laws and the establishment of a network of Marine Protected Areas.

Contributed by Sheila A. McKenna

New Caledonia: Province Nord (June and October – November, 1996)

In 1996, Province Nord government of New Caledonia collaborated with Conservation International and the Maruia Society to undertake a biological and socioeconomic RAP survey of five key sites selected by the Commission de l'Environnement: Mont Panié (5,000 hectares), Aoupinié (5,400 ha), Ouaté (6,400 ha), Néoua (1,865 ha) and Pindaï (2,320 ha). The first two sites had protection status but were not being managed effectively, while the three other sites were not protected by public regulations.

Plants, birds, reptiles and invertebrates (butterflies, moths, long-legged flies, flies and barklice) were surveyed to generate species lists and abundances for each of the five sites. The socioeconomic survey led to significant recommendations, especially toward the implementation of co-management principles that would result in local tribes working in conjunction with the

government and NGOs to manage the sites. The final report was delivered in 1998 with sound recommendations for conservation of the sites.

Beyond the valuable scientific gains of this RAP survey for the government of Province Nord, a sustainable relationship was built with the Maruia Society and Conservation International. Indeed, Province Nord has started to implement conservation actions for terrestrial biodiversity and Protected Areas, while the authorities have become convinced that co-management principles are both indispensable and realistic. This institutional vision of co-management was realized in 2002 in the Mont Panié Special Botanical Reserve which gathered again the three partners in collaboration on a sustainable and ongoing initiative.

Contributed by François Tron and Van Duong Dang

Siamese crocodile (*Crocodylus siamensis*)

The Central Cardamoms lies within the mid-section of the Cardamom Mountain range in southwestern Cambodia. The Central Cardamoms consists of a vast, forest-covered mountain plateau from which narrow valleys extend. The monsoon rains fall heavily on the Cardamom Mountains, with annual rainfall often exceeding 4,000 mm. The main habitat is evergreen forest, much of which is in primary condition due to the remoteness of the mountain range and its relative inaccessibility. There are also dry deciduous forests to the north of the mountain range, and pine forest and grasslands on the peaks. The Cardamoms are a center of floral endemism, where over half of Cambodia's known 2,300 species of plants and half of its estimated 230 endemic plant species have been recorded.

A mini-RAP survey was conducted in 2001 to provide an overview of species diversity in the Central Cardamoms and to evaluate the area's conservation importance, with the ultimate goal of providing sufficient information to support the development of a Protected Forest. The RAP survey also aimed to identify threats and conservation targets for the proposed protected area.

The RAP survey results highlight the exceptional biodiversity and ecosystem services values of the area which are fostered by a wide range of elevations and high diversity of habitats. This survey and subsequent surveys by CI recorded at least 66 mammal species, 174 bird species, 74 reptile species, 32 amphibian species and 44 fish species. Of these, more than 40 are globally threatened species. Threatened mammal species include Asiatic Black Bears, Clouded Leopards, Asian Elephants, and Dhole (Asiatic wild dogs). The Central Cardamoms hold one of the last remaining breeding populations of Critically Endangered Siamese Crocodiles, as well as seven globally threatened turtle species such as the Endangered Elongated Tortoise, making it one of the region's most important sites for reptile conservation. Many rare freshwater-dependent species were found associated with clear rivers flowing from the Cardamoms watershed, including the Endangered Asian Arowana and White-winged Duck.

This RAP survey confirmed that the Central Cardamoms is a site of extraordinary biodiversity and watershed conservation value, leading to the official designation in 2002 of the Central Cardamoms Protected Forest for Biodiversity Conservation and Watershed Management. Covering an area of 401,313 hectares, this is one of the largest protected areas in Southeast Asia. The Central Cardamoms Protected Forest is now widely recognized as one of the most important protected areas in the region, both for biodiversity and also as a watershed upon which a third of Cambodia depends. The rivers flowing from this protected area provide drinking water for thousands of downstream communities, as well as water for irrigation to allow year-round agriculture. In addition, the rivers contain migratory fish populations that support the world's most productive fishery – the Tonle Sap Lake. The protected area is also a vast carbon sink. This protected area therefore provides a perfect combination of biodiversity conservation, support for human wellbeing through water and food security, and management of standing forests to reduce the impacts of climate change.

Contributed by David Emmett

Bengal Loris *(Nycticebus bengalensis)*

Terrestrial flatworm

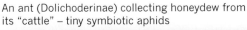

An ant (Dolichoderinae) collecting honeydew from its "cattle" – tiny symbiotic aphids

Indonesia: Northwest Mamberamo Basin (April 27 – May 18, 2007)

During April and May 2007, a RAP survey in northwestern Papua Province documented a rich flora and fauna in the lower reaches of the Mamberamo River. The RAP expedition surveyed eight sites during 22 days in mangrove forest, mixed sago swamp forest and lowland rainforest. The survey was initiated by and received support from Nations Petroleum, a company exploring for gas in the region with an interest in minimizing their impact on the environment. The RAP expedition aimed to generate information that could be used by Nations Petroleum to guide environmental management in their concession area. The team found good populations of cassowaries, crowned pigeons and wallabies, and discovered about eight new plants and four new ant species. Diversity was particularly high in largely undisturbed mixed rainforest above Baitanisa Village compared to the logged forest near Gesa and the naturally poorer swamp and mangrove forests. Careful management of the Mamberamo Basin is critical because logging operations, development for agriculture, and the associated influx of people from elsewhere threaten the integrity of this major freshwater

Mamberamo River

catchment. Although Nations is no longer working in the area, large-scale logging has already had a major impact in the foothill forests on the northern side of the Van Rees Mountains. The RAP team recommended that a conservation awareness program be initiated in the area to counter an anticipated increase in demand for bushmeat in the future.

Contributed by Stephen Richards

By joining the RAP surveys in Suriname, I got the chance to work on an international basis and was exposed to different research methods because of the different taxa that we focused on. It was a way for me to get to see and understand how different elements are connected in nature, especially in the areas where we worked. Very impressing was the indescribable breathtaking beauty of these areas. It is therefore very painful and heartbreaking sometimes that governments do not understand that these places can bring more revenue for their countries compared to the very destructive activities of mining and forestry. The RAP surveys have shown that there are still numerous unknown species on earth. We have not focused on mushrooms but especially the Natives in Suriname use many mushrooms for nutritional and medicinal purposes. A lot is still unknown about earth's biodiversity and its potential in serving humans. I consider the RAP results as a guide and eye opener for institutions and governments to choose a proper way of managing biodiversity rich areas from which the country and its people can benefit without destroying it.

- Haydi J. Berrenstein, Suriname

The villages of Matuku in northeast Fiji rely greatly on the forest ecosystem services

RAP joined up with a team from the Herbarium of the University of the South Pacific to conduct a biodiversity survey in the Nakorotubu mountains of northeastern Viti Levu, Fiji in December 2009. The scientific team included mostly scientists and students from Fiji, who were joined by experts from Solomon Islands, Bulgaria, Venezuela, Singapore and the United States. The team surveyed a range of taxa including birds, amphibians, several insect groups (ants, dragonflies, fruit flies, stick insects), snails, aquatic crustaceans, fishes, and invasive plants and animals.

On northeastern Viti Levu – Fiji's largest island – the Nakorotubu mountain range comprises one of the largest tracts of forest in the country, connecting crucial ecosystems and providing water, food security and resources for the residents of indigenous communities who own the land and its forests.

The RAP survey will provide essential baseline information on the forest's biodiversity to show just how closely its species are linked to human livelihoods. It aimed to increase knowledge of species distributions and demonstrate the value of species and ecosystems for human well-being, with a particular focus on the interconnectivity of ecosystems. For example, one fish species that spawns in a mountain river may be eaten miles away in a coastal community. This information will assist in national and community planning and management that facilitate sustainable ag-

ricultural production, more effective forest management and the identification of special areas for protection.

The RAP team visited three field sites near the villages of Matuku, Soa and Nasau, home to about 90, 300 and 200 people respectively. Led by guides from these villages and from the sister village of Verevere on the coast, the researchers explored the mountains every day to document native and invasive species. Preliminary results from the survey indicate that the number of rare species found in the mountains is very high. In Fiji, as many as 75% of the plant species and 63% of ant species are endemic to the islands, illustrating the uniqueness of Fiji's ecosystems.

While the biologists were out netting insects and counting birds, the RAP team's socioeconomic team worked to bring this data closer to home for nearby villagers. The goal was to verify how much the community depends on these natural resources, and how they can maintain them as a part of their culture. Also joining the expedition was a researcher from the Fiji Museum who identified and recorded sites of cultural significance and the community stories linked to those sites. Through interviews and "mind-mapping" – a methodology where villagers were split into groups and asked to draw maps of their village and surrounding landmarks and resources – the socioeconomic team collected a list of more than 40 non-timber products used for food, medicine, building materials and other purposes. They also created a list of animal species that are regularly used for food sources – species such as crabs and fish from freshwater sources, and feral pigs from the forest.

Although data are still being compiled, preliminary findings suggest what was already evident to local people: the region's species play a large role in everyday life for forest villages. These forests also have a wider global impact: they absorb carbon from the atmosphere, playing a crucial role in climate change mitigation. Local researchers are continuing to collect data on regional resource use.

CI-Fiji and its partners plan to use these new findings to make recommendations for increased protection of regional ecosystems and an expanded role in conservation efforts for local communities. CI is focused on establishing a Viti Levu Islandscape based around a core corridor of protected terrestrial and marine areas with integrated watershed and resource management areas linking these protected areas. CI is promoting a co-management approach where the indigenous land-owning communities, resource users, government and other stakeholders manage as partners to ensure that Fiji meets its national and international conservation obligations while at the same time assisting communities to meet their livelihood and wellbeing aspirations.

Contributed by Leeanne Alonso, Molly Bergen, and Sefanaia Nawadra

Winkler traps used by biologists to collect small arthropods from the soil and leaf litter

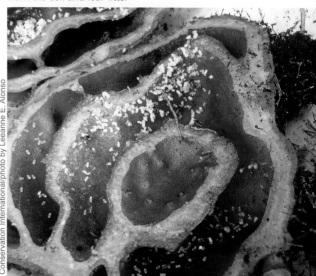

A cross-section of an ant-plant *(Myrmecodia* sp.)

An endemic Fiji katydid *(Diaphlebus* sp.)

Bolivia: Pando (June 23 – July 21, 1992)

The 1992 RAP expedition to the Pando region in northern Bolivia collected information for future decision-making on research and conservation, highlighting the conservation values of this region which has two main biogeographic influences: the southwest Amazon Basin, and the Brazilian Shield. The RAP survey underscored the importance of the northeast region of Pando for conservation, proposed creation of a protected area, and had other impacts as well. Following the 1992 RAP survey, Pando became an attractive area for biological assessment: in 1996 an AquaRAP survey was conducted, and between 1999 and 2002 there were three Rapid Biological Inventories with support from The Field Museum. In 1997, the Department of Pando Land Use Plan provided for the creation of the Federico Román Reserve, which in 2005 gave rise to the Bruno Racua Departmental Wildlife Reserve, encompassing 74,054 hectares of intact forest. Likewise, it highlighted the conservation value of the areas between the Tahuamanu and Muyumanu rivers, both tributaries of the Río Orthon which is now part of the Bolpebra Filadelfia Integrated Natural Management Area created in 2009 with 1.4 million hectares. Finally, the forests of Pando are relatively well-preserved thanks to the presence of Brazil Nuts, the wild fruits of the tree *Bertholletia excelsa*, an essential component of the economy of the region, the exports of which provide over US $40 million, benefiting more than 10,000 households in Pando.

Contributed by Eduardo Forno

Stories from the field...

My first experience with RAP was during the Coppename RAP in 2004. I was still a student 'Environmental Management' at the Anton de Kom University of Suriname. I always knew I wanted do something with the 'green' side of environment, but it was all still vague. The RAP was also my first opportunity to go that far in the interior of Suriname. It was like a new world opening for me. I still remember one experience. As I was assisting Dr. Paul Ouboter with water quality measurements one day, I told him: 'Now I understand the geography lectures I got in primary school.' The lectures were about the intrusion of rivers through the high lands (bedrock) of the interior. I could never visualize that lecture in my head and my question was always: how would that look like? Seeing the Coppename River with all the rocks in it, brought back that lecture to my mind and made the process more clear to me.

RAP has shaped my whole career. After my participation with the Coppename RAP in 2004 in which I assisted Dr. Paul Ouboter, who I didn't know before, he offered me a job at the National Zoological Collection of Suriname/Center of Environmental Research. I started working there while I was finishing my bachelors degree, did my bachelors thesis there, for which I went back to the Coppename basin. Now I have a Masters degree in Ecology, working as a researcher at the same institute (doing research on using amphibians as indicator for disturbance). I also participated recently (August-September 2010) as a leading scientist for water quality in the South Suriname (Kwamalasamutu) RAP.

- Gwen Landburg, University of Suriname

The Mountains of Southwest China reach from the Tibetan Plateau to the central Chinese plain. Some of the largest remaining blocks of contiguous forest in China are located within this mountainous zone. The wide range of ecosystems from temperate to alpine harbors the richest biodiversity of any temperate forest region in the world. An extraordinary 230 rhododendron species are found here, half of which are endemic to the region. The diverse vegetation provides habitat for many endangered and endemic wildlife species, including Giant Panda, Red Panda, Golden Monkey, Snow Leopard, and Takin.

The region is also culturally rich, inhabited by Kampa Tibetans, who are strong believers in Tibetan Buddhism, which teaches unique cultural values and perceptions toward life and the natural world. In Ganzi Prefecture, western Sichuan, Tibetan villages and monasteries have designated more than 2,000 sacred natural sites that provide critical refuge for wildlife. This non-material value system presents a unique opportunity for biodiversity conservation and is especially important in promoting sustainable development and livelihoods, not only for Tibetan communities but also for the rest of Chinese society. Unfortunately, this cultural tradition currently faces great challenges from rapid social and economic development, including grazing, roads, and tourism.

A RAP team of Chinese and international biodiversity experts surveyed the diversity of plants, several insect groups including ants, beetles, and orthoptera (grasshoppers, crickets and katydids), reptiles and amphibians, birds, and mammals in three remote valleys in the Mountains of Southwest China,

Sichuan Province in 2005. The aims of the RAP survey were to collect biodiversity data to assist in guiding conservation activities and management of Tibetan Sacred sites in the region, and to enhance scientific capacity in the Himalayan region by developing collaborations between international and local scientists and by providing training to students.

The RAP survey revealed that all three RAP survey sites contained a rich and interesting biodiversity, each presenting unique opportunities for biodiversity conservation. In Danba County, the RAP team found the habitat fragmented, with much of the vegetation degraded or destroyed due to natural or human causes. However, they also documented many globally threatened species, including Critically Endangered and Endangered small mammal species and several threatened bird species including the Chinese Monal (*Lophophorus lhuysii,* Vulnerable) and the Sichuan Jay (*Perisoreus internigrans,* Vulnerable). The RAP survey took place near the Sacred Dingguoshan Mountain which contains forests in good condition, a low population density of local people, and vegetation recovering well from past logging. Therefore this site has high protection value.

Highest diversity values were recorded in the lower elevation site in Kangding County with several species possibly new to science, including two amphibian species. Higher diversity of plants (1,227 species) and ants (34 species) was documented at this site compared to the two others. The Alpine Stream Salamander (*Batrachuperus tibetanus,* Vulnerable) was recorded here. Interviews with local people revealed the possible presence of a total of 25 species of large mammals at Kangding, including Red Panda (*Ailurus fulgens*, Endangered), Serow (*Capricornis milneedwardsii*, Near Threatened), Asian Black Bear (*Ursus thibetanus*, Vulnerable), and Tufted Deer (*Elaphodus cephalophus,* Data Deficient).

The third site in Yajiang County was at the highest elevation and in best condition, and featured a surprisingly high diversity of mammals and birds, as well as high habitat heterogeneity. Twelve threatened plant species, eight beetles endemic to Sichuan Province, and 104 species of birds were documented. More primary vegetation remains in this area, as the scale and intensity of commercial logging is less than that of the other two sites. A new subspecies of Qinghai Vole *(Microtus fuscus)* and a range extension for the Greater Brown Vole *(Eothenomys miletus)* were documented. The RAP team recorded the presence of 12 species of large mammals (with 30 species likely) including White-lipped Deer (*Cervus albirostris,* Vulnerable), and Asian Golden Cat (*Catopuma temminckii,* Vulnerable).

After the RAP survey, two nature reserves were established following RAP's conservation recommendations to conserve the endangered species and the alpine and sub-alpine ecosystems: Yongzhonglin nature reserve (40,100 hectares, established in 2005) in Danba County, and Shenxianshan nature reserve (39,100 ha, established in 2009) in Yajiang County. A Conservation Stewardship Program was carried out at the survey site in Danba County during 2006 to 2008, facilitated by Conservation International. Local communities were authorized to conduct patrolling and monitoring activities to protect the surrounding 5,000 ha of forest and wildlife to augment protection by the Danba Forestry Department. The lessons learned from Danba County have contributed to the other nine sites with ongoing Conservation Stewardship Programs in Tibetan areas, which demonstrate that conservation stewardship is an effective way to integrate Tibetan cultural values and traditional land management into the government conservation network.

Contributed by Leeanne Alonso, Xiaoli Shen, and Piotr Naskrecki

The Alpine stream salamander (*Batrachuperus tibetanus*)

Prominent moth caterpillar (*Furcula* sp.)

Entomologist Derek Sikes, a member of the RAP team, collecting data

Madagascar: Réserve Naturelle Intégrale d'Ankarafantsika (February 3 – 24, 1997)

The first RAP survey in Madagascar was conducted in the Réserve Naturelle Intégrale of Ankarafantsika, located within the Complex of Protected Areas of Ankarafantsika. The forests of the plateau of Ankarafantsika, located in the northwestern part of Madagascar between the Mahajamba and Betsiboka Rivers, contain one of the largest remaining dry forests in the west with an area of more than 134,000 hectares. These forests protect the watershed of the second largest rice-growing region in Madagascar, Marovoay. Despite recognized national importance for conservation, the reserve is visibly threatened and subject to strong pressures from the production of charcoal, logging, expansion of grazing and collecting forest products. Every dry season, the reserve is also exposed to severe fires. A RAP survey was conducted in 1997 to provide information on the diversity within the reserve and how it is impacted by human activities. Ankarafantsika houses rich floral diversity with 287 species of vascular and 154 species of herbaceous plants, many endemic, within different habitats such as swamp forest and dry forests. Among the fauna, eight species of lemurs were observed, one of them new to science. Fourteen species of small mammals and a total of 69 species of birds were documented. Forty-seven species of reptiles and 12 amphibians, including one snake, two lizard and two frog species new to science, were also recorded. The RAP team recommended that management be improved in order to reduce the effects of human incursions into the reserve, and that a sustainable alternative for people, possibly in the form of an ecotourism project in the reserve, be created. Zoning of a national park has since been proposed based on biological data obtained through the RAP survey and ecotourism infrastructure is now well established at the station.

Contributed by Harison Randriansolo and Jessica Deichmann

Madagascar: Andrafiamena (June 16 – 26, 2007)

Andrafiamena Forest, located in northern Madagascar, is part of the transitional complex between the eastern rain and western dry forest. It represents a crossroads in a corridor which includes Ankarana Special Reserve, the Analamera Classified Forest and the forest of Andavakoera. This corridor has a total area of about 29,000 ha and rises to 310-760 m. Andrafiamena Forest is home to Perrier's Sifaka *(Propithecus perrieri)*, one of the 25 most threatened species of primates in the world, and the main reason for conducting this RAP survey. The inventory also aimed to identify key areas for conservation, which may lead to the establishment of a new protected area.

The RAP team identified 214 species in 146 genera of plants (25 of which are endemic). Three species of mammals were recorded including two endemic rats *(Eliurus minor, E. webbi)* and the invasive *Rattus rattus*; however, many more species are expected to occur at the site and likely were not observed because they were not active during the season in which the survey took place. Additionally, 49 bird (36 endemic), 28 reptile and 5 amphibian species were documented. The prevalence of reptiles in relation to amphibians suggests that the site belongs to the western dry domain; however, the presence also of typical rainforest species indicates the transitional character of the forest corridor.

Logging, uncontrolled bush fires and clearing, and hunting for bushmeat are the major threats to Andrafiamena Forest. In the future, change in traffic following the improvement of the national road from Ambondromamy into Antsiranana may have a negative effect on the forest as well. The conservation of this site is a great hope for people surrounding Andrafiamena Forest. The forest operates as a reservoir of water in this region, so loss of this forest would significantly decrease the amount of water available for irrigation. Andrafiamena Forest also has great potential for ecotourism which would benefit local populations. As of 2010, Andrafiamena Forest is part of a complex of forests being considered for incorporation in the New Protected Areas system of Madagascar.

Contributed by Michele Andrianarisata and Harison Randrianasolo

Solomon Islands
Rennell Island and Indispensable Reefs
June 15 – 26, 1994

Midnight snapper *(Macolor macularis)*, adult phase

Situated southeast of the main chain of the Solomon Islands, Rennell Island, Bellona Island, and their sister reefs, the Indispensables, are located a considerable distance from any of the country's major islands. Rennell and Bellona are of special interest because they are the world's finest examples of uplifted atolls and contain the Pacific's largest lake, Lake Te-Nggano. The area of islands, lagoons and coral reefs here covers approximately 128,000 hectares in total. The islands of Rennell and Bellona are almost identical in size and orientation to the Indispensable Reefs complex, which constitutes the Solomon Islands' largest tracts of coral reefs.

This MarineRAP survey, requested by the Rennell and Bellona Provincial Government, had four main objectives: 1) assess and establish a baseline of information on habitat types and biodiversity in these reef ecosystems; 2) assess the level to which reef ecosystems are affected by human activities or natural disturbances; 3) assess and estimate the abundance of select species with particular importance as marine resources; and 4) identify and assess sites of particular importance for the maintenance of biodiversity, ecological viability and economic value among the fringing reefs of Rennell Island and the Indispensable Reefs.

The MarineRAP survey assessed 15 study sites over an estimated 17,000 ha of fringing reefs. A team of seven scientists and officials led by the University of Auckland Leigh Marine Laboratory in New Zealand carried out surveys to describe the coral and fish communities, and to obtain quantitative estimates of coral cover, abundance of large fish, as well as stocks of economically important shellfish and invertebrate species (giant clams, pearl oysters, sea snails and sea cucumbers).

Coral diversity at Rennell and the Indispensable Reefs, a total of 194 species in 52 genera, is consistent with previously recorded diversities from the Solomon Islands, although the habitats visited did not include more turbid coastal locations. The reef ecosystems of these areas are relatively pristine and retain a high level of integrity.

Over 170 species of fish were recorded during the survey, including 28 species of butterflyfish (Chaetodontidae) and 17 species of surgeonfish (Acanthuridae). The taxonomic composition of fish communities at the Indispensable Reefs and Rennell Island was quite similar, with no clear patterns in fish species present at each site or the overall number of species recorded. Among the three families of demersal reef fish that are the main targets of fishing activity (groupers, breams and snappers), there is a consistent trend for more fish and larger fish to be found at Indispensable Reefs than at Rennell Island.

A survey of the shellfish resources revealed that many large and important species were either absent or very rare. Sea snails in the genus *Trochus* were not recorded anywhere at the Indispensable Reefs, while among giant clams, the Saffron-colored Clam *(Tridacna crocea)*, was found at Rennell Island only, the Horse's Hoof Clam *(Hippopus hippopus)* was seen in low numbers at the Indispensables only, the Southern Giant Clam *(Tridacna derasa,* Vulnerable) was rarely seen, and no live specimen of the Giant Clam *(Tridacna gigas*, Vulnerable) was recorded during the surveys. There is clear evidence of the impact of large-scale removal of commercially valuable clam species. This indicates that it would be timely for resource owners to initiate a management plan for these reefs.

Coral reefs of this region are valuable as sources of food and income, and as tourist attractions. The influence of human activities on Rennell and the Indispensables has begun to have observable impacts on coral reef resources, despite the remaining integrity and high diversity of marine species. The survey team recommended that the sites warrant international recognition for their high biodiversity, and that both the Island and the Reefs should be nominated as a World Heritage Site, should this be desired by the resource owners and the provincial Government. Also recommended was the development of a community-based management program for commercial shellfish species (including re-seeding and population monitoring, particularly of giant clams) to ensure viability of future resources.

The MarineRAP results and recommendations were used in the decision that inscribed East Rennell Island on the World Heritage List of Natural Sites in 1998 as the first such site in the South Pacific. This illustrates how improving knowledge of biodiversity and marine resource use through RAP can bring about meaningful conservation efforts.

Contributed by François Martel

Bluestripe Snapper school *(Lutjanus kasmira)*

Sea cucumber *(Thelenota rubralineata)*

Saffron-colored Clam *(Tridacna crocea)*

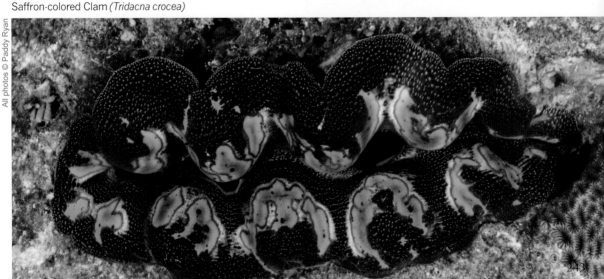

I got to know RAP 6 years ago when I started my graduate studies in a Tibetan region. RAP came to the Mountains of Southwest China, one of the 34 global biodiversity hotspots identified by Conservation International, for an explorative journey with scientists from all over the world. We conducted a three-week comprehensive survey in a remote mountainous Tibetan area in Sichuan Province, where I was impressed by the crystal clear rivers, surrounding snow-capped peaks and great smiles on local Tibetan faces. Later that year, I joined another RAP exploration on the southern slopes of the Himalayas in Nepal as an avian team member. Both surveys were part of Mission Himalayas, a scientific and outreach collaboration between Conservation International, The Walt Disney Company and Discovery Network.

RAP offered me the greatest experience I ever had! It was the first time I worked with world class ornithologists, searching for birds in remote forests and alpine meadows for weeks. I learned how to make "pishing" sounds to attract birds. I was astonished by groups of tits and warblers rushing towards us when Hem Baral, the Nepalese bird specialist, imitated the call of the Collared Owlet. I clearly remember the fluttering of a tiny Yellow-rumped Honeyguide hunting for honey on a cliff hundreds-of-meters high and the loud whistle of Chestnut-headed Tesias along the trail in the dense rhododendron forest. I was like a little kid exposed to the great nature and suddenly seeing all these incredible creatures, excited and anxious. It was also the first time I stayed with more than 20 scientists in the remote camps, listening to their stories from around the world. I was learning new skills and techniques as well as from their dedication to the scientific work, inspired and motivated.

The network that RAP built remains in China although the field journey has ended. Two new nature reserves have been established following the recommendations from RAP. In 2007, the Rapid Biodiversity Assessment Program aimed at exploring the biodiversity in China was founded by the Center for Nature and Society, Peking University. Another 4 rapid biodiversity assessments have been organized and conducted in China, and more than 30 new species of plants, rodents, amphibians, and insects have been discovered. I grew with RAP, beginning as a young student and local RAP participant and becoming a scientist and organizer of the rapid assessments in China.

The Tube-nosed Fruit Bat and the hundreds of other species recently discovered in Papua New Guinea by RAP remind us about "how much we still don't know about Earth's hidden secrets and important natural resources". Our planet is currently suffering a rapid biodiversity loss, and an unprecedented number of species are threatened with extinction due to human pressure and global changes. RAP quickly collects valuable biodiversity data and uses this information to guide conservation efforts and raise public awareness of the global decline in biodiversity. RAP lives by its motto So many species....So little time. I would like to further develop this motto, adding So many contributions for RAP's efforts building local networks, and So much value for "safeguarding the unknown and as-yet undiscovered benefits that nature provides."

- Xiaoli Shen, Center for Nature and Society
Peking University, Beijing, China

New Caledonia
Northeast Lagoon (Touho to Ponérihouen)
November 14 – December 7, 2009

Plate coral (*Montipora* sp.)

Athird MarineRAP survey was conducted in New Caledonia along the northeast coast from Touho to Ponérihouen. This region lies just south of the area surveyed during the 2004 Mont Panié MarineRAP expedition. Forty-eight sites were assessed from Grand Récif Mengalia in the north to Ugue Pass in the south. The inscribed World Heritage marine cluster, Zone Côtière Nord–Est, encompasses the area between Grand Récif Mengalia and Cap Bayes Pass that is speckled with several uninhabited small islands and cays. For the entire survey area, the corresponding incorporated municipalities included Touho, Poindimié and Ponérihouen. There are 44 Kanak tribes in this area comprising approximately 75% of the population. Only the most southerly municipality surveyed, Ponérihouen has nickel mining activity that occurs in Monéo and the neighboring commune of Houaïlou. Therefore some of the reef sites assessed are subject to sediment stress.

Similar in scope to two previous MarineRAP surveys, the main focus was to identify the biodiversity, critical species and areas for protection. Forty-seven reef sites and one mangrove site were surveyed. During scuba diving and snorkeling surveys, the scientists evaluated the biodiversity of fish, invertebrates (e.g., hard corals, nudibranchs or sea slugs, and starfish), commercially important species (e.g., sea cucumbers and fish)

and the health of the site. Sea turtles were also observed and recorded during the survey. An *in situ* evaluation of marine mammals was planned for this survey, but unfortunately was cancelled due to inclement weather. Nevertheless, a compilation of various past marine mammal studies is to be included in the final report. The socioeconomic scientists conducted extensive on-site interviews with the local stakeholders to assess their needs, beliefs and concerns regarding marine resource use. This included approximately 25 tribes or settlements living on the coast.

MarineRAP scientists documented remarkable biodiversity with 338 coral and 433 fish species. For corals, 25 species were documented to have range extensions with the most notable being that of *Acropora rudis,* a species only previously reported from the Indian Ocean. Range extensions were also documented for fish: *Chlorurus japanensis* (parrotfish) and *Halichoeres richmondi* (Richmond's Wrasse). The latter was first observed, but not verified during the Mont Panié survey. Moreover, several species possibly new to science (nine corals and 10 fish) were discovered and are currently undergoing further study. For other invertebrates, a total of 14 starfish and 21 nudibranch species were observed. For sea cucumbers, 18 species targeted by fishermen were found with an additional five non-targeted species. There were very few sightings of apex predators such as sharks, and no observations of large size classes of commercially important fish species.

The condition of the reefs varied with a trend for fringing reefs (those closest to shore) to be the most impacted, especially by sedimentation stress. Alarmingly, symptoms indicative of disease were noted on some corals (both hard and soft) and sponges at just over half the sites visited. Three species of sea turtle, Hawksbill *(Eretmochelys imbricata),* Green *(Chelonia mydas),* and Loggerhead *(Caretta caretta)* are known from this area. The last two species have been documented to nest on the islets in the area. A review of sightings data for cetaceans (e.g., dolphins and whales) in the Touho to Ponérihouen area confirmed that nine of the 24 species known to be from New Caledonia occur there.

The socioeconomic component indicated that the stakeholder tribes interviewed recognize the importance of their marine resources and the need to protect them through various methods (e.g., fish catch quotas and no–take areas). Interviewees confirmed other observations made by the MarineRAP team, including the problem of sedimentation degrading especially the fringing reefs.

Although sediment loading did not appear to be as severe on the reef sites here as that observed during the Yandé to Koumac MarineRAP survey, the need to undertake activities to mitigate land erosion and land run off is certainly required. Restoring the watershed by replanting native plants is a recommended start. Sediment from road based work was also mentioned by the stakeholders as contributing to the problem. This can be lessened by placing sediment screens as a barrier to collect the sediment before it reaches the reefs. Restoring, maintaining and monitoring the watersheds of the three municipalities as part of an integrated coastal zone management plan would be most beneficial.

Further study is recommended for several taxa (e.g., sea cucumbers, clams, fish) to provide better estimates of species population over time. The diagnosis and cause of the diseases noted on several of the reefs sites also warrants further investigation. As this survey finished recently (2009), synthesis of the data is still in progress. Report of the findings back to the local stakeholders is the next step in continuing to develop realistic conservation and management measures.

Contributed by Sheila A. McKenna, Schannel van Dijken, and François Martel

Clown fish *(Amphiprion perideraion)*

Papua New Guinea: Milne Bay Province I (September 27 – October 18, 1997)

Milne Bay, a poorly known region within the area known as the 'Coral Triangle,' is a large maritime province (~25 million hectares) of eastern Papua New Guinea. It contains 1.3 million ha of coral reefs, much of which is still in near pristine condition, unlike other areas of the Indo-Pacific. Milne Bay Province is sparsely populated, but 70% of the population lives on the coast. Coastal villagers are interested in maintaining their traditional rights and artisanal fishing of their marine resources, while finding ways to benefit from them economically. On September 27, 1997, a MarineRAP team took off aboard the Black Adder yacht to survey 53 sites that had been carefully selected to maximize the number of different habitats included in the sampling. The scuba-diving team encountered 362 species of coral including 14 new species; 637 species of marine mollusks; and 1,039 species of reef and shore fishes, three of which were new to science. Large marine vertebrates like sharks, dugongs and turtles were abundant. Two members of the expert RAP team documented higher diversity at these sites than anywhere they had ever surveyed previously! As a result of this MarineRAP survey, Milne Bay Province was identified by the RAP team as a valuable coral reef wilderness area. RAP scientists recommended that Marine Protected Areas (MPAs) and/or Wildlife Management Areas (WMAs) be established in Milne Bay Province because of its unusually high biodiversity coupled with traditional community management and rights to these resources. They also suggested that steps be taken to reduce the effects of human activities on the nearly pristine areas of the province, that economic incentives be developed to support marine conservation, and that capacity be strengthened for monitoring and managing potential MPAs and WMAs. The results of this RAP, reinforced by a second RAP survey in 2000, generated initial conservation interest that led to a community-based coastal and marine conservation project, which ran from 2003-2006. This project was instrumental in raising awareness among communities about the value of their marine resources, and the importance of their sustainable management.

Contributed by Jessica Deichmann and David Mitchell

Papua New Guinea: Milne Bay Province II (May 30 – June 24, 2000)

Encouraged by the incredible diversity observed during the first MarineRAP survey of Milne Bay Province in 1997, the Milne Bay Provincial Government invited a second MarineRAP expedition in 2000 to document 57 additional sites in the province. Researchers recorded 418 species of coral, confirming Milne Bay as one of the richest places on the globe for corals. Much of the observed coral cover was live, with 50% of reefs surveyed in good to extraordinary condition. The results of this second MarineRAP survey increased the number of mollusk species known from Milne Bay to 954 and the number of fish species to 1,109, the highest fish diversity of any area previously surveyed in Melanesia. Abundant stocks of most edible reef fish were observed, but stocks of giant clams and sea cucumbers appeared to be depleted as a result of overharvesting. The RAP team recommended continued education and awareness of the area's conservation importance. Based on the MarineRAP data collected in Milne Bay Province and follow-up work led by Conservation International, Community Managed Marine Areas off the eastern tip of PNG have been proposed. These areas, which are covered under

Sea slug (*Ceratosoma magnifica*)

© Gerald Allen

local management plans, will be monitored and formally recognized under the innovative Local Level Government law by 2011. Other coastal communities have shown an interest in participating in this process for managing their own marine resources. Since 2006 the Milne Bay Seascape has been on PNG's tentative list for selection as a World Heritage Site.

Contributed by Jessica Deichmann and David Mitchell

Madagascar
Coral Reefs of the Northwest
January 11 – 26, 2002

Cushion star (*Culcita* sp)

Coral reefs along Madagascar's coast are best developed in the northeast, far north, northwest and southwest. For this MarineRAP survey, 30 coral reef sites off the northwestern coast of Madagascar were surveyed from 11 to 26 of January, 2002. The survey area extended along the far northwestern coast from Nosy Hao, near the northern tip of Madagascar, to Nosy Iranja, lying approximately 220 km to the south. The main areas assessed included Andranomaimbo Bay, Cape Saint Sebastian, Mitsio Islands, Nosy Be (including Sakatia and Nosy Tanikely), Ambavatoby Bay, and Nosy Iranja. The charter dive boat "Inga Viola" served as a base of operations and individual sites were accessed by a pair of small motor boats. Sites for assessment were selected based on lack of pre-existing biodiversity information in the area, importance of the area for existing and proposed protected or managed areas and logistical feasibility.

The main objectives were to assess 1) the biodiversity of three focal taxa (coral, mollusks and fish) 2) fish targeted for consumption 3) the health of the reef and 4) use, needs and concerns of local communities for their marine resources. Highlights of the survey included a total of 323 species of corals documented, of which nine were new to science. A total of 525 species of mollusks were recorded. Two new species of damselfish (family Pomacentridae) were discovered among the 463 total species of fish documented during the survey. Fifty-five species of fish are targeted

by local fishermen. The majority of reef areas surveyed were in good condition. The most frequently observed damage was predation by the coral predator *Acanthaster planci* or Crown of Thorns Starfish. Evidence of overfishing and destruction to mangrove trees was also observed in the survey area.

Recognizing that reefs can only be sustained and managed when there is strong community-based support, the community liaison team visited 15 villages in the survey area. Initial contacts were made with the head of the village and approximately three to four fishermen from each village were then interviewed. As expected, findings indicated that fishing is important in all the villages with an estimated 60-75 % of adult males engaged in this activity. Women fish from the beach and participate in fish drying. Seasonal immigrant fishermen account for about 80% of the fishing activity in the area. Fishing is mainly from dugout canoes (with sails) and small motor boats. The primary methods include hook and line, fish traps, nets, and beach seines. There is a feeling among fishermen that fish stocks are declining both in size and abundance.

Based on biodiversity and aesthetic qualities, three sites were identified as deserving special conservation protection during the survey. These included Nosy Hoa, Nosy Ankarea and Nosy Tanikely. Many species of fishes and corals not seen during other portions of the RAP suvey were recorded in Nosy Hoa. Near the northern tip of Mitsio Island, Nosy Ankarea was an excellent site with spectacular reef development full of fish, and the above water scenery was equally impressive with steep cliffs, lush forest and white sand beaches. The area is also a nesting ground for the rare and endangered Madagascar Fish Eagle. Nosy Tanikely was the best location in the Nosy Be area, and although it does not have official status as a reserve, it is "semi-protected" by local regulations. For example, no fishing is allowed on the surrounding reefs. Interestingly, this level of protection has been incredibly successful. The density of fish around the island was the best observed at any locality during the RAP survey. This is an excellent indication of the sort of results that can be expected if certain key reef areas are set aside as reserves and properly managed.

In general, all sites appear to be of biological and ecological importance and should be preserved. Unlike many terrestrial sites in Madagascar, the natural state of most reef habitats in the country remains intact. Thus, there is a real opportunity to protect and ensure the preservation of high levels of biodiversity. As of 2007, one of the surveyed sites, Nosy Hara archipelago, received temporary protection status. This area covers over 180,000 hectares and this new temporary protection status has brought wide publicity about the initiative to establish a formal protected area at the site.

Contributed by Harison Randrianasolo, Sheila A. McKenna, and Jean Maharavo

Periophthalma prawn goby *(Amblyeleotris periophthalma)*

Pomacentrus caeruleopunctatus, a new species found during the RAP survey

Nosestripe anemonefish *(Amphiprion akallopisos)*

After lugging 97 kilos of canned sauerkraut deep into the heart of the Surinamese rain forest, I decided it was my duty to catch a fish or two. Of course, I pretended to be motivated only by scientific research, and jokingly promised to deliver a new species for the fish biologists on the expedition. As our native Trio guide steered the dugout canoe away from camp, the setting sun illuminated a giant kapok tree, crowned by the brilliant rainbow of a passing thunderstorm. We scrambled onto a pair of large boulders in the middle of the river and I tossed a hook baited with a chunk of piranha into the water.

I breathed in the musty air mingling from the river and the forest and began to tune into all five senses, which had been dulled by too much time in Washington, DC. Clouds of aquatic insects rose wispily from the river's surface, taking to wing after months of life underwater. Deep, throaty croaks of gladiator frogs (among the world's largest tree frog species), punctuated the songs of thousands of crickets and katydids. A spectral pair of glowing yellow eyes danced eerily amongst the dark trees at the water's edge. I recognized the lights as the sexual display of a large male click beetle, one of thousands of insect species in the region, many of which remain undiscovered by scientists.

Just as I watched a meteoroid's fiery plummet into the Earth's atmosphere, I felt a quick tug at the fishing line in my hand and instinctively yanked back. I excitedly pulled in a striped catfish with long whisker-like barbels. The fish specialists informed me that the catfish was a new species for our current expedition. The specimen was preserved for the museum collection, leaving my dinner plate free for extra sauerkraut atop my rice that evening.

Although the catfish species was not new to science, our expedition discovered several previously unknown species, including fish and my own specialty, scarab beetles. RAP expeditions such as this have uncovered hundreds of new species over the years, but we have a long way to go and not enough time. It's critical that we understand which species exist and where they live if we are to prevent them from going extinct, a problem facing thousands of species in a rapidly changing world.

- Trond Larsen, Senior Research Scientist, Biodiversity Assessment
& Ecosystem Health, Conservation International

Brazil
Abrolhos Bank
February 11 – 28, 2000

Juvenile French angelfish *(Pomacanthus paru)*

Off the coast of Brazil, about halfway between Rio de Janeiro and Salvador, a 200 km wide expansion of the continental shelf forms the Abrolhos Bank, an area comprised of small volcanic islands, coral reefs, mangroves, algae bottoms and sea grass beds. Waters in the Abrolhos Seascape are heavily affected by coastal runoff and riverine inputs. Most marine areas affected by this kind of turbidity cannot support high biodiversity; however, the Abrolhos Seascape is home to more corals and endemic reef fish than anywhere else in the Southern Atlantic. Its mosaic of habitats along with unusually high biodiversity make the Abrolhos an important focus for marine conservation.

Threats to this unique and vulnerable seascape are ever-present and include illegal and overfishing, oil and natural gas exploitation, proposed shrimp farming and coastal deforestation which causes excess sedimentation to build up in the water. A MarineRAP in February 2000 was one step in CI's strategy, in partnership with several Brazilian governmental and non-governmental organizations, to mitigate coastal and marine environmental degradation in the Abrolhos. Part of the Abrolhos Seascape (88,250 hectares) has been protected in the Abrolhos Marine National Park since 1983, but the majority of the region's biodiversity remained unprotected. One of the main goals of the MarineRAP survey was to demonstrate the importance of the region for marine conservation in Brazil and the Southern Atlantic. The MarineRAP survey called attention to the re-

gion and the importance of the creation of other Marine Protected Areas in the Abrolhos.

Nineteen MarineRAP expert scientists surveyed 45 sites within a diversity of reefal habitats in the Abrolhos Bank. RAP scientists conducted underwater surveys of corals, fishes, algae, polychaete (bristle) worms, mollusks and crustaceans. These groups were selected as indicator species – those which would help scientists determine the relative biodiversity and health of the surveyed sites in the Abrolhos Bank.

RAP scientists recorded over 1,300 species, confirming Abrolhos as the South Atlantic's most biodiverse marine domain. Some of the most interesting findings included the discovery of 17 new mollusks and one new fish species. This MarineRAP survey also revealed 15 algae, two coral, 86 polychaete (95% of all polychaetes found on this RAP survey), 23 crustacean and nearly 100 fish species never before observed in the Abrolhos region. RAP scientists even observed three algae, 17 mollusks and 11 crustaceans that had never previously been seen in all of Brazil!

RAP experts recommended that the network of protected areas in the Abrolhos should be expanded to include other key biodiversity areas.

Proper enforcement of protected areas and improved partnerships between the government, non-governmental organizations and local communities in planning and management of coastal resources should also be established. They also advocated for continued biological surveys in other areas of the Abrolhos to determine the source and extent of environmental degradation in the region.

Since the 2000 RAP survey, CI-Brazil's Marine Program has been working with local communities and the Brazilian government to design and implement a conservation management plan for and increase the number of protected areas in the Abrolhos Seascape. Approximately 370,000 hectares have been effectively protected so far through a series of multiple-use and no-take Marine Protected Areas.

Ocean surgeon *(Acanthurus bahianus)*

Through a comprehensive monitoring program initiated after the RAP survey, the diligent work of CI-Brazil, CI's Marine Management Areas Science (MMAS) Program and other partners demonstrated the spillover contribution of no-take reserves to maintaining stable fish populations and continuing to provide locals with the food resources they have been depending on for generations. The information provided by the MarineRAP survey was critical for the creation of two additional extractive reserves in the region, adding 200,000 hectares to the Marine Protected Area network. Additionally, using data accumulated from the RAP survey and the MMAS Program, Abrolhos Marine National Park was designated a Ramsar site in 2010, joining the list of the world's most important wetlands. These are concrete examples of how scientific data can contribute to biodiversity conservation outcomes.

Contributed by Jessica Deichmann and Guillherme Dutra

Bleny *(Malacoctenus* sp.) on reef coral *(Mussismilia hispida)*

Firecoral *(Millepora* sp.)

Regional Profile: Venezuela
Record of RAP Surveys
2000 – 2008

Venezuelan Guyana region

© Conservation International/photo by Anabel Riol

2002

2008

2008

2000

2003

2005

The RAP program in Venezuela

Through six RAP surveys conducted in 2000 – 2008 in unexplored and threatened areas of Venezuela, the RAP program has recorded and distributed new data of global interest, and created an indispensible biological reference for the country.

The six RAP expeditions in Venezuela represent the greatest contribution to the knowledge of biodiversity and the threats it faces in the country in recent history. In fact, they constitute the only examples of continued, multidisciplinary and inter-institutional evaluations of this dimension not only in Venezuela, but also probably in the region. Taking into account that they studied difficult to access sites which necessitated complex logistics, requiring large budgets and effective scientific and logistic coordination, the program was a great contribution as much in its development as in its results.

The RAP surveys recorded some 5,000 species of flora and fauna in six large river valleys in Venezuela (Table 1).

© Josefa C. Señaris

A new species of *Anomaloglossus*

257

Table 1. Species documented during Venezuela RAP surveys

	Guiana Shield Wilderness					Andes Hotspot
	Caura 2000	Delta 2002	Ventuari 2003	Paragua 2005	Cuyuní 2008	Calderas 2008
Plants	399	N	357	589	480	579
Aquatic invertebrates	>105	>110	>64	112	82	77
Fishes	278	106	470	95	130	9
Amphibians	N	44	29	26	27	17
Reptiles	N	91	51	31	23	16
Birds	N	202	157	127	254	294
Mammals	N	N	N	48	47	74
New regional records	116	50	20	66	19	296
New VZ records	11	14	20	0	8	10
New to science	11	9	14	15	7	14

N - not included in the survey

Rió Paragua

Caura (2000)

One of the most pristine watersheds in the world - home of the Ye´kuana

Discovering unknown aquatic biodiversity and the threats it faces, including overfishing, indiscriminate use of natural resources, agricultural expansion and a possible water diversion project in the upper Caura, was the motivation for this first AquaRAP survey in Venezuela. The results show an extremely rich aquatic biodiversity within the watershed, including 10 decapod crustaceans and 278 fish species, 11 of which are new to science.

Para Waterfall

Orinoco Delta - Gulf of Paria (2002)

Richness and productivity of the Orinoco Delta and Gulf of Paria estuarine ecosystem

The enormous productivity and biotic richness of the Orinoco Delta and Gulf of Paria estuarine ecosystem faces a great threat: use of trawl nets for catching shrimp and fish. Additional threats include deforestation within mangrove forests and increased sedimentation caused by dredging. RAP and CI-Venezuela partnered with ConocoPhillips on an AquaRAP survey in the Orinoco Delta and the Gulf of Paria. The survey highlighted high diversity in the region with 30 species of decapod crustaceans, more than 100 fish species, 44 amphibians, 91 reptiles and approximately 200 species of birds. Additionally, in this region, the Warao indigenous population is basically completely dependent on these natural resources, which makes the design of conservation programs for the sustainable use of biodiversity an urgent priority. Recommendations from this AquaRAP survey promoted the first aquatic biodiversity monitoring program in Venezuela with participation from local communities (Creole and indigenous) in the Pedernales, Mánamo, and Manamito river branches and adjacent areas; this also established a basis for replication of this program in the Macareo tributary and Punta Pescador, including monitoring of fishing grounds and aiming for responsible use of aquatic resources in the Orinoco Delta.

Channel and river mouth in the Orinoco Delta

Two great rivers, one continental delta

The union of the Orinoco and Ventuari Rivers forms an internal delta with islands of flooded moriche swamps, savannas and a great variety of bodies of water, which are unique habitats due to their distinct physiographic, limnotic and biodiversity characteristics. This framework of pristine landscapes has a latent, but near and dangerous threat: illegal mining in adjacent zones, including in Parque Nacional Yapacana itself. The RAP survey of this continental delta revealed more than 500 vascular plants in coastal forests which provide habitat for 29 species of amphibians, 51 reptiles and more than 150 birds. On the aquatic side, the survey uncovered 470 fish species – 13 new to science – and 14 decapods including one new species of shrimp. This makes this delta one of the most species rich areas, in both flora and fauna, in South America. This internal delta is also home to 10 species of aquatic turtles and it still maintains a significant number of threatened species including the Orinoco caiman, the Arrau turtle and the Yapacana poison dart frog. As recommended as a result of this AquaRAP survey, the Fundación La Salle de Ciencias Naturales is currently developing a program backed by the Venezuelan government and within the framework of the Statutory Law of Science Technology

and Innovation, focused on the education and training of local personnel to monitor turtle populations and their sustainable use, including *ex situ* conservation actions like incubation of eggs and monitoring of mercury contamination.

Ventuari River

Three million hectares of life, culture and hydroelectric potential

The Paragua River is the main tributary to one of the country's major rivers, the Caroní, which supplies 70% of the hydroelectric power in Venezuela. The upper basin of the Paragua River is one of the least known and most pristine areas on the planet. The hydroelectric potential of its rivers and its biological and cultural diversity combine to make this a key area for priority protection. The Upper Paragua RAP survey in 2005 revealed 16 species that were new to science: one plant, four amphibians, one reptile and at least 10 fish. As a result of the survey, there was a remarkable increase in the knowledge of the region's biodiversity, as well as extensions of the known distributions of more than 60 species. The upper basin of the Paragua River

Ichún Waterfall

remains in almost pristine condition, with healthy populations of threatened species. Nevertheless, the growing mining activity in other areas of the basin presents an imminent danger, not only for the natural biodiversity, but also for the native people of this zone. Sapé speaking indigenous people still survive here, but apparently there are no Uruak speaking people remaining. This last group is in alarming danger of disappearance and with it, a part of our universal cultural heritage.

Upper Cuyuní (2008)

The threat of mining against what is still unknown

The Cuyuní River valley includes approximately 10% of Venezuela's Guyanan region. Harboring great diversity resulting from the juxtaposition of species from the Amazon, the Guyanas and the river valley itself, it forms an important part of the extensive Essequibo River basin, shared with the country of Guyana. The biological richness of this area continues to be threatened by small and large scale gold mining activities that have historically been carried out in the zone. The Upper Cuyuní RAP survey in 2008, conducted in partnership with Gold Reserve Inc., registered a high diversity of invertebrate, aquatic and terrestrial vertebrate, as well as plant species, despite the deforestation and degradation of the river. The headwaters of the Cuyuní River, however, remain in nearly pristine condition, protected by the geography of the Sierre de Lema and the Parque Nacional Canaima, but face the latent threat of invasion by illegal miners. The recommendations from this RAP survey include developing a monitoring plan for threatened species, mercury contamination and deforestation; an action plan for environmental education; and establishment of a biological station to fulfill the imminent need for monitoring the biota and the territory of the Cuyuní River Basin.

The Cuyuní RAP Documentary *"El Dorado existe"*, (45 min. MiniDV Pro Digital) shows the preparation, development and conclusion of this extraordinary expedition in Venezuela.

Uey River Waterfall

© Conservation International/photo by Anabel Rial

A natural Andean conservation corridor, unprotected and highly valuable

The Ramal de Calderas comprises a strip of 547 km^2 in the piedmont and the vertical llanos of the Venezuelan Andes. Its strategic value is fundamental given its hydrologic resources and its potential as a natural biological corridor capable of connecting adjacent protected natural areas (Sierra Nevada, La Culata and General Cruz Carrillo [Guaramacal] National Parks, Teta de Niquitao-Güirigay Natural Monument and the Protective Zone of the hydrological basins of the Guanare, Boconó, Tucupido, La Yuca and Masparro rivers). Current agricultural activities strongly threaten its forests and its hydrologic potential. Continued work in this area over four years and the results of this RAP survey offered effective alternatives to stop the fragmentation of wooded habitat as well as the consequential impacts of fragmentation on human well-being. Creation of a conservation area, development of sustainable use of natural resources projects and initiation of conservation education are currently in progress. The Ramal Calderas RAP survey incited the National Electric Corporation's interest in the area as well as economic support for the installation of the first GLORIA site for global climate change monitoring in Venezuela. Also, Project GEF Terrandina and the National Government support the evaluation of biodiversity in shade coffee plantations, plantations that mix in natural landscape but still conform to coffee production.

Shade-grown coffee plantations

© P. Soriano

New Species Discovered

Sixty five species new to science were discovered (Table 2), thanks to the collaboration and team work of a network of more than 50 scientists and 20 institutions with experience and commitment to the work of biodiversity conservation under the RAP scheme.

Rivulus sape, a new species of killifish

A new species of *Trichomycterus* catfish

A new species of *Astroblepus* catfish

© Josefa C. Señaris

Gontaodes alexandermendesi, a new gecko species

Table 2. New species discovered during Venezuela RAP surveys						
Caura RAP 2000	**Delta RAP 2000**	**Ventuari RAP 2000**	**Paragua RAP 2005**	**Cuyuní RAP 2008**	**Calderas RAP 2008**	**Perija Mini RAP 2008**
Decapods	**Decapods**	**Decapods**	**Flora**	**Fishes**	**Flora**	**Amphibians**
Pseudopalaemon	*Alpheus* sp. 1	*Macrobrachium* sp.	*Ilex* sp.	*Rivulus* sp. 1	*Ilea* sp.	*Cochranella* sp.
Fishes	*Alpheus* sp. 2	Fishes	Amphibians	*Rivulus* sp. 2	*Xanthosoma* sp.	*Cryptobatrachus* sp.
Apareidon sp.	*Palaemonetes* sp.	*Potamotrygon* sp.	*Anomaloglossus* sp. 1	*Trichomycterus* sp. 1	*Frailejón*	*Pristimantis* sp. 4
Aphyocharax sp.	*Upogebia* sp.	*Schizodon* sp.	*Anomaloglossus* sp. 2	*Trichomycterus* sp. 2	*Coespeletia*	*Pristimantis* sp. 5
Astyanax sp.	*Armases* sp.	*Brittanichthys* sp.	*Dendrosophus* sp.		Fishes	
Bryconops sp.	Fishes	*Serrasalmus* sp.	*Cecilia;* gen. and sp.		*Astroblepus* sp.	
Harttia sp.	*Potamotrygon* sp. 1	*Characidium* sp.	Fishes		*Trichomycterus* sp. 1	
Imparfinis sp.	*Potamotrygon* sp. 2	*Hoplias* sp.	*Cyphocharax* sp.		*Trichomycterus* sp. 2	
Moenkhausia sp.		*Trachelychthys* sp.	*Erythrinus* sp.		Amphibians	
Paravandellia sp.		*Hemiancistrus* sp.	*Lebiasina* sp.		*Adenomera* sp.	
		Batrachoglanis sp.	*Brachyglanis* sp.		*Aromobates* sp.	
		Paracanthopoma sp.	*Ituglanis* sp. 1		*Pristimantis* sp.	
		Tricomycteridae; gen. and sp.	*Ituglanis* sp. 2			
		Crenicichla sp.	*Trichomycterus* sp. 1			
		Laetacara sp.	*Trichomycterus* sp 2			
			Aequidens sp.			
			Rivulus sape			

264

What's new about Venezuela RAP surveys?

CI-Venezuela and its closest scientific collaborators from the Fundación La Salle de Ciencias Naturales introduced additional elements to the RAP program in order to optimize the information gathered in the field. This information can also be found in the following volumes of the *RAP Bulletin of Biological Assessment*: 28 (Caura), 37 (Orinoco Delta and Gulf of Paria), 30 (Ventuari), 49 (Paragua), 55 (Cuyuní) and 56 (Calderas).

Elements of RAP Surveys in Venezuela

Aqua-terrestrial RAPs: As of 2003, we have united explorations in aquatic and terrestrial ecosystems, including transitional zones (estuaries and deltas), using multidisciplinary teams from a number of institutions, applying different methodologies that produce effective results within a short time frame.

Key biodiversity areas (KBAs): Venezuelan scientists and CI together selected priority areas for study based on KBAs, representing the holes in biodiversity information and threats, and together they took charge of the technical and logistic coordination of exploration of these areas.

Local people: Surveys encouraged active participation from local communities, indigenous people or farmers in the design, field work and formulation of recommendations for the responsible use of resources and area, and continued monitoring.

Biodiversity use: Surveys included the study of the use of wild flora and fauna by the local communities.

Context analysis: Surveys included socioeconomic aspects and valuation of natural resources. The analyses were done under an ecosystemic concept.

Bibliographic Reference: The RAP Bulletin became a reference publication so that other authors that had not participated in the survey but that had unpublished data on the area covered

© Conservation International/photo by Anabel Rial

Venezuelan Guiana Shield

© Douglas Rodriguez-Olarte

AquaRAP team members

© Bruce Holst

RAP team meeting in camp

© Cesar Barrio-Amorós

RAP herpetologists at work

265

in the survey were invited to publish and divulge this information in the RAP Bulletin.

National Fundraising: Financial support was obtained from public and private businesses in Venezuela, and important counterparts of associates in Venezuela in order to complete the expeditions.

Continuity: The frequency and continuity of the RAP program in Venezuela is maintained by an attentive and enthusiastic Venezuelan team. We recognize the extraordinary support by Conservation International and its allies toward the understanding and conservation of Venezuelan biodiversity and its global importance.

Threatened Species: Sixty-seven threatened species were detected during the six RAP surveys in Venezuela. This information has allowed updates

Fishery resources

Fishery resources

Herpetologists examining specimens

266

and provided additional knowledge about species status for cases in which a species has rarely been seen since its original description.

Species	Category	
	IUCN 2007	Venezuela RED BOOK
Amaurospiza carrizalensis	CR C2a(ii); D	DD
Crocodylus intermedius	CR A1c, C2a	CR C2a(i)
Minyobates steyermarki	CR B2ab(ii)	EN B2ab(iii)
Chiropotes israelita	EN A2cd; B2ab(i,ii,iii); C2a(i)	VU A2d
Pteronura brasiliensis	EN B1ab	EN A2cd
Neusticomys venezuelae	EN B1+2c	DD
Ateles belzebuth	VU A2acd	VU A2cd
Cochranella riveroi	VU D2	NT
Colostethus murisipanensis	VU D2	VU D3
Diclidurus ingens	VUA2c	DD
Eleutherodactylus marahuaka	VU D2	DD
Geochelone denticulata	VU A1cd+2cd	NT
Inia geoffrensis	VU A1cd	VU A2acde+3de
Trichechus manatus	VU C1	CR A2cd
Lonchorina fernandezi	VU A2cd+3cd	EN A3c
Metaphryniscus sosae	VU D2	NT
Oreophrynella cryptica	VU D2	NT
Oreophrynella huberi	VU D2	VU D2
Oreophrynella macconnelli	VU D2	DD
Oreophrynella nigra	VU D2	VU D2
Oreophrynella quelchii	VU D2	VU D2
Oreophrynella vasquezi	VU D2	VU D2
Pauxi pauxi	VUc2a(i)	EN C2a(ii)
Peltocephalus dumerilianus	VU A1acd	VU A2abd
Podocnemis erythrocephala	VU A1bd	NT
Podocnemis unifilis	VU A1acd	VU A2abcd
Priodontes maximus	VU A2cd	EN A2cd
Speothos venaticus	VU C2a(i)	VU A2c
Sphiggurus vestitus	VU C2a	VU C1
Stefania riveroi	VU D2	VU D2
Stefania schuberti	VU D2	NT
Tapirus terrestris	VU A2cd+3cd+4cd	VU A2cd
Tepuihyla rimarum	VU D2	VU D2
Thripophaga cherriei	VU D2	VU D2
Podocnemis expansa	LR/cd	CR A2abd
Myrmecophaga tridactyla	NT	VU A2cd
Podoxymys roraimae	LR/nt	VU D2
Leopardus pardalis	LC	VU A2c
Leopardus tigrinus	NT	VU A2c
Leopardus wiedii	LC	VU A2c
Panthera onca	NT	VU A1cd+2c;C1
Lontra longicaudis	DD	VU A2c
Harpia harpyja	NT	VU C2a(ii); D1
Morphnus guianensis	NT	VU C2a(ii); D1
Podocnemis expansa	LR/cd	CR A2abd

Table 3. Venezuelan Guiana Shield. List of threatened species observed on the RAP surveys

Species	Category	
	IUCN 2007	Venezuela RED BOOK
Aburria aburri	NT	VU
Allobates humilis		DD
Dendroica cerulea	VU	NT
Doryfera ludovicae	LC	DD
Dysithamnus leucostictus	NE	DD
Grallaria guatimalensis	LC	NT
Hyloscirtus platydactilus		DD
Ichthyomys hydrobates		CA
Leopardus sp		VU
Lonchophylla robusta		CA
Lontra longicaudis		VU
Mannophryne cordillerana		DD
Ochthoeca cinnamomeiventris	NE	NT
Odontophorus columbianus	NT	NT
Oryzoborus angolensis	LC	DD
Pauxi pauxi	VU	EN
Pristimantis yustizi		DD
Rupicola peruviana	LC	NT
Scytalopus atratus	LC	NT
Speothos venaticus		VU
Sphiggurus pruinosus		VU
Terenura callinota	LC	DD
Tremarctos ornatus	VU	EN
Vermivora chrysoptera	NT	DD

Table 4. Venezuelan Andes. List of threatened species observed on the RAP surveys

Capacity Building/Training

The RAP surveys fortified institutional capacity in Venezuela. More than 20 institutions and 50 national scientists along with six invited foreign institutions participated in the six RAP surveys and some of the national scientists were then invited on RAP surveys in other countries. The national press has maintained interest in our results and partnerships have grown over the years.

A RAP scientist explaining mammal identification

© Simón Ortiz

Table 5. The evolution of RAP partners in Venezuela

Caura RAP 2000	Delta RAP 2002	Ventuari RAP 2003	Paragua RAP 2005	Cuyuni RAP 2008	Calderas RAP 2008
CI Vzla	CI Vzla	CI Vzla	CI Vzla	CI Vzla	CI Vzla
CABS	CABS	CABS	CABS	CABS	FUNDATADI
UCV	FLSCN	FLSCN	FLSCN	FLSCN	ULA
FMNH	ConocoPhillips Vzla.	Fund. Cisneros	CVG-EDELCA	Gold Reserve-Brisas del Cuyuni	FLSCN
Organización Kuyujani	UCV	CoP	CoP	CoP	CoP
ACOANA	E&E	UCV	FIU	ABT	ABT
			MPPA	Fundación Andigena	Fundación Andigena
		Fundación Terra Parima	A.C. Proiectum	FIU	UCV
		FIJBV	IVIC	UCV	UNELLEZ
				UNC	INTI
				INPA	MPPAT- CIARA
				MBG	PAT
				IVIC	GEF TERRANDINA
					ICAE
					IVIC

CI Vzla: Conservación Internacional Venezuela, **CABS:** CI's Center for Applied Biodiversity Science, **UCV** Universidad Central de Venezuela, **FMNH:** Field Mus. Nat. Hist. **FLSCN:** Fundación La Salle de Ciencias Naturales, **E&E:** Ecology and Environment, **CoP:** Colección Ornitológica Phelps, **FIJBV:** Fund. Inst. Jardín Botánico de Vzla., **CVG EDELCA:** Corporación Venezolana de Guayana, Electrificación del Caroní., **MPPA:** Ministerio del Ambiente, **IVIC:** Inst. Venezolano Invest. Científicas, **ABT:** Ascanio Birding Tours, **FIU:** Florida International University, **UNC:** Universidad Nacional de Colombia, **INPA:** Inst. Nacional de Pesquisas Amazónicas (Brasil), **MBG:** Missouri Bot. Gard., **FUNDATADI:** Fund. Agricultura Tropical y Desarrollo- Universidad de los Andes, **ULA:** Universidad de los Andes, **INTI:** Instituto Nacional de Tierras, **MPPAT-CIARA:** Ministerio de Agricultura y Tierras- Fund. Ciara, **ICAE:** Instituto de Ciencias Ambientales y Ecológicas.

Calderas RAP team

© Simón Ortiz

Conservation Impacts

Protected areas - *More than 300,000 hectares of protected forest in the most important electricity-providing river basin in the country*

The Alto Paragua RAP survey promoted the formation of the Paraguata National Park. This was originally a project of EDELCA that CI-Venezuela took over and carried out along with the National Institute of Parks and the local indigenous communities. Currently all the necessary documentation is in the hands of the National Government so that it can decide on the area's official designation as a National Park.

Conservation Priority Setting - Corridor strategy - *Understanding the global importance of the site*

The Andean RAP survey in Calderas confirmed the conservation priority that this site has in the Andes and affirmed our conservation proposal before national players. Projects already in progress or ready to begin include 1) first GLORIA monitoring site for global climate change, 2) Cooperativa Aromas de Calderas, 3) proposal for a conservation area, 4) training natural history guides and bird watchers, 5) Project GEF Terrandina – Evaluation of Shade Coffee Plantation Biodiversity and 6) rural community tourism.

Guiding Industry - *Protecting the essential*

The Upper Cuyuní RAP represented the first alliance with the mining industry in the country. Gold Reserve Inc. and its branch, Compañía Aurífera Brisas del Cuyuní, C.A., along with Conservation International (CI) promoted the integral development of the influence of business operations in the area. Gold Reserve Inc. is a mining company that has worked more than 15 years in Venezuela. This alliance with CI-Venezuela demonstrated the possibility of carrying out concrete actions with benefits for all sides: 1) a RAP survey in the previously unexplored upper Cuyuní river valley; 2) an audiovisual documentary showing the biological potential of the area and the importance of its preservation to the world; 3) a biodiversity moni-

toring plan based on the findings of RAP surveys; and 4) a sustainable natural resource management plan. The final results convinced the mining company of the RAP survey's great impact, not only in the extent of the results, but also in the scope of the recommendations and the possibilities of putting them into practice.

Demonstrating links between species and human well-being - *To understand in order to care for, to care for in order to survive*

The Orinoco Delta and the Gulf of Paria RAP Bulletin made recommendations to administrators and managers of the country's continental and marine fishery resources with respect to the conservation of species utilized by humans. The result was the immediate implementation of the first scientific and community long-term monitoring program involving local participation of the aquatic resources of the Orinoco delta: sustainable use through knowledge and for the good of humankind. This experience with ConocoPhillips Venezuela and the Fundación La Salle de Ciencias Naturales was extrapolated to other areas of the delta and coordinated later by other organizations and oil companies (StatoilHydro and Chevron) that used our recommendations and experience as an example.

The Ventuari RAP survey demonstrated the extraordinary richness of freshwater and terrestrial turtles that inhabit this internal delta – 10 species. Their overexploitation by the indigenous communities and Creoles of the area has prompted the "Conservation and sustainable use of freshwater Chelonians program", an idea developed by the current coordinators of the Fundación La Salle de Ciencias Naturales with financial support from the Organic Law of Science, Technology and Innovation (Ley Orgánica de Ciencia, Tecnología e Innovación) of the state of Venezuela. This initiative, the only one of its kind in the country, works in two geographic areas – the lower Rio Caura river valley in Bolívar state and the confluence of the Orinoco-Ventuari rivers in Amazonas – and includes systematic monitoring of turtle populations, including the Arrau (*Podocnemis expansa*) which is in danger of extinction. Currently, local communities are being trained through workshops and environmental sensitivity courses and an ex-situ hatchery and nursery center is maintained which releases juvenile turtles at the end of each year, all under the guise of responsible resource management on the part of the local communities – knowledge in action for conservation and the well-being of humans.

The success of the Rapid Assessment Program in Venezuela was due to effective support from our partners and confidence in our team, which permitted us to introduce new methods, make decisions based on local expertise, increase effectiveness in the field and produce more chapters with previously unpublished information in the RAP Bulletins.

Contributed by Anabel Rial, Carlos A. Lasso, J. Celsa Señaris, and Ana Liz Flores

Turtle hatchery and nursery centre

School children helping to release community-reared juvenile turtles

Cooperativa Aromas de Caldera

Regional Profile: Indonesia
Bird's Head Seascape
2001 – 2009

Patrol vessel *FRS Monaco*, purchased with funds raised by "Blue Auction"

Summary of Bird's Head Seascape, Indonesia MarineRAP results

Over the past decade, CI conducted a series of three ground-breaking MarineRAP surveys in the Bird's Head Seascape (BHS) of Indonesia, including the Raja Ampat MarineRAP (March-April 2001; McKenna and Rylands 2001; McKenna et al. 2002), Teluk Cenderawasih MarineRAP (February 2006), and the Fakfak-Kaimana Coastline MarineRAP (April-May 2006). These surveys, augmented by a Raja Ampat rapid ecological assessment by partner The Nature Conservancy in November 2002 and five follow-up reef fish surveys across the BHS between 2007-2009, have shown conclusively that this area ranks as a top global priority for marine conservation and served as a catalyst to initiate one of CI's largest marine investments to date.

Biodiversity Results

Taken together, the results of these surveys clearly indicate that the Bird's Head Seascape sits at the global epicenter of known shallow-water marine biodiversity. In synthesizing the survey results, Allen and Erdmann (2009) record a total of 1,511 species of BHS coral reef fish from 451 genera and 111 families (that total has now risen to over 1,600 species!) – easily the highest diversity ever recorded for an area of this size. Similarly, in their comprehensive delineation of the Coral Triangle region, Veron et al. (2009) highlight the BHS as the only coral ecoregion in the world to reach nearly 600 hard coral species – approximately 75% of the global coral species complement.

These MarineRAP surveys also revealed an area of incredible endemism – otherwise considered rare in the marine realm. Approximately 40 new coral species were discovered on the BHS RAP surveys, most of which appear endemic to the seascape. Of the world record 57 species of stomatopod crustaceans recorded during the RAP surveys, 11 are new and eight of these appear endemic to the BHS. Among reef fishes, the BHS is home to at least 31 endemic species, 29 of which were discovered during these surveys and have now been described (Table 1).

Endemic goby (*Calumia papuensis*)

Endemic jawfish (*Opistognathus rufolineatus*)

The walking shark "Kalabia" (*Hemiscyliium galei*), an international media celebrity!

273

© Gerald Allen

Endemic tilefish (*Hoplolatilus erdmanni*)

Table 1: New Reef Fish Species described from CI's Bird's Head MarineRAP and related surveys	
Raja Ampat	*Apogon leptofasciatus* Allen, 2001
	Apogon oxygrammus Allen, 2001
	Chromis athena Allen & Erdmann, 2008
	Chrysiptera arnazae Allen, Erdmann & Barber, 2010
	Diancistrus niger Schwarzhans, Moller & Nielsen, 2005
	Eviota raja Allen, 2001
	Pentapodus numberii Allen & Erdmann, 2009
	Pseudochromis sp.n. Gill, Allen & Erdmann, in press
	Pseudochromis matahari Gill, Allen & Erdmann, 2009
Teluk Cenderawasih	*Calumia eilperini* Allen & Erdmann, 2010
	Calumia papuensis Allen & Erdmann, 2010
	Chromis unipa Allen & Erdmann, 2009
	Cirrhilabrus cenderawasih Allen & Erdmann, 2006
	Hemiscyllium galei Allen & Erdmann, 2008
	Paracheilinus walton Allen & Erdmann, 2006
	Pictichromis caitinae Allen, Gill & Erdmann, 2008
	Pseudanthias charlenae Allen & Erdmann, 2008
	Pterocaesio monikae Allen & Erdmann, 2008
	Pterois andover Allen & Erdmann, 2008
Fak Fak – Kaimana Coastline	*Chrysiptera giti* Allen & Erdmann, 2008
	Corythoichthys benedetto Allen & Erdmann, 2008
	Hemiscyllium henryi Allen & Erdmann, 2008
	Heteroconger mercyae Allen & Erdmann, 2009
	Hoplolatilus erdmanni Allen, 2007
	Manonichthys jamali Allen & Erdmann, 2007
	Opistognathus rufilineatus Smith-Vaniz & Allen, 2007
	Paracheilinus nursalim Allen & Erdmann, 2008
	Pomacentrus fakfakensis Allen & Erdmann, 2008
	Pseudochromis jace Allen, Gill & Erdmann, 2008

Conservation Impacts

While the MarineRAP surveys certainly succeeded in revealing the tremendous marine biodiversity of the Bird's Head Seascape, their overall conservation impacts in the region have far surpassed simple species lists, and they continue to play a catalytic role to this day.

As a direct result of the BHS RAP surveys, a total of seven new MPAs totaling over 1.7 million hectares in area were gazetted (six in Raja Ampat and one in Kaimana). Combined with existing MPAs in the seascape, the BHS now boasts a network of 10 MPAs nearly 3.6 million hectares in total area – over one-third of the entire Indonesian national MPA system. Importantly, the Cenderawasih RAP survey also resulted in a significant increase in annual budget allocation to Teluk Cendrawasih National Park and reinvigorated park rangers with a new sense of pride in their work.

Even today, as the individual MPAs in the BHS network strive to complete their management and zonation plans, data from the BHS RAP surveys continue to be a primary driver – especially information on habitat type distribution, location of spawning aggregation sites and turtle nesting beaches, and genetic connectivity between reefs. A comprehensive analysis of coral community types conducted using the data collected from the three BHS RAP surveys has provided a clear blueprint for designing an overall zonation system for the MPA network which prioritizes representation of all community types in strict protection zones.

Positive publicity from the BHS RAP surveys (which were covered in hundreds of newspapers, magazines and TV news programs around the world and reached an estimated 50 million people in the US alone) produced a dramatic increase in the awareness and pride of community members and local and national governments of the unique natural heritage in the Bird's Head. This in turn has ensured that BHS MPAs are prioritized in spatial plans and annual governmental budget allocations.

This widespread publicity was also a key factor in the success of the "Blue Auction", wherein the naming rights to 10 new fish species discovered during the BHS RAP surveys were auctioned off in a charity auction in Monaco. The auction, hosted by Prince Albert of Monaco, raised just over $2 million in funding for three priority marine conservation programs in the Bird's Head.

The media buzz created by the BHS RAP surveys was also responsible for launching the rapid expansion of marine tourism in the seascape. Prior to the 2001 Raja Ampat MarineRAP survey, less than 300 guests visited the seascape each year and were limited to a choice of one eco-resort and one live-aboard dive vessel; in 2010, Raja Ampat alone will host over 4000 guests and there are now six eco-resorts and at least 25 live-aboard dive vessels offering itineraries in the BHS (and hundreds of local jobs to coastal communities). Importantly, CI has helped local governments to devise a tourism entrance fee system which now collects approximately $200,000/year, proceeds of which fund an urgently-needed healthcare program for pregnant and nursing mothers in Raja Ampat.

Marine conservation education vessel *MV Kalabia* also funded by the "Blue Auction"

Children learning on board *MV Kalabia*

© Burt Jones

High fish biomass in the Bird's Head Seascape

Data from the BHS RAP surveys have also been used in developing national and regional policies. In late 2009, Indonesia's Ministry of Marine Affairs and Fisheries asked CI to lead a national process to define geographic priorities for marine biodiversity conservation. Using data from the BHS RAP surveys and other similar assessments conducted across the Indonesian archipelago, an expert team of 20 marine taxonomists concluded that the BHS is the number one priority region nationally for marine conservation investment by the government. These prioritization results are now directly influencing both national budget allocations and investments by international development assistance programs including those in the six-country, multi-donor Coral Triangle Initiative.

Taken in total, the influence of these three strategic MarineRAP surveys in the Bird's Head has far surpassed expectations, leading directly to development of the largest MPA network in Indonesia and a conservation investment in the BHS of nearly $25 million over the past 9 years by a wide range of donors. Based on this experience, CI-Indonesia adheres strictly to the principle that any proposed expansion of our work in other areas of Indonesia must begin with a properly-conducted MarineRAP survey as the basis of all future conservation investment in that area.

Literature Cited

Allen G.R. and M.V. Erdmann. 2009. Reef fishes of the Bird's Head Peninsula, West Papua, Indonesia. Check List: Journal of Species Lists and Distribution 5: 587-628.

McKenna S.A., G.R.Allen and S. Suryadi (eds). 2002. A marine rapid assessment of the Raja Ampat Islands, Papua Province, Indonesia. RAP Bulletin of Biological Assessment 22. Center for Applied Biodiversity Science, Conservation International. Washington, DC, USA.

McKenna S.A. and A.B. Rylands. 2001. Unparalleled species richness found on the coral reefs of Raja Ampat Islands. Oryx 35:355.

Veron J.E.N., L.M. Devantier, E. Turak, A.L. Green, S. Kininmonth, M. Stafford-Smith and N. Peterson. 2009. Delineating the Coral Triangle. Galaxea: Journal of Coral Reef Studies 11: 91-100.

Contributed by Mark Erdmann

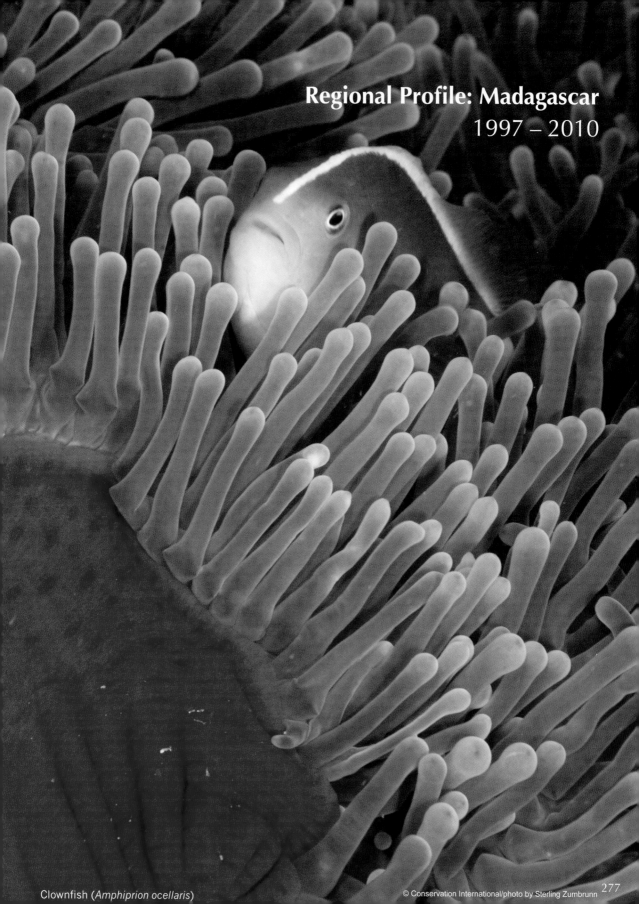

Clownfish (*Amphiprion ocellaris*)

Baobab trees

Madagascar treefrog (*Boophis luteus*)

Introduction

During the past 15 years, terrestrial and marine rapid biological assessments have been undertaken in Madagascar. Terrestrial assessments include those in the Réserve Naturelle Intégrale of Ankarafantsika (February 1997), the Mantadia Zahamena Corridor (November 1998 - January 1999), the Special Reserve of Bora (August 1999), the Special Reserve of Tampoketsa Analamaintso (September 1999), the Special Reserve of Marotandrano (September 1999), the Classified Forest of Bongolava (December 2004), the Nosivolo River (December 2006) and the Andrafiamena Forest (June 2007). Marine assessments include those in the North West (January 2002) and North East (2006 and 2010) part of the islands. Other biological inventories have been funded by Conservation International and carried out by partners, including ZICOMA in Mahavavy Kinkony Complex (2002), Missouri Botanical Garden in the Mountain of Ibity and Itremo (2004), Institute for the Conservation of Tropical Environments in the Classified Forest of Vondrozo (2005), and The Peregrine Fund (2008) in the Complex of Bemanevika.

Biodiversity

The island of Madagascar is home to five endemic plant families and about 14,000 plant species, of which nearly 90% are endemic (Ramananjana-hary et al. 2010). Primate biodiversity and endemism are also very high, placing Madagascar among the world's highest priorities for primate conservation: 99 species and subspecies are all endemic (Mittermeier et al. 2008). There are five endemic families of birds with 209 breeding species, of which 51% are endemic to Madagascar (Goodman and Hawkins 2008). In addition, there are 370 species of reptiles (Glaw and Vences 2007) and Madagascar's amphibians are almost entirely unique to the country, with 244 species of which 99% are endemic (Vieites et al. 2009). The discovery of species new to science is one of the strengths of the RAP process (McKenna et al. 2005, Schmid and Alonso 2005). Sometimes species long considered extinct in the wild are rediscovered (Randrianasolo et al. 2009).

Madagascar Moon moth (*Aegema mittrei*)

Degraded landscape in the highlands

The Rapid Assessment Program (RAP) can collect maximum information at a given site in a very limited time. Various characteristics of each habitat type and threats are noted and flora and fauna species are identified and recorded. One problem is that sometimes it takes time for foreign researchers to send the results of their study, especially taxonomic identifications, back to the country. However, data collected through the RAP are extremely valuable for conservation because they are quickly available and usable for decision-making.

Conservation Impacts

The areas of global importance for conservation of wildlife must be well identified, but the information required is not always available because some areas are inaccessible and therefore are not assessed adequately. The lack of data in the form of taxonomic inventories is a problem, especially for tropical ecosystems.

The results of the assessment are applied to conservation in different ways, including the expansion of known extent of occupation of a given species (for example - *Mantella cowani*, Critically Endangered; *Prolemur simus*, Critically Endangered); identifying an area of priority for conservation because of the presence of exceptional biodiversity (rare, endemic, vulnerable, and/or restricted range species); and also the justification for an extension or a creation of a new protected area.

Contribution to IUCN status assessment

Population trends and species distributions are part of the criteria used to determine whether a species is threatened or not (IUCN Standards and Petitions Working Group 2008). The geographic range of the species and the level of habitat fragmentation can be identified through a RAP survey. The different RAP surveys conducted and the results of various research projects generate an idea of the distribution of a given species. Such information is crucial in the mechanism of evaluating the conservation status of species of fauna and flora through the IUCN process. Some examples of evaluations for which RAP results were used directly or indirectly for Madagascar include: i) Global Amphibian Assessment (IUCN et al. 2006); ii) Global Mammal Assessment (Shipper et al. 2008); iii) Fish Assessment (Scheduled October 2010); iv) Reptile Assessment (Scheduled January 2011); and v) Plant Species Assessment by the Madagascar Plant Specialist Group (GSPM). Results of these assessments have been used for identifying sites of biological importance (Rasoavahiny et al. 2008).

The Endangered Coquerel's Sifaka (*Propithecus coquereli*)

Documentation of the ocean's hidden biodiversity

MarineRAP helps by recording species that take refuge in the coral reefs, and evaluating the health and state of the reef. It is also used to assess tourism potential, to identify causes of marine biodiversity degradation, to assess stocks of marine resources (commercial fish, octopus, etc.), to establish an indicator for monitoring the status of biodiversity, and finally to propose a measure of conservation based on scientific data collected during underwater observations.

Identification of Key Biodiversity Areas

It is difficult to attempt to conserve all the threatened species in a protected area without knowing in advance their distribution and abundance in different parts of the island. RAP surveys provide essential information on the presence and distribution of species in a given site. The concept of Key Biodiversity Areas (KBA) was designed to identify appropriate sites for biodiversity conservation (Eken et al. 2004). The approach is to identify the location of the most endangered species in the world; actions in conservation efforts and priorities should then be focused in these areas. For Madagascar, 164 terrestrial KBA sites have been identified throughout the island, hosting 532 globally threatened species (IUCN 2008).

Following a rapid biological assessment of a given site, zoning can be performed. The core of the protected area is the area requiring absolute protection, and areas with lower biodiversity will be the buffer zone. Currently about 60 of these KBAs have official protection status (temporary or permanent protection). Forty of these sites have received technical and financial support from Conservation International.

The Endangered Diademed Sifaka (*Propithecus diadema*)

Marine diversity in northeast Madagascar

Protected areas and their role in mitigation of the effects of climate change

The forest, in addition to its biological and ecological significance, provides many ecosystem services. The forest serves as a water reservoir and it also absorbs carbon dioxide which mitigates the effects of climate change. As an example, in the Zahamena-Mantadia corridor known also as the Ankeniheny Zahamena corridor, reforestation and restoration contributes to mitigating climate change through carbon sequestration: a) reforestation of 1,100 hectares of native forest will sequester carbon and b) the maintenance of forest cover through the protection of the forest corridor of 371,000 hectares will help avoid carbon dioxide emissions from deforestation. The local community benefits directly from payments for these ecosystem services.

Limiting or prohibiting deforestation (by creating a protected area, for example) can help species to adapt to climate change. Restoration will reconnect forest fragments and expand habitat for many species. This forest can then serve as a bridge in the case of any biological habitat modification.

Creation of a Ramsar site

The scientific studies made by the Department of Animal Biology, University of Antananarivo in partnership with Conservation International and the South African Institute for Aquatic Biodiversity (SAIAB) have concluded that the Nosivolo river is very important in terms of biodiversity. Nosivolo is home to at least 19 endemic species of fish, four of which are locally endemic, including: the Katria (*Ptychochromoides katria*, Vulnerable), the Songatana (*Oxylapia polli*, Critically Endangered) and two more undescribed species of Madagascar Rainbowfish (*Bedotia* and *Rheocles*).

The Secretariat of the Ramsar Convention and the Ministry of Environment and Forests in Madagascar have just declared the Nosivolo River as the seventh Ramsar Site in Madagascar and the first river in the country to be included in this international convention. This new Ramsar site of 358,500 hectares includes the Nosivolo River and its watersheds.

Summary

The Rapid Assessment Program (RAP), a scientific tool performed by CI and its partners, has contributed to biodiversity conservation in Madagascar. It has served as a lever for investment. In the Ankeniheny Mantadia Zahamena Corridor, CI and donors such as USAID have supported activities leading to the creation of a new protected area. The tourism sector should benefit from the presence of charismatic species typical of a region.

Species records for any natural site will be useful for promoting biodiversity and local community awareness. The availability of information on the presence and distribution of fauna and flora in a given site can leverage conservation and promote ecotourism. There was a considerable increase in tourism infrastructure in Andasibe, from three hotels in 1994 to eight in 2010.

Families of Malagasy fisherman

Ambodivahibe coral reef

Giant Leaf-tailed Gecko *(Uroplatus fimbriatus)*

Literature Cited

Eken G., L. Bennun, T.M. Brooks, W. Darwall, L.D.C. Fishpool, et al. 2004. Key biodiversity areas as site conservation targets. BioScience 54: 1110-1118.

Goodman S.M. and A.F.A. Hawkins. 2008. Les oiseaux. Pp 383-434 in Goodman S. M. (ed). Paysages Naturels et Biodiversité de Madagascar. Muséum National d'Histoire Naturelle, Paris.

Glaw F. and M. Vences. 2007. A field guide of the amphibians and reptiles of Madagascar, 3rd edition. Vences & Glaw Verla, Cologne.

IUCN 2008. IUCN Red List of Threatened Species. <http://www.iucnredlist.org/>.

IUCN, Conservation International and Nature Serve. 2006. Global Amphibian Assessment. <http:// www.iucnredlist.org/initiatives/amphibians>.

IUCN Standards and Petitions Working Group. 2008. Guidelines for Using the IUCN Red List Categories and Criteria. Version 7.0. Prepared by the Standards and Petitions Working Group of the IUCN SSC Biodiversity Assessments Sub-Committee in August 2008.

McKenna S.A., G.R. Allen and H. Randrianasolo (eds). 2005. Une évaluation rapide de la biodiversité marine des récifs coralliens du Nord-Ouest de Madagascar. RAP Bulletin of Biological Assessment 31. Conservation International. Washington, DC, USA.

Mittermeier R.A., J.U. Ganzhorn, W.R. Konstant, K. Glander, I. Tattersall, et al. 2008. Lemur diversity in Madagascar. International Journal of Primatology 29: 1607-1656.

Pachypodium sp from the Madagascar spiny forest

CI freshwater team releasing *Erymnochelys madagascariensis*

Parson's Chameleon (*Calumma parsonii*)

The Near Threatened Tomato Frog (*Dyscophus antongilii*)

Randrianasolo H., L. Alonso, M. Andrianarisata, J. Maharavo, N. Rabibisoa, D. Rakotondravony, L. Ramiandrarivo and V. Randrianjafy. 2009. Définir l'évaluation biologique rapide (RAP): Outil scientifique fondamental dans le processus de création d'une aire protégée. Pp 185-204 in Triplet P. (ed). Manuel de gestion des aires protégées d'Afrique francophone. Awely, Paris.

Ramananjanahary R.H., C.L. Frasier, P.P. Lowry II, F.A. Rajaonary and G.E. Schatz. 2010. Madagascar's Endemic Plant Families Species Guide. Missouri Botanical Garden. Antananarivo, Madagascar.

Rasoavahiny L., M. Andrianarisata, A. Razafimpahanana and A.N. Ratsifandrihamanana. 2008. Conducting an ecological gap analysis for the new Madagascar protected area system. Pp 12-21 in P. Goriup (ed). IUCN. Gland, Switzerland.

Schipper J., J.S. Chanson, F. Chiozza, N.A. Cox, M. Hoffman, et al. 2008. The status of the world's land and marine mammals: Diversity, threat, and knowledge. Science 322: 225.

Schmid J. and L.E. Alonso (eds). 2005. Une évaluation biologique rapide du corridor Mantadia-Zahamena, Madagascar. RAP Bulletin of Biological Assessment 32. Conservation International. Washington DC, USA.

Vieites D.R., K.C. Wollenberg, F. Andreone, J. Köhler, F. Glaw and M. Vences. 2009. Vast underestimation of Madagascar's biodiversity evidenced by an integrative amphibian inventory. Proceedings of the National Academy of Sciences 106: 8267–8272.

Contributed by Harison Randrianasolo, Luciano Andriamaro, Zolalaina Rakotobe, and Leon Rajaobelina

Regional Profile: New Guinea
The best (and most difficult) place for RAP expeditions
1996 – 2010

Rugged southern slopes of the Foja Mountains,
Papua Province, Indonesian New Guinea

Background

CI's RAP survey program in mainland New Guinea began in the Lakekamu Basin of southern Papua New Guinea in 1996, but New Guinea was home to RAP-style expeditions long before that. Some of the first RAP-style field surveys anywhere in the world were those of the Archbold Expeditions to New Guinea from 1933 to 1976. These expeditions, which penetrated deep into what is now Indonesian New Guinea in the west, and Papua New Guinea in the east, brought together teams of experts to intensively survey remote and biologically important areas that were poorly known. The Archbold expeditions pioneered the use of support aircraft, a feature that is almost standard for any terrestrial RAP now. When CI's RAP program began working in New Guinea, the information accumulated by the Archbold Expeditions and a handful of surveys by other museums was still pretty much the state of knowledge for the entire region. New Guinea was, and remains, one of the poorest-known major terrestrial biotic provinces in the world. Little is known of New Guinea for a good reason - even with support from aircraft, it is incredibly difficult for even a lone biologist, much less a RAP team, to access many parts of the island. There is little infrastructure within large, rugged and sparsely-populated blank spaces on the map. In terms of biology New Guinea is an ideal place for RAP surveys, but in terms of logistics it can be the toughest.

Biodiversity Results

New Guinea is the world's largest and highest tropical island. Best known biologically for its spectacular birds of paradise, egg-laying mammals and tree-climbing kangaroos, the region is also part of the famous 'coral triangle', harboring spectacular and diverse marine ecosystems. The rich diversity of New Guinea's plants and animals, and the relatively high proportion of its forests that remain intact led to the island's recognition as a High Biodiversity Wilderness Area, one of just five such areas on earth.

To better understand this diversity, Conservation International's Rapid Assessment Program has conducted nine terrestrial RAP surveys across the island. Results of these surveys consistently

Striped Possum (*Dactylopsila trivirgata*), Muller Range

Undescribed microhylid frog (*Oreophryne* sp.), Muller Range

reinforce the fact that New Guinea's biodiversity remains among the poorest documented anywhere. Several MarineRAP surveys have identified reef ecosystems in Milne Bay and in the Bird's Head Seascape around the Raja Ampat islands as among the most diverse in the world, focusing international attention on this globally significant marine realm.

Numerous new fish and invertebrate species were discovered during MarineRAP expeditions around New Guinea, including 10 species reported in a single publication dedicated to the description of new fishes discovered in the Bird's Head region in 2006 (Erdmann 2008).

Terrestrial RAP surveys have also documented many hundreds of new species including dozens of plants, hundreds of insects and spiders, more than 50 frogs, several new mammals and the first new bird species discovered in New Guinea for nearly 70 years (Beehler et al. 2007).

Of course most of these species were already known to the local Papua New Guineans who are enormously knowledgeable regarding their local flora and fauna, particularly about species that have cultural or dietary significance. As a result local communities have always added considerably to the knowledge base of RAP researchers who visit their lands.

Conservation Outcomes

In a society where local communities own the land and its resources, and where cultural and linguistic diversity rival the region's rich biodiversity, conservation outcomes will differ from those strived for in the west. While the documentation of spectacular biodiversity and new species is unlikely to result in the formal protection of critical habitats in New Guinea, the presence of RAP scientists gives rise to interest within the local communities about the flora and fauna of a surveyed area. Modi Pontio, former Country Director of CI-Papua New Guinea, reflects that "Growing up in the village, we often do not recognize the value of the animals and plants around us; we take that for granted, but

© Conservation International/photo by Stephen Richards

Juvenile tree kangaroo (*Dendrolagus inustus*), raised by villagers at Kwerba Village, Foja Mountains

© Conservation International/photo by Stephen Richards

Male King Bird of Paradise (*Cicinnurus regius*), Tualapa, Papua New Guinea

© Piotr Naskrecki

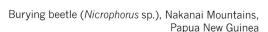
Burying beetle (*Nicrophorus* sp.), Nakanai Mountains, Papua New Guinea

Lake Tawa, Kaijende Highlands, Papua New Guinea

© Conservation International/photo by Stephen Richards

when somebody comes from a long way and shows an interest in a plant or animal, that raises the importance of the plant or animal and as a result we (communities) start to value the plant or animal."

RAP information is also very useful in raising the profile of a site. Good examples are Milne Bay where RAP expeditions recorded 1,300 of the 1,400 species of reef fish known from PNG and found that Nuakata holds the highest fish and mollusk diversity in PNG; and the Foja Mountains of Indonesia's Papua Province where reports of a 'Lost World' generated enormous interest globally in New Guinea's poorly-known biodiversity.

RAP results have helped CI to secure funding for focal conservation sites in the region by informing our partners about the importance of the contribution they are making to biodiversity conservation. For example support from Porgera Joint Venture for conservation activities in the Kaijende Highlands has continued to flow partly due to an improved understanding of the biological importance of the area following the 2005 RAP survey. Data collected during the 2005 Kaijende RAP expedition are currently being used in a GIS modeling project to help define the boundaries of a proposed protected area in this vast montane wilderness area.

The RAP program in New Guinea has provided the opportunity for local scientists to work along-side, and learn from, world class international scientists. These capacity building opportunities are invaluable for a region that is still developing its own local scientific capacity. Many long-term collaborations between foreign and PNG scientists and students have begun with RAP surveys, and these partnerships will allow local scientists to broaden their skills and knowledge, to have exposure to the wider world, and ultimately to take over RAP-style projects from visiting scientists.

Sociocultural Influences on Conservation in New Guinea

Stuart Kirsch is a sociocultural anthropologist who worked in the Lakekamu Basin of southern Papua New Guinea where CI conducted the first New Guinea RAP survey. The Lakekamu RAP exercise was organized in conjunction with a proposed Integrated Conservation and Development (ICAD) project, and Stuart observed the relationships among four groups of landowners in the basin and their attitudes towards the project (Kirsch 1997). His observations are pertinent for understanding the success or otherwise of conservation projects in the New Guinea region and are described below.

At the time of the Lakekamu RAP survey and training exercise in 1996, the four groups at Lakekamu differed significantly in their aspirations for the future. The group with the strongest ties to the cash economy and the capital city wanted to sell their resource rights in return for the opportunity to live a modern, urban lifestyle. Another group lived in the mountains and used lowland resources to supplement their highlands subsistence practices; its members were also willing to auction off the resources of the Lakekamu basin. A third group lived on the edge of the basin and expressed support for the conservation and development project provided that it did not interfere with the economic ventures of its members. The fourth and largest group of people living in the Lakekamu basin was the strongest supporter of the conservation project because its members realized that their livelihoods depended on their continued access to the rain forest. One conclusion from this research is that attitudes towards conservation and development in Papua New Guinea are influenced by regional histories and expectations for the future. In addition, when people see rain forest conservation as important to their economic well-being, they may be more inclined to support such initiatives. An important caveat was that the project did not restrict access to subsistence use of natural resources in the basin. At Lakekamu the primary threats to biodiversity were from proposed logging projects, oil palm plantations, and gold mining.

The inability of the four groups in the basin to reach agreement on how to share property rights initially delayed progress towards a conservation agreement in the area, suggesting that conservation organizations should pay greater attention to local property rights when designing projects. Indeed the challenges at Lakekamu and the mixed record of success for conservation projects in New Guinea reinforce the need for new conservation models in the region. However by fostering the growing conservation awareness of all four of the landowning groups, Conservation International, through the dedication of the PNG Field Team, has brought Lakekamu to the verge of a Conservation Area declaration. The four groups have been working closely together for 5-6 years now, and are dedicated to establishment of the conservation area.

Ceratobatrachid frog (*Platymantis boulengeri*) in Nakanai Mountains rainforest

Literature Cited

Beehler B.M., D.M. Prawiradilaga, Y. de Fretes, N. Kemp and N. S. Sodhi. 2007. A new species of smoky honeyeater (Meliphagidae: Melipotes) from western New Guinea. The Auk 124:1000-1009.

Erdmann M. 2008. "Blue Auction" Special Edition: Preface. Aqua Special Publication 13:89-90.

Kirsch S. 1997. Regional dynamics and conservation in Papua New Guinea: The Lakekamu River Basin Project. The Contemporary Pacific 9(1):97-121.

Contributed by Stephen Richards and Andrew Mack

Papua New Guinean scientists identify a bird netted during the Muller Range RAP survey

289

"Bog Camp", Foja Mountains RAP survey

Tribute to Paul Igag

At the time of our twentieth anniversary, we also note the sad loss of one of the first RAP trainees in Papua New Guinea. Paul Igag had a productive career as a conservationist and the nation's first ornithologist. Initially he trained with Andrew Mack, but moved on to be a teacher himself, mentoring and guiding research of younger Papua New Guinean students. The RAP training has a multiplier effect when the former trainees go on to become trainers themselves, usually independent of CI. Paul was a researcher for the PNG Institute of Biological Research, an organization he helped found. Paul's life mirrors the commitment and hazards faced by conservationists working at the areas where biodiversity is high. Every RAP scientist has a history of close brushes with death – from botched landings in jungle clearings, to nearly every tropical disease known, and a few still without names. Like Paul, most gracefully endure these hazards as part of the cost of business and a worthwhile risk in exchange for the honor of experiencing some of the most beautiful and wondrous natural places left on the planet.

- Andrew Mack

Eustace Alexander
Conservation International - Guyana,
Georgetown, Guyana
e.alexander@conservation.org

Gerald Allen
Western Australia Museum, Welshpool, WA,
Australia
tropical_reef@bigpond.com

Leeanne E. Alonso
Conservation International, Arlington, VA, USA
l.alonso@conservation.org
leeannealonso@yahoo.com

Luciano Andriamaro
Conservation International - Madagascar,
Antananarivo, Madagascar
l.andriamaro@conservation.org

Michèle Andrianarisata
Conservation International - Madagascar,
Antananarivo, Madagascar
m.andrianarisata@conservation.org

Nathalie Baillon
Environmental and Natural Resources
Service, Province Nord, New Caledonia
n.baillon@province-nord.nc

Bruce Beehler
Conservation International, Arlington, VA, USA
b.beehler@conservation.org

Molly Bergen
Conservation International, Arlington, VA, USA
m.bergen@conservation.org

Enrico Bernard
Universidade Federal de Pernambuco, Recife
Antigo - Pernambuco, Brazil
enricob2@gmail.com

Henri Blaffart
deceased

Jean-Jérôme Cassan
Environmental and Natural Resources
Service, Province Nord, New Caledonia
dde-com@province-nord.nc

Bayron Castellanos
Asociación Balam, Ciudad Flores, Petén,
Guatemala
baycas@intelnett.net.gt

Miriam Castillo
Conservación Internacional - Guatemala, San
Jose, Guatemala
m.castillo@conservation.org

Jessica L. Deichmann
Conservation International, Arlington, VA, USA
jessiedeichmann@gmail.com

Giuseppe DiCarlo
Conservation International, Arlington, VA, USA
gius.dicarlo@gmail.com

Van Duong Dang
Environmental and Natural Resources
Service, Province Nord, New Caledonia
v.dang@province-nord.nc

Guilherme Dutra
Conservation International - Brazil,
Caravelas, Brazil
g.dutra@conservation.org.br

David Emmett
Conservation International - Cambodia,
Phnom Penh, Cambodia
d.emmett@conservation.org

Mark Erdmann
Conservation International - Indonesia,
Jakarta, Indonesia
m.erdmann@conservation.org

Luis Espinel
Conservación Internacional - Peru, Lima, Peru
l.espinel@conservation.org

Peter J. Etnoyer
Coastal Center for Environmental Health
and Biomolecular Research, National
Oceanographic and Atmospheric
Administration (NOAA), Charleston, SC, USA
Peter.Etnoyer@noaa.gov

Cristina Félix
Conservación Internacional - Ecuador, Quito,
Ecuador
m.felix@conservation.org

Ana Liz Flores
Independent Consultant
analizflores@gmail.com

Eduardo Forno
Conservación Internacional - Bolivia, La Paz,
Bolivia
e.forno@conservation.org

Juan Manuel Guayasamin
Pontificia Universidad Católica del Ecuador,
Quito, Ecuador
jmguayasamin@gmail.com

Paul Hoetjes
National Department Caribbean
Netherlands, Caribbean Netherlands
Paul.Hoetjes@rijksdienstCN.com

Tim Killeen
Conservation International, Arlington, VA, USA
t.killeen@conservation.org

Stuart Kirsch
Department of Anthropology, University of
Michigan, Ann Arbor, MI, USA
skirsch@umich.edu

Yéo Kolo
University of Abobo-Adjamé, Abidjan, Côte
d'Ivoire
koloyeo@yahoo.com

Carlos A. Lasso
Instituto de Recursos Biológicos Alexander
von Humboldt, Bogotá, Colombia
classo@humboldt.org.co

Juan Carlos Ledezma
Conservación Internacional - Bolivia, La Paz,
Bolivia
j.ledezma@conservation.org

Andrew Mack
Powdermill Nature Reserve, Carnegie
Museum of Natural History, Rector, PA, USA
macka@carnegiemnh.org

James MacKinnon
Conservation International - Madagascar,
Antananarivo, Madagascar
j.mackinnon@conservation.org

Jean Maharavo
Centre National de Recherches sur
l'Énvronment, Antananarivo, Madagascar
maharavo@simicro.mg

François Martel
Polynesian Xplorer Ltd, Apia, Samoa
francois@polynesianxplorer.com

Sheila A. McKenna
SEAlliance, Alameda, CA, USA
sheilamckenna@yahoo.com

Roan Balas McNab
Wildlife Conservation Society, Bronyx, NY, USA
mcnab@wcs.org

David Mitchell
Conservation International - Papua New
Guinea, Alotau, Papua New Guinea
d.mitchell@conservation.org

Russell A. Mittermeier
Conservation International, Arlington, VA, USA
r.mittermeier@conservation.org

Piotr Naskrecki
Museum of Comparative Zoology, Harvard
University, Cambridge, MA, USA
pnaskrecki@oeb.harvard.edu

Sefanaia Nawadra
Conservation International - Fiji, Suva, Fiji
s.nawadra@conservation.org

Carmen Noriega
Conservación Internacional - Peru, Lima, Peru
c.noriega@conservation.org

Nirhy Rabibisoa
Conservation International - Madagascar,
Antananarivo, Madagascar
n.rabibisoa@conservation.org

Léon Rajaobelina
Conservation International - Madagascar,
Antananarivo, Madagascar
l.rajaobelina@conservation.org

Zo Lalaina Rakotobe
Conservation International - Madagascar,
Antananarivo, Madagascar
z.rakotobe@conservation.org

Harison Randrianasolo
Conservation International - Madagascar,
Antananarivo, Madagascar
h.randrianasolo@conservation.org

Hanta Ravololonanahary
Conservation International - Madagascar,
Toamasina, Madagascar
h.ravololonanahary@conservation.org

Anabel Rial
Museo de Historia Natural La Salle, Caracas,
Venezuela
anabel.rial@fundacionlasalle.org.ve

Stephen J. Richards
Conservation International, Atherton,
Australia
s.richards@conservation.org

Josefa Celsa Señaris
Museo de Historia Natural La Salle, Caracas,
Venezuela
josefa.senaris@fundacionlasalle.org.ve

Xiaoli Shen
Center for Nature and Society, Peking
University, Beijing, China
xlshen.09@gmail.com

Jérôme Spaggiari
Independent Consultant
jerome.spaggiari@wanadoo.fr

Luis Suárez
Conservación Internacional - Ecuador, Quito,
Ecuador
l.suarez@conservation.org

Suer Suryadi
Destination Management Center for Tourism
and Conservation
suerdipapua@yahoo.com

Jeanne G. Tabangay
Conservation International - Philippines,
Palawan, Philippines
j.tabangay@conservation.org

Annette Tjon Sie Fat
Conservation International - Suriname,
Paramaribo, Suriname
a.tjonsiefat@conservation.org

François Tron
Conservation International - New Caledonia,
Province Nord, New Caledonia
f.tron@conservation.org

Schannel van Dijken
Conservation International, Apia, Samoa
s.vandijken@conservation.org

Philip Willink
The Field Museum, Chicago, IL, USA
pwillink@fieldmuseum.org

Appendix I. RAP survey participants

Aalangdong, Oscar I.
Abban, Kofi
Abedi-Lartey, Michael
Absalão, Ricardo S.
Abu-Juam, Musah
Acevedo, Romina
Acosta, Arturo
Acosta, Raul
Adjedu, Ebenezer
Aduse-Poku, Kwaku
Agnarsson, Ingi
Agossou Bruno, Djossa
Aguinagalde, Mercedes
Agyei, Alex
Aké-Assi, Laurent
Akwada, Gilijen
Alassane Bangoura, Mohamed
Alban Castillo, J.
Albarrán, Esperanza
Albarran, Irene
Alberca, Edison
Alberca, Milton
Albuja V., Luís
Aldás, Silvia
Alexander, Eustace
Alió, José
Allen, Gerald R.
Allen, Mark
Allison, Allen
Almendáriz, Ana
Alonso, Alfonso
Alonso, Leeanne E.
Alpert, Gary
Alvarado, Italo
Amanzo, Jessica
Amarumollo, Jabz
Amegbe, Godwin
Ampadu-Agyei, Okyeame
Anawoe, Nicholas
Anda, Redempto
Anderson, Kayce (Casner)
Andrews, Amos
Andriamampianina, Lanto
Andriamampianina, Lantoniaina
Andriambelo, Lanto
Andriambelo, Lanto Herilala
Andrianarisata, Michèle
Angle, J. Phillip
Ansah, Frederick
Antiko, Samuel

Antone, Vitus
Anwar, Khaerul
Aparicio, James
Aplin, Ingi
Aplin, Ken
Appleton, Chris
Arakaki Marishi, Mónica
Araújo Pereira, Luciano
Araujo, Enmanuel
Armstrong, Kyle
Arroyo Padilla, Luzmilla
Arzamendia de Montiél, Gladys
Asamoah, Augustus
Asato, Lani
Ascanio, David
Ascorra, César
Asheja, Aritakosé
Ashton, Peter J.
Assi Yapo, Jean
Astrongatt, Stéphane
Ataroff, Michelle
Auccca, Constantino
Awbrey, Kim
Awotwe-Pratt, Vincent
Aymard, Gerard
Ayzama, Serio
Babcock, Russell
Badal, Ryan
Badger, Philip
Badu, Kwesi
Bailey, Ana Cristina
Bailey, Brent
Baillon, Nathalie
Bakarr, Mohamed I.
Bakary, Giséle
Bakary, Gisèle
Bakowski, Marek
Balagawi, Solomon
Baldeon, Severo
Bánki, Olaf
Baral, Hem
Barbosa, Francisco Antonio R.
Barkley, Linda J.
Barré, Nicolas
Barreira e Castro, Clóvis
Barrera, Soraya
Barrie, Abdulai
Barrientos, Christian
Barrière, Patrick
Barriga, Ramiro

Barrio-Amorós, César L.
Bart, Theresa
Bastidas, Lindolfo
Bates, John M.
Battista, Fiocco Giovanni
Baudat-Franceschi, Julien
Bautista, Jaime
Bawole, Roni
Becerra, Egmidio
Beck, Stephan
Beehler, Bruce M.
Belton, Lorien
Beltrán, Hamilton
Benjamin, Cheyne
Bermudez, Alexis
Bernabé, Tra Bi Gabo
Bernal, Nuria
Bernard, Curtis
Bernard, Enrico
Berrenstein, Haydi J.
Berrú, Melva
Berry, Paul
Bestelmeyer, Brandon T.
Bevilacqua, Mariapia
Bhihki, Chequita
Bhuju, Dinesh
Bickford, David P.
Bigilale, Ilaiah
Bills, Roger
Billy, Madison G.
Birnbaum, Philippe
Bladholm, Sharon
Blaffart, Henri
Blanco-Belmonte, Ligia
Boada, Carlos
Boeadi
Bol, Modesto
Boli, Paulus
Bonaccorso, Elisa
Bonnéhin, Léonie
Boomdijk, Dennis
Boseto, David
Botchway, Kwame
Botshelo, Oikantswe
Bouarat, Sylvain
Boucher, Timothy
Bourget, Edouard
Boyle, Brad
Branch, William Roy
Braun, Holger

Briceño, Ehiro
Briceño, Henry O.
Briceño, Régulo
Brodie, Gilianne
Brodie, Gillian
Brooks, Barrett
Brown, Jerry
Buhlmann, Kurt
Buitrón, Galo
Bungabong, Victoria
Burke Burnett, John
Butler, Coreen
Butynski, Thomas M.
Caballero, Andy
Cadle, John
Calcaño Lanz, Ludovico
Callmander, Martin
Camara, Mamadi 3
Campbell, Patrick
Campos, Liliana
Capelo, Juan Carlos
Capriles, Carlos
Carbajal, José Luis
Carpenter, Kent
Carr, John L.
Carroll, Nathaniel
Cartaya, Vanesa
Castañeda Moya, Francisco
Castaño, John Harold
Castillo Villeda, Miriam Lorena
Castillo, Abel
Castro, Edgardo
Catella, Agostinho
Cavero, Moices
Celestin, Keulay Minty
Chagall, Veira
Chang, Fonchii
Chernoff, Barry
Chicchón, Avecita
Chonati, Ana Maria
Christie, W. Tyler
Christy, Patrice
Chunping, Liang
Chuquihuanca, Martin
Clarke, David
Clemens, Raymond
Cole, Russell
Coleman, James
Colonnello, Giuseppe
Coltro, Jr., Luiz Antônio
Comer, Marnee
Comiskey, James
Contreras, Elba

Contreras, Laura
Contreras, Mónica
Cooper, Anderson
Cooperman, Michael
Copeland, Lekima
Córdova, Saida
Cornejo Farfán, Arturo
Cornuet, Nathaniel
Couch, Charlotte
Creese, Robert
Crothers IV, Samuel
Cumberlidge, Neil
Curran, Sarah
Curtis, Barbara
da Silva, Cláudia Regina
Dabo, Jonathan
Dahl, Chris
Dalino, Hay
Dallmeier, Francisco
Damasceno, Jr., Geraldo Alves
Daniels, Amandu K.
Davis, Jr., Lloyd R.
de Abreu Vianna, Juliana
De Dijn, Bart P.E.
de Freitas, Justin
de Freitas, Sr., Duane
de Fretes, Yance
De Greef, Stephane
de la Colina, Rafael
de la Cruz, Alicia
de O. Figueiredo, Márcia A.
de Oliveira, Marcia Divina
de Salis, Suzana Maria
de Silva, Naamal
de Souza Gama, Cecile
de Toledo Piza, Mônica
Decher, Jan
Deichmann, Jessica L.
Delamou, Nicolas Londiah
DeMetro, Andrew
Demey, Ron
Denis, Toto Seki
Derveld, Iwan
Deschner, Tobias
Devantier, Lyndon
Diallo, Mamadou Saliou
Díaz, Wilmer
DiCarlo, Giuseppe
Dijkstra, Klaas-Douwe B.
Do Nascimiento, Carlos
Doku-Marfo, Ernestina
Donahue, Paul K.
Donovan, Foort

Dutra, Guilherme F.
Dutra, Leo X. C.
Duval, Thomas
Eason, Nicolas
Ebigbo, Njikoha
Ekpe, Patrick
Elizeche, Karen
Ellenbogen, Keith
Ellenreider, Natalia
Ellery, W. N.
Elmendorf, Byron
Emmett, David
Emmons, Louise H.
Encarnación, Filomeno
Erdmann, Mark
Eriksson, Jonas
Ernst, Raffael
Espinel, Luís
Estenssoro, Silvia
Etnoyer, Peter
Evans, Richard
Evans, William
Fabian, Lingaard
Fábregas, Glenda
Fahé, Jérome
Fahr, Jakob
Fajardo, Carlos
Falconí, Lorena
Famolare, Lisa
Faria Pereira, Marcos Callisto
Farina, Oriana
Farino, Julio
Felix, Ble Gbo
Félix, Cristina
Fenner, Douglas
Feragotto, Wiliam
Fernández, Ángel
Fernández, Enrique
Ferreira, Carlos E. L.
Ferreira, Vanda Lúcia
Ferrer, Arnaldo
Fietz, Joanna
Finch, Brian
Finch, Davis W.
Fisher, Brian
Fitzgerald, Kelly
Flores, Ana Liz
Flores, Danny
Flynn, Adrian
Folger, Djaek
Foon, Klassie Etienne
Forsyth, Adrian B.
Foster, Robin B.

Francini-Filho, Ronaldo B.
Franquet, Romain
Freed, Paul
Freeman, Theo
Freile, Juan Fernando
Friedman, Kim
Froehlich, Otávio
Fuentes, Alfredo
Fuming, Shi
Funi, Cláudia
Gabaldón, Arnoldo
Gajapersad, Krisna
Gámez, Jorge
Gamui, Banak
Gamys, Joel
Garcete, Bolívar
García Díaz, José Vicente
Garcia Esquivel, Javier
Garcia V., Roosevelt
García, Juvencia
García, Manuel
García-Amado, María Alexandra
Gardner, Henry
Garrigue, Claire
Gassman, Dirk
Gentry, Alwyn H.
Gerber, Attie
Gibbs, David
Gill, Bruce
Giraldo, Alejandro
Goerck, Jaqueline
Gonto, Reina
González, José Tomás
González, Nelson
Goodman, Steven M.
Gorpudolo, Moses G.
Gould, Howard
Gourène, Germain
Gowensmith, Debbie
Grace, Roger
Gracia, Simeon
Grados, Juan
Granier, Nicolas
Gregory, L. Tremaine
Griffith, Frances
Guayasamin, Juan Manuel
Guerra S., Juan Fernando
Guerra, Fernando
Guinand, Lupe
Gutierrez, Luis
Hagedorn, Mary
Hamada, Márcia Orie
Hancock, Pete

Hannah, Lee
Hao, Tang
Hao, Wang
Hardjoprajitno, Mercedes
Haripersaud, Paddy
Harris, Mônica
Hart, Rob
Harvey, Michael B.
Hatine, Bernard
Hedemark, Michael
Heinemann, Amy
Helgen, Kristofer M.
Hemphill, Arlo Hanlin
Hequet, Vanessa
Herbinger, Ilka
Hernández-Acevedo, Jaime
Herrera, Karin
Hesse, Alan
Hiandodimat, Jacob
Hidalgo, Max
Hillers, Annika
Hinds, Wilshire
Hinojosa, Flavo
Hoetjes, Paul
Hoffman, Bruce
Hoke, Peter
Holié, Jean-Louis
Holst, Bruce K.
Hongping, Deng
Hopkins, Michael John Gilbert
Hormenyo, Augustine
Hosken, Malo J.
Hurrell, Sue
Ibarra, Omaira
Icochea, Javier
Igag, Paul
Ignacio, Leroy
Ilha, Henrique H.
Imirizalidu, Mael
Ingles, Jose
Inskipp, Carol
Ipu, Rodney T.
Irham, Mohammad
Isaacs, Bemner
Iskandar, Djoko T.
Jadán Maza, Angel Oswaldo
Jaffé, Rudolf
Jairam, Rawien
Jammes, Lois
Jankipersad, Reshma
Jantz, Ted
Jaomanana
Jaramillo, Nubia

Jeffers, Jennifer
Jenkins, Aaron
Jiménez, Robert
Joemratie, Sahieda
Johnkind, Carel C. H.
Josse, Carmen
Jourdan, Hervé
Jozua, Sheik
Juhn, Daniel
Justiniano, Hermes
Kabiay, Marthen Helios
Kadjo, Blaise
Kadosoe, Vanessa
Kalamandeen, Michelle
Kale, Enock
Kalkman, Vincent
Kalo, David
Kamara, Morris S.
Kameubun, Conny
Kante, Soumaoro
Kaonga, Martin
Kasanpawiro, Cyndi
Kasmir, Leslie (Rice)
Kataoui, Jean-Pierre
Kawanamo, Miller
Kawatu, Paul Johan
Keith, Philippe
Kelly, Brian
Kemp, Neville
Kerr, Vince
Keulaï, Minty Célestin
Kibikibi, Edward
Kiem, Ary P.
Kigl, Michael
Kihn, Herman A.
Killeen, Timothy J.
Kinbag, Felix
Kinch, Jeff
Kipping, Jens
Kirsch, Stuart
Kobli, Gnali
Kofi Abban, Eddie
Kofi Sam, Moses
Kolding, Jeppe
Kollie, Charles
Kolo, Yéo
Kon, Masahiro
Konaté, Souleymane
Konie, John
Kosi, Tommy
Kota, Sr., Aaron N.
Kouakou, Gilbert N.
Kouamé, N'Goran Germain

Kouassi Konan, Edouard
Kouassi, Kouassi
Kpelle, David Guba
Kpewor, Mawolo
Kpoghomou, Elie
Kpolo, Ouattara
Kratter, Andrew
Krey, Keliopas
Krishar, Aditya
Kruger, Masego
Kulang, Joel
Kulmoi, Paulus
Kuro, Dink
Kutoro, Kelejwang
Kutoro, Kisego
Kwao Ossom, William
Laboute, Pierre
Lai, Joelle
Laime, Manuel
Lajones, N.
Laman, Tim
Lamas, Gerardo
Landburg, Gwen
Lara, Oscar
Larsen, Torben
Larsen, Trond
Lasso, Carlos A.
Lasso-Alcalá, Oscar M.
Lauginie, Francis
Lazuardi, Muhammad
Le Nagard, Ghyslaine
Leaché, Adam
Leão de Moura, Rodrigo
Leão, Zelinda M. A. N.
Lebbie, Aiah
Ledesma, Rene
Legendre, Hervé
Legra, Leo
Lekhuru, Merepelo
Lentino, Miguel
León Alvarez, Ronald Fernando
León, Blanca
León, Luís
León, Rocío
León-Mata, Oscar
Letsara, Rokiman
Lew, Daniel
Lezama, Zaqueo
Lianxian, Han
Lim, Burton K.
Lima, Flávio C. T.
Lima, Jucivaldo Dias
Linárez, Luís Alberto

Lindsay, Stephen
Littler, Diane
Littler, Mark
Llosa, Gonzalo
Lohnes, Edward
Loja, Juan
López Ordaz, Adriana
López, Lawrence
Loua, Néma Soua
Lourenço, Wilson R.
Lourival, Reinaldo
Love, Greg
Lowry, Porter P.
Lozada, Tannya
Lucky, Andrea
Luger, Martina
Luke, Roger
Luke, W. R. Quentin
Luna, Alfredo
Luna, Lucía
Luo, Miaway
Machado-Allison, Antonio
Mack, Andrew L.
Mackintosh, Angelique
Maco Garcia, José
Mac-Quhae, Cesar
Magalhães, Célio
Maharavo, Jean
Mancilla, Mario
Mandelburger, Darío
Marawanaru, Elisha
Marcano, Alberto
Marcel, Zabi Kourame
Marinov, Milen
Marquet, Gérard
Marquez, Josmar
Márquez, Phecda
Marshall, Christopher
Martín, Ricardo
Martinez, Raffy
Martínez-Escarbassiere, Rafael
Martowitono, Kemisem
Marty, Christian
Márvez, Pablo
Masalila, Mathilda
Masibalavu, Vilikesa
Masundire, Hilary
Matararaba, Sepeti
Mattié, Nelson
Maxted, Nigel
McCallum, Rob
McCullough, Jennifer
McGarry, Tessa

McKenna, Sheila A.
McKeon, Sea
Meadows, Martin
Medard, Jules
Medeiros, Marcelo S.
Medina, Mirta
Mehlomakulu, Mandla
Mendoza, Carlos
Menezes, Naércio
Mensoh, Nyumah
Mereles, María Fátima
Merg, Kurt F.
Mesa, Lina
Michelangeli, Fabián
Michiyo Takeda, Alice
Milani, Nadia
Mille, Christian
Missa, Olivier
Mitro, Sutrisno
Mittermeier, Russell A.
Moeljosoewito, Rosita
Mogea, Johanis P.
Mogea, Yohanes
Mojica, José Iván
Mokgosi, Johannes
Mokunki, Loago
Mol, Jan H.
Molgo, Iwan E.
Molina Rodríguez, César
Molubah, Flomo
Monadjem, Ara
Monente, José A.
Montambault, Jensen R.
Montaña, Carmen
Moore, Bruce
Moore, Michael
Mora Polanco, Abraham Rafael
Mora-Day, Julián
Morales Can, Julio
Moreira Martins, Ana Carolina
Moreno Souza Paula, Pablo
Moreno, Gilberto
Morón, Antonio
Mosepeli, Belda Q.
Moskovits, Debra
Mostacedo, Bonafacio
Motaloate, Seteng
Mothibi, Tumi
Moussa Condé, Mohamed Balla
Muchoney, Doug
Muir, Paul
Munzinger, Jérôme
Murdoch, Jed

Murillo, Jhonny
Murphy, Pitz
Naikantini, Alifereti
Naipau, Opon
Nakajima, Jimi Naoki
Nakoro, Elia
Naraine, Gurudatt
Narvaez, Alexis
Nasiu, Ajilon
Naskrecki, Piotr
Nauray, William
Naven, Heng
Neles, Erwin
Nengu, Shaft
Neyra, Daniel
Ngadino, Lucille F.
Nico, Leo G.
Nicolait, Lou
Nicolalde-Morejón, Edison
Nicolas, Violaine
Nielsen, Clare
Niño, Miguel
Niukula, Jone
Noonan, Brice
Norconk, Marilyn A.
Nordin, Lee-Ann
Nordin, Mark
Norman, Zacharias
Norris, Ryan
Nuamah, Collins
Nugroho, Julius
Núñez, Gabriela
Núñez, Percy
Obura, David
Ochi, Teruo
Ochoa, Alejandra
Ochoa, Diana
Oduro, Kwaku Lokko
Oedeppe, Sheinh A.
Ofori Boateng, Caleb
Ohee, Hendrite L.
Ohee, Henni
Olijfveld, Lucien
Oliver, Paul
Oliver, Tom
Olong, Kasim
Olssen, Annette
O'Neill, Elizabeth
Opiang, Muse
Oppong, James
Ordoñez, Jorge
Ordóñez, Leondardo
Oremus, Marc

Orihuela, Gabriela
Orsak, Larry
Ortaz, Mario
Ortega, Alfonso
Ortega, Hernán
Ortiz, Rosa
Osei-Owusu, Yaw
O'Shea, Brian
Osuna, Aurelio
Osuna, Carlos
Osuna, José Luis
Ouattara, Allassane
Ouattara, Soulemane
Ouboter, Paul
Ouillate, Edmond
Ousmane Tounkara, Elhadj
Owusu, Emmanuel
Oyakawa, Osvaldo
Pacheco, Victor
Pada, Defy
Paiva, Paulo C.
Palacios, Bernabé
Palacios, Carolina
Palacios, César
Palacios, Graciano
Palacios, José Luis
Palacios, Vanesa
Palacios, Walter
Palacios, William
Paniagua, Narel
Pantodina, Napoti
Pardede, Shinta
Parinding, Zeth
Parker, Theodore A. III
Pattiselanno, Freddy
Payan, Esteban
Peal, Alex
Peña, Marielos
Penner, Johannes
Pequeño, Tatiana
Peralta de Almeida Prado, Cynthia
Peralta, Carmen
Pereira, Guido A.
Perez Mora, Edward Enrique
Peréz Zúñiga, José
Pérez, Edgar Selvin
Peréz, Ester
Pérez, Sergio G.
Perozo Diaz, Abel
Perozo, Laura
Perry, Alan
Peterson, Leroy

Peterson, Stanley
Petkoff, Irene
Petts, Geoffrey
Phillips, Oliver
Piedrahita, Paolo
Pierce, Andy
Pilgrim, John
Pinto, Miguel
Pique, Martino
Pires, Débora O.
Pisapia, Daniel
Plavsic, Militsa
Poitilinaoute, Hervé
Polhemus, Dan A.
Polo, Roberto
Pombo, Carlos
Ponce, Carlos
Ponce, Elias
Ponciano, Ismael
Pontillas, John
Portilla, Alfredo
Pott, Vali
Pradhan, Rebecca
Prado, Manuel
Prika, Orlando
Prince-Nengu, Jane
Provenzano-Rizzi, Francisco
Pupuka, Phillip
Quawah, Joshua
Queral-Regil, Alejandro
Quimillo, Ramón
Quiñonez, Tomiche
Quintella Lobão, Adriana
Quintero, Eugenia
Quirroga O., Carmen
Quispitupac, Eliana
Rabemananjara, Falitiana
Rabevohitra, Raymond
Rabibisoa, Nirhy
Rachman, Ismail A.
Radilofe, Sahondra
Rafamantanantsoa, Casimir
Rafanomezantsoa, Jeannot
Raga, Tau Teeray
Rahajasoa, Grâce
Raharimalala, Jeannine
Raherilalao, Marie Jeanne
Rainey, Hugo J.
Rajaobelina, Serge
Rajaran, Anand
Rajoelison, Gabrielle
Rakotobe, Zo Lalaina
Rakotomanana, Hajanirina

Rakotondraparany, Felix
Rakotondravony, Daniel
Rakotoniana, Johnson
Ramanamanjato, Jean-Baptiste
Ramcharan, Serano
Ranaivojaona, Rolland
Randriamanantsoa, Bemahafaly
Randrianarison, Jean Victor
Randrianasolo, Harison
Randrianirina, Jasmin
Randrianjafy, Volomboahangy
Randrianjanaka, Marson Lucien
Ranjakason
Rasoloarison, Rodin
Ratelolahy, Fèlix
Ratsimbazafy, Rémi
Ratsirarson, Helian
Rawa, Agnieszka
Razafimahatratra, Bertrand
Razafindrianilana, Norbert
Razafinjatovo, Philippe
Razakamalala, Richard
Reich, Alexandra
Remetwa, Herman
Remsen, J. V.
Rentz, David
Renyaan, Samuel
Reyes, Daisy
Reynel, Carlos
Reynolds, Robert
Rezende, Ubirazilda Maria
Rhodes, Jaye
Rial, Anabel
Richards, Stephen J.
Ricket, Arwen
Rico-Arce, Lourdes
Ridsdale, Colin
Ringler, Max
Riseng, Karen J.
Rivas, Belkis
Rivas, Gilson
Rivera, Carlos
Rivera, Francis
Rizqon, Seha
Rocha, Omar
Rödel, Mark-Oliver
Rodriguez Olivet, Carlos
Rodríguez, Carlos A.
Rodríguez, Fernando
Rodríguez, Francisco
Rodríguez, Juan
Rodríguez, Juan Carlos
Rodríguez, Juan José

Rodríguez, Leyda
Rodríguez, Lily
Rodríguez-Olarte, Douglas
Rogow, Todd
Rojas, Ángel
Rojas-Runjaic, Fernando
Rojas-Suárez, Franklin
Romo, Mónica
Rondeau, Guy
Roque, José Eduardo
Rosales, Aníbal
Rosales, Judith
Rosariyanto, Edy Michelis
Ross, Karen
Rounds, Isaac
Rowley, Jodi
Rumahorbo, Basa T.
Ruzicka, Jan
Sabino, José
Sackie, Zinnah
Safran, Sharon
Sagata, Katayo
Salazar, Edwin
Salcedo M., Norma J.
Salcedo, Marcos
Salimo
Samanez, Iris
Sambolah, Richard
Samman, James
Samoilys, Melita
Sampson, María A.
Samudio, Héctor
Sanabria, Nelson
Sanchez Riveiro, Homero
Sánchez, Javier
Sanchez, Luzmila
Sanderson, James G.
Sant'Agostino, Luís Henrique
Santisteban, Jose
Sapa, Jonathang
Sarmiento, Jaime
Satyawan, Dharma
Savage, Anne
Schargel, Richard
Schenkers, Maikel
Schmid, Jutta
Scholes, Ed
Schulenberg, Thomas S.
Schultz, Ted R.
Seele, Letlhogomolo
Seeto, Pamela
Segal, Bárbara
Seing, Sam The

Señarìs, Josefa Celsa
Serejo, Cristiana S.
Serrano, Martha
Servat, Grace
Sethunya, Kobamelo
Setio, Pujo
Shah, Karan
Shaoying, Liu
Shepard, Jr., Glenn H.
Shikoei, Tedde
Shine, Robert
Shoni, Romel
Short, Andrew
Short, Carla A.
Shrestha, Tej Kumar
Shunqing, Lu
Shu-Shu, Anthony
Siaw, D. E. K. A.
Sidlauskas, Brian
Sikes, Derek S.
Silka Innah, Henry
Simmons, Armand (Picky)
Sine, Robert
Singadan, Rose
Sitha, Som
Skelton, Paul
Skipwith, Phillip
Smith, Kent
Smith, Michael
Snelling, Roy R.
Solaga, Mônica
Solari, Sergio
Somaa, Nana Abena
Somua Amakye, Joseph
Song, Huang
Sophak, Sett
Soriano, Pascual
Sosa-Calvo, Jeffery
Soumah, Kadiatou
Spaggiari, Jérôme
Spanó, Saulo
Sparks, John S.
Spector, Sacha
Steene, Roger
Stergios, Basil
Stotz, Douglas F.
Struhsaker, Thomas
Strüssmann, Christine
Stuart, Bryan
Suartana, Ketut G.
Subedi, Indra
Surjadi, Purbassari
Suryadi, Suer

Suyanto, Agustinus
Swope, Evangeline
Tacheba, Budzanani
Taillebois, Laura
Takeuchi, Wayne
Tanda, La
Taphorn, Donald
Tapia, Elicio
Tapilatu, Ricardo
Tardy, Emmanuel
Tauna, David
Teimpouène, Ghislain
Téimpouenne, Matthias
Téimpouenne, Thomas
Tein, Ronald
Tello, José
Tenege, Sylvester
ter Steege, Hans
Thacker, Robert
Thaman, Baravi
Theodorakis, Christopher W.
Theuerkauf, Jörn
Thomas, Nunia
Thomsen, Jørgen
Thy, Neang
Tianjian, Gong
Timo, Oscar
Tirado Chamorro, Milton Fabian
Tjappa, Petrus
Tjaturadi, Burhan
Tjon, Kenneth
Tlotlego, Shex
Toha, Hamid
Tombolahy, Monica
Toney, Corletta
Torr, Geordie
Torres Vergara, Irene Lucia
Tron, François
Trotz, Maya
Tuiwawa, Fiona
Tuiwawa, Marika
Turak, Emre
Tweddle, Denis
Tylol, Innocent
Udvardy, Shana
Uetanabaro, Masao
Ulloa, Roberto
Unggul Nugroho, Irba
Valdes, Armando
Valdivieso, Javier
Valencia, Gorky
Valero, Félix
Valero, Isidoro

Valero, Rafael
Valle, Darwin
van Balen, Bas
van Balen, S. (Bas)
van Bergen, Marieke
van der Lugt, Frank
van der Waal, Ben
van Dijken, Schannel
van Mastrigt, Henk
van Tassell, James
Vandrot, Hervé
Vargas, Lourdes
Velazco, Paul
Veles, Segundo
Veron, J. E. N.
Vieira, Inácia Maria
Vierhaus, Henning
Vieux, Caroline
Villamizar, Rosa
Villanueva, Sérgio
Vivar, Elena
Vrede, Ingrid
Vreedzaam, Arionene
Waldron, Neville
Walker, Nathaniel
Wally, Elisa
Wan Tong, Kenneth
Wanguenne, Maurice
Waqa, Hilda
Waqa-Sakiti, Hilda
Warikar, Evie L.
Warpur, Maklon
Watcher, Tyana
Watling, Dick
Watling, James I.
Weber, Natalie
Wellington, Kabelo Brenda
Wells, Fred E.
Werner, Timothy
Whistler, Arthur
White, Mel
Wiakabu, Joseph
Wickel, Antoine
Widodo, Wahyu
Willem, Joeheo
Williams, Claude Thomas
Williams, Jeff
Willink, Philip W.
Wirjosentono, Jan
Wolf, Edward
Womsiwor, Daud
Wright, Debra D.
Wright, Heather E.

Wust, Walther
Xiaoli, Shen
Yanez, Patricio
Yang, Liu
Yapi, Kouassi
Yaynochi, Reuben
Yeboué, Lucie N'Guenan
Yéo, Kolo
Yohanita, Aksamina M.
Yoteni, Hugo
Young, Paulo S.
Youssouf, Kone
Yukuma, Charakura
Yusuf, Syafyudin
Zanata, Angela Maria
Zarza, Heliot
Zhengdong, Fang
Zhenghui, Xu
Zhongming, Wang
Zhumei, Li
Zwuen, Sormongar

A Rocha International
Afrique Nature Internationale, Côte d'Ivoire
Alcan Inc., Canada
Alcoa World Alumina LLC (ALCOA), USA
Anton de Kom University, Suriname
Ascanio Birding Tours, Venzuela
Asociación Guatemalteca para la Conservación Natural (CÄNAN K'AAX), Guatemala
Asociación para la Conservación del Patrimonio del Cutivireni, Peru
Association Maruia Trust Nouvelle Calédonie, New Caledonia
Association Nationale pour la Gestion des Aires Protégées (ANGAP), Madagascar
Australian Institute of Marine Science, Australia
Australia's Commonwealth Scientific and Industrial Research Organisation (CSIRO), Australia
Badan Pengembangan Dan Pembangunan Daerah (BPPEDA), Indonesia
Bandung Technology Institute (ITB), Indonesia
Belize Center for Environmental Studies, Belize
Bernice P. Bishop Museum, USA
BHP Billiton Maatschappij Suriname (BMS), Suriname
BIOCENTRO - Universidad Experimental de los Llanos Ezequiel Zamora (UNELLEZ) - Guanare, Venzuela
Biological Diversity of the Guianas Program, Smithsonian Institution, USA
Center for Applied Biodiversity Science (CABS), USA
Centre for Study of Biological Diversity (Biodiversity Centre) (University of Guyana), Guyana
Centre Forestier N'Zérékoré, Guinea
Centro de Datos para la Conservación de Bolivia, Bolivia
Centro de Estudios Conservacionistas (CECON), Guatemala
La Colección Boliviana de Fauna (CBF), Bolivia
Colección de Vertebrados de la Universidad de Los Andes (CVULA), Venzuela
Colección Ornitológica Phelps, Venzuela
La Comisión Nacional del Medio Ambiente (CONAMA), Guatemala
ConocoPhillips, Venzuela
Consejo Nacional de Areas Protegidas (CONAP), Guatemala
Coral Reef Initiatives for the Pacific (CRISP), New Caledonia
CORDIO East Africa, Kenya
Dayu Biik, New Caledonia
Department of Conservation, New Zealand
Department of Fisheries, Botswana
Department of Water Affairs, Botswana
Dewan Masyarakat Adat Mamberamo Raya (DMAR), Indonesia
Direction de la Protection de la Nature, Côte d'Ivoire
Direction du Développement Économique et de L'Environnement de la Province Nord (DDEE), New Caledonia
Discovery Communications, USA
Disney Worldwide Conservation Fund (DWCF), USA
EcoCiencia, Ecuador
Ecology and Environment (E & E), Venzuela

Economic Development Agency of New Caledonia (ADECAL), New Caledonia
ECOSYN, Netherlands
El Instituto de Zoología Tropical (IZT), Universidad Central de Venezuela, Venezuela
Empresa Brasileira de Pesquisa Agropecuária (EMBRAPA), Brazil
Environment and Conservation Management Committee - East New Britain, Papua New
    Guinea
Environmental Protection Agency (EPA), Guyana
Escuela Politécnica Nacional, Ecuador
Estación Biológica las Guacamayas, Guatemala
The Field Museum, USA
Fiji Department of Forestry, Fiji
The Fiji Museum, Fiji
Florida International University, USA
Foibe Fampandrosoana sy Fikarohana ny eny Ambanivohitra (FOFIFA)/Direction des
    Recherches Forestieres et Piscicoles, Madagascar
Forestry Development Authority (FDA), Liberia, Liberia
Foundation for People and Community Development, Papua New Guinea
Fundación Amigos de la Naturaleza, Bolivia
Fundación AndígenA, Venezuela
Fundación CIARA, Venezuela
La Fundación Cisneros, Venezuela
Fundación Ecológica Arcoiris, Ecuador
Fundación Ecuatoriana de Investigación y Manejo Ambiental, Ecuador
La Fundación Instituto Botánico de Venezuela (FIBV), Venezuela
Fundación Jardín Botánico del Orinoco (FJBO), Venezuela
Fundación Jatún Sacha, Ecuador
Fundación La Salle de Ciencias Naturales (FLSCN), Venezuela
Fundación Natura - Guayaquil Chapter, Ecuador
Fundación para la Agricultura Tropical Alternativa y el Desarrollo Integral (FUNDATADI),
    Venezuela
La Fundación Programa Andes Tropicales (PAT), Venezuela
Fundación Terra Parima, Venezuela
Gold Reserve - Compañía Aurífera Brisas del Cuyuní, C.A., Venezuela
Guinée Ecologie, Guinea
Guyana Agency for Health Sciences Education, Environment and Food Policy, Guyana
Harry Oppenheimer Okavango Research Centre, Botswana
Hasanuddin University, Indonesia
Herbario Nacional de Bolivia, Bolivia
Herbarium, Pontificia Universidad Católica de Ecuador, Ecuador
Indonesian Institute of Sciences (LIPI), Indonesia
Institut Congolais pour la Conservation de la Nature (ICCN), Democratic Republic of the Congo
Instituto Brasileiro do Meio Ambiente e dos Recursos Naturais Renováveis (IBAMA), Brazil
Instituto de Biología Experimental (IBE), Universidad Central de Venezuela, Venezuela
Instituto de Ciencias Ambientales y Ecológicas (ICAE), Venezuela
Instituto de Ciencias Naturales, Universidad Nacional de Colombia, Colombia
Instituto de Ecología de Bolivia, Bolivia
Instituto de Estudos do Mar Almirante Paulo Moreira (IEAPM), Brazil
Instituto de Investigaciones de Amazonía Peruana, Peru

Instituto de Pesquisas Jardim Botânico do Rio de Janeiro, Brazil
Instituto de Zoología y Ecología Tropical (IZET), Universidad Central de Venezuela, Venzuela
Instituto Nacional de Pesquisas da Amazônia (INPA), Brazil
Instituto Venezolano de Investigaciones Científicas (IVIC), Venzuela
Kreditanstalt für Wiederaufbau, Germany
Laboratório de Estudos Costeiros, Instituto de Geociências, Universidade Federal da Bahia, Brazil
Louisiana State University, USA
Marie Selby Botanical Gardens, USA
Milne Bay Provincial Government, Papua New Guinea
Ministère des Eaux et Forêts (MEF), Madagascar
MIRAY project, Madagascar
Missouri Botanical Garden, USA
The Mountain Institute, USA
Museo de Historia Natural "Noel Kempff Mercado", Bolivia
Museo de Historia Natural, Universidad Nacional Mayor de San Marcos (MHN-UMSM), Peru
Museo de la Estación Biológica Rancho Grande, Venezuela
Museo de Zoologia, Pontificia Universidad Católica de Ecuador, Ecuador
Museo Nacional de Historia Natural, Bolivia
Museo Nacional de Historia Natural del Paraguay, Paraguay
Museu de Zoologia, Universidade de São Paulo, Brazil
Museu Nacional, Universidade Federal do Rio de Janeiro, Brazil
National Center for Environmental Research, Madagascar
National Geographic Society, USA
National Trust of Fiji, Fiji
Nations Petroleum, Canada
NatureFiji-MareqetiViti, Fiji
Newmont Ghana Gold, Ltd., Ghana
Organization Kuyujani, Venezuela
Palawan Council for Sustainable Development, Philippines
The Papua Environment Foundation (YALI–Papua), Indonesia
Papua New Guinea Department of Environment and Conservation, Papua New Guinea
Papua New Guinea Institute of Biological Research, Papua New Guinea
Papua New Guinea National Museum and Art Gallery (PNGNM), Papua New Guinea
Papua State University, Indonesia
Parc Botanique et Zoologique de Tsimbazaza, Madagascar
Parque Nacional Marinho dos Abrolhos, Brazil
Perlindungan Dan Konservasi Alamb (PKA), Indonesia
PGRR/Centre Forestier de N'Zérékoré, Guinea
Research and Development Center for Oceanology (RDCO), Indonesia
Rio Tinto Mining and Exploration Limited, Australia
Secretaria Estadual do Meio Ambiente do Amapá, Brazil
Secretariat of the Pacific Regional Environment Program, New Caledonia
Shell Prospecting and Development, Peru
Smithsonian Institution, National Museum of Natural History (NMNH), USA
Société Calédonienne d'Ornithologie (SCO), New Caledonia
Société de Développement des Siège SocialForêts (SODEFOR), Côte d'Ivoire
Society for the Conservation of Nature in Liberia (SCNL), Liberia

South African Institute for Aquatic Biodiversity, South Africa
South Australian Museum, Australia
South Pacific Regional Herbarium, Fiji
Stichting Natuurbehoud Suriname (Stinasu) - Foundation for Nature Conservation in Suriname,
    Suriname
Suralco (Suriname Aluminum Company LLC), Suriname
Tropenbos International, Netherlands
United Nations Mission in Liberia (UNMIL), Liberia
United States Department of State, USA
Universidad Centroccidental Lisandro Alvarado, Colección Regional de Peces (CPUCLA),
    Venzuela
Universidad Nacional de Asunción, Paraguay
Universidad Nacional de Loja, Herbario Reinaldo Espinosa (LOJA), Ecuador
Universidade de São Paulo, Brazil
Universidade Federal de Mato Grosso do Sul, Brazil
Université d'Abobo Adajamé, Côte d'Ivoire
Université d'Antananarivo, Madagascar
Université de Cocody, Côte d'Ivoire
Université de Mahajanga, Madagascar
University of Aukland, Leigh Marine Laboratory, New Zealand
University of Botswana, Botswana
University of Cenderawasih (UNCEN), Indonesia
University of Florida, USA
University of Illinois, Illinois Natural History Survey, USA
University of Liberia, Liberia
University of the South Pacific, Biology Division, Fiji
Western Australia Museum, Australia
Wetlands International - Oceania
Wildlife Conservation Society, USA

Appendix III. RAP donors and supporters

The Rapid Assessment Program thanks the following individuals, foundations and organizations for their generous financial support over the past 20 years.

3-M Corporation
A Rocha International
Alcan Inc.
Alcoa Foundation
Alcoa World Alumina LLC (ALCOA)
Dr. Janis Alcorn
Allen & Company, Inc.
Arcadia Foundation
Neil Baer
Barker Foundation
Beneficia Foundation
BHP Billiton Maatschappij Suriname (BMS)
BIOCENTRO-UNELLEZ-Guanare, Venezuela
Biodiversity Support Program
Kim L. Bishop
blue moon fund (formerly W. Alton Jones Foundation)
Brevard Community College, USA
Randy Brooks
Colección Ornitológica Phelps, Venezuela
The Comer Science and Education Foundation
Commission for Environmental Cooperation
Compañía Aurífera Brisas del Cuyuní C. A. (CABC), Venezuela
ConocoPhillips-Venezuela
Conselho Nacional de Desenvolvimento Científico e Tecnológico (CNPq), Brazil
Conservation Stewards Program, Conservation International
The Leon and Toby Cooperman Family Foundation
Critical Ecosystem Partnership Fund
Curtis Woods Investments
CVG Electrificación del Caroní, C.A. (EDELCA)
Direction du Développement Économique et de L'Environnement de la Province Nord (DDEE), New Caledonia
Disney Worldwide Conservation Fund
Disney Worldwide Services, Inc.
Ecology and Environment (E & E), Venezuela
Economic Development Agency of New Caledonia (ADECAL)
Empresa Cemento Nacional, SA, Ecuador
Environ UK Limited
European Union
Jay Fahn
The Field Museum (Department of Zoology: Environmental and Conservation Programs), USA
Fiji Water Foundation

Fundação Carlos Chagas Filho de Amparo à Pesquisa do Estado do Rio de Janeiro (FAPERJ),
  Brazil
Fundação de Amparo à Pesquisa do Estado de São Paulo (FAPESP), Brazil
Fundação O Boticário de Proteção à Natureza, Brazil
Fundação Universitária José Bonifácio, Brazil
Fundación La Salle de Ciencias Naturales (FLSCN), Venezuela
Fundación para la Agricultura Tropical Alternativa y el Desarrollo Integral (FUNDATADI),
  Venezuela
La Gerencia de Investigación orientada del FONACIT, Venezuela
The Giuliani Family Foundation
Global Conservation Fund
Global Environmental Facility
Global Environmental Protection Institute
Joan and Selma Goldstein
Howard Gould
Ann-Eve Hazen
The Headley Trust
The Henry Foundation
Alan Hixon
The Home Depot
Indonesian Institute of Sciences (LIPI)
Kreditanstalt für Wiederaufbau (KfW)
Molly Kux
Iara Lee and George Gund Foundation
Leslie Lee
The John D. and Catherine T. MacArthur Foundation
Marshall Field Funds
John E. McCaw
McDonald's Corporation
John S. McIlheny
Richard Menzel
Ministry of Environment, Cambodia
Bonnie Mitsui
Moore Charitable Foundation
Gordon and Betty Moore Foundation
Mount Holyoke College, USA
The Mulago Foundation
National Geographic Society
National Science Foundation
Nations Petroleum
Netherlands Committee for IUCN
New England Aquarium, USA
New England Biolabs Foundation
New Horizons Fund at the University of North Carolina at Asheville, USA
Newmont Ghana Gold, Ltd.
Newmont Mining Corporation
The North Face
Fabian and Nina Oberfeld

One World/Weavers Apparel LLC
Overseas Economic Cooperation Fund of Japan (now Japan Bank for International Cooperation)
The David and Lucile Packard Foundation
Porgera Joint Venture (PJV)
Power Foods of Berkeley, CA, USA
Ramada Inn Belize City
Reserva Ecologico El Refugio, Bolivia
Grace Jones Richardson Trust
Rio Tinto
Royal Ontario Museum, Canada
The Rufford Foundation (formerly The Rufford Maurice Laing Foundation)
Sainsbury Foundation
Tom and Miriam Schulman
Secretaría Nacional de Ciencia y Tecnología del Ecuador (SENACYT)
Shell International
David and Janet Shores
Ken F. Siebel
Smart Family Foundation
Miranda Smith
Smithsonian Institution
Richard and Jessica Sneider
Suralco (Suriname Aluminum Company LLC)
John F. Swift
William W. and Mary Lee Tennant
William P. Tennity
Tinker Foundation Incorporated
Total Foundation
Tropical Wilderness Protection Fund
United Nations Food and Agriculture Organization
United Nations Trust Funds subcontract UNTS/MAG/001/GEF (FAO)
United Nations Development Programme
United States Department of State
Universidad de los Andes, Colombia
Universidade Federal do Rio de Janeiro, Brazil
The University of Chicago, USA
USAID (Global Bureau: Guatemala Bureau)
Walt Disney Company
The Walton Family Foundation
Alan Weeden
The William P. Wharton Trust
Harold C. Whitman
Hans Wilsdorf Foundation
Wolfensohn Family Foundation

CENTRAL AND SOUTH AMERICA

Belize: Columbia River Forest Reserve. Parker, T.A. III. (ed.). 1993. A Biological Assessment of the Columbia River Forest Reserve, Toledo District, Belize. RAP Working Papers 3. Conservation International, Washington, DC.

Bolivia: Alto Madidi Region. Parker, T.A. III and B. Bailey (eds.). 1991. A Biological Assessment of the Alto Madidi Region and Adjacent Areas of Northwest Bolivia May 18 - June 15, 1990. RAP Working Papers 1. Conservation International, Washington, DC.

Bolivia: Lowland Dry Forests of Santa Cruz. Parker, T.A. III, R.B. Foster, L.H. Emmons and B. Bailey (eds.). 1993. The Lowland Dry Forests of Santa Cruz, Bolivia: A Global Conservation Priority. RAP Working Papers 4. Conservation International, Washington, DC.

Bolivia/Peru: Pando, Alto Madidi/Pampas del Heath. Montambault, J.R. (ed.). 2002. Informes de las evaluaciones biológicas de Pampas del Heath, Perú, Alto Madidi, Bolivia, y Pando, Bolivia. RAP Bulletin of Biological Assessment 24. Conservation International, Washington, DC.

Bolivia: South Central Chuquisaca. Schulenberg, T.S. and K. Awbrey (eds.). 1997. A Rapid Assessment of the Humid Forests of South Central Chuquisaca, Bolivia. RAP Working Papers 8. Conservation International, Washington, DC.

Bolivia: Noel Kempff Mercado National Park. Killeen, T.J. and T.S. Schulenberg (eds.). 1998. A biological assessment of Parque Nacional Noel Kempff Mercado, Bolivia. RAP Working Papers 10. Conservation International, Washington, DC.

Bolivia: Río Orthon Basin, Pando. Chernoff, B. and P.W. Willink (eds.). 1999. A Biological Assessment of Aquatic Ecosystems of the Upper Río Orthon Basin, Pando, Bolivia. Bulletin of Biological Assessment 15. Conservation International, Washington, DC.

Brazil: Rio Negro and Headwaters. Willink, P.W., B. Chernoff, L.E. Alonso, J.R. Montambault and R. Lourival (eds.). 2000. A Biological Assessment of the Aquatic Ecosystems of the Pantanal, Mato Grosso do Sul, Brasil. RAP Bulletin of Biological Assessment 18. Conservation International, Washington, DC.

Brazil: Abrolhos Bank. Dutra, G.F., G.R. Allen, T. Werner and S.A. McKenna (eds.). 2005. A Rapid Marine Biodiversity Assessment of the Abrolhos Bank, Bahia, Brazil. RAP Bulletin of Biological Assessment 38. Conservation International, Washington, DC.

Brazil: Amapá. Bernard, E. (ed.). 2008. Rapid Biological Inventories in the Tumucumaque Mountains National Park, Amapá, Brazil. RAP Bulletin of Biological Assessment 48. Conservation International, Arlington, VA.

Ecuador: Cordillera de la Costa. Parker, T.A. III and J.L. Carr (eds.). 1992. Status of Forest Remnants in the Cordillera de la Costa and Adjacent Areas of Southwestern Ecuador. RAP Working Papers 2. Conservation International, Washington, DC.

Ecuador/Peru: Cordillera del Condor. Schulenberg, T.S. and K. Awbrey (eds.). 1997. The Cordillera del Condor of Ecuador and Peru: A Biological Assessment. RAP Working Papers 7. Conservation International, Washington, DC.

Ecuador/Peru: Pastaza River Basin. Willink, P.W., B. Chernoff and J. McCullough (eds.). 2005. A Rapid Biological Assessment of the Aquatic Ecosystems of the Pastaza River Basin, Ecuador and Perú. RAP Bulletin of Biological Assessment 33. Conservation International, Washington, DC.

Ecuador: Nangaritza Tepuyes. Freile, J.P., Moscoso, and C. Felix. 2010. La Magia de los Tepuyes del Nangaritza: una guía para conocer a sus habitantes. Conservación Internacional Ecuador. Quito, Ecuador.

Ecuador: Nangaritza Tepuyes. Guayasamin, J.M. and E. Bonaccorso (eds.). 2011 (*in press*). Evaluación Ecológica Rápida de la Biodiversidad de los Tepuyes de la Cuenca Alta del Río Nangaritza, Cordillera del Cóndor, Ecuador. Bulletin of Biological Assessment 58. Conservation International, Arlington, VA.

Guatemala: Laguna del Tigre National Park. Bestelmeyer, B. and L.E. Alonso (eds.). 2000. A Biological Assessment of Laguna del Tigre National Park, Petén, Guatemala. RAP Bulletin of Biological Assessment 16. Conservation International, Washington, DC.

Guyana: Kanuku Mountain Region. Parker, T.A. III and A.B. Forsyth (eds.). 1993. A Biological Assessment of the Kanuku Mountain Region of Southwestern Guyana. RAP Working Papers 5. Conservation International, Washington, DC.

Guyana: Eastern Kanuku Mountains. Montambault, J.R. and O. Missa (eds.). 2002. A Biodiversity Assessment of the Eastern Kanuku Mountains, Lower Kwitaro River, Guyana. RAP Bulletin of Biological Assessment 26. Conservation International, Washington, DC.

Guyana: Kanuku Mountains. Rapid Assessment Program. 2003. Biodiversity in the Kanuku Mountains. Conservation International, Washington, DC.

Guyana: Southern Guyana. Alonso, L.E., J. McCullough, P. Naskrecki, E. Alexander and H.E. Wright (eds.). 2008. A Rapid Biological Assessment of the Konashen Community Owned Conservation Area, Southern Guyana. RAP Bulletin of Biological Assessment 51. Conservation International, Arlington, VA.

Guyana: Southern Guyana. Rapid Assessment Program. 2008. Biodiversity in the Konashen Community-owned Conservation Area, Guyana. Conservation International, Arlington, VA.

Paraguay: Río Paraguay Basin. Chernoff, B., P.W. Willink and J. R. Montambault (eds.). 2001. A biological assessment of the Río Paraguay Basin, Alto Paraguay, Paraguay. RAP Bulletin of Biological Assessment 19. Conservation International, Washington, DC.

Peru: Tambopata-Candamo Reserved Zone. Foster, R.B., J.L. Carr and A.B. Forsyth (eds.). 1994. The Tambopata-Candamo Reserved Zone of southeastern Perú: A Biological Assessment. RAP Working Papers 6. Conservation International, Washington, DC.

Peru: Cordillera de Vilcabamba. Alonso, L.E., A. Alonso, T. S. Schulenberg and F. Dallmeier (eds.). 2001. Biological and Social Assessments of the Cordillera de Vilcabamba, Peru. RAP Working Papers 12 and SI/MAB Series 6. Conservation International, Washington, DC.

Suriname: Coppename River Basin. Alonso, L.E. and H.J. Berrenstein (eds.). 2006. A Rapid Biological Assessment of the Aquatic Ecosystems of the Coppename River Basin, Suriname. RAP Bulletin of Biological Assessment 39. Conservation International, Washington, DC.

Suriname: Lely and Nassau Plateaus. Alonso, L.E. and J.H. Mol (eds.). 2007. A Rapid Biological Assessment of the Lely and Nassau Plateaus, Suriname (with additional information on the Brownsberg Plateau). RAP Bulletin of Biological Assessment 43. Conservation International, Arlington, VA.

Venezuela: Caura River Basin. Chernoff, B., A. Machado-Allison, K. Riseng and J.R. Montambault (eds.). 2003. A Biological Assessment of the Aquatic Ecosystems of the Caura River Basin, Bolívar State, Venezuela. RAP Bulletin of Biological Assessment 28. Conservation International, Washington, DC.

Venezuela: Orinoco Delta and Gulf of Paria. Lasso, C.A., L.E. Alonso, A.L. Flores and G. Love (eds.). 2004. Rapid assessment of the biodiversity and social aspects of the aquatic ecosystems of the Orinoco Delta and the Gulf of Paria, Venezuela. RAP Bulletin of Biological Assessment 37. Conservation International, Washington, DC.

Venezuela: Los Ríos Orinoco y Ventuari. Lasso, C.A., J.C. Ceñaris, L.E. Alonso and A.L. Flores (eds.). 2006. Evaluación Rápida de la Biodiversidad de los Ecosistemas Acuáticos en la Confluencia de los ríos Orinoco y Ventuari, Estado Amazonas, Venezuela. RAP Bulletin of Biological Assessment 30. Conservation International, Washington, DC.

Venezuela: La Cuenca Alta del Río Paragua. Ceñaris, J.C., C.A. Lasso and A.L. Flores (eds.). 2008. Evaluación Rápida de la Biodiversidad de los Ecosistemas Acuáticos de la Cuenca Alta del Río Paragua, Estado Bolívar, Venezuela. RAP Bulletin of Biological Assessment 49. Conservation International, Arlington, VA.

Venezuela: La Cuenca Alta del Río Cuyuní. Lasso, C.A., J.C. Ceñaris, A. Rial and A.L. Flores (eds.). 2010. Evaluación Rápida de la Biodiversidad de los Ecosistemas Acuáticos de la Cuenca Alta del Río Cuyuní, Guyana Venezolana. RAP Bulletin of Biological Assessment 55. Conservation International, Arlington, VA.

Venezuela: Ramal Calderas. Rial B., A., J.C. Ceñaris, C.A. Lasso and A.L. Flores (eds.). 2010. Rapid assessment of the biodiversity of the Ramal Calderas, Venezuelan Andes. RAP Bulletin of Biological Assessment 56. Conservation International, Arlington, VA.

AFRICA AND MADAGASCAR

Botswana: Okavango Delta. Alonso, L.E. and L. Nordin (eds.). 2003. A Rapid Biological Assessment of the aquatic ecosystems of the Okavango Delta, Botswana: High Water Survey. RAP Bulletin of Biological Assessment 27. Conservation International, Washington, DC.

Côte d'Ivoire: Marahoué National Park. Schulenberg, T.S., C.A. Short and P.J. Stephenson (eds.). 1999. A Biological Assessment of Parc National de la Marahoué, Côte d'Ivoire. RAP Working Papers 13. Conservation International, Washington, DC.

Côte d'Ivoire: Two Classified Forests. Alonso, L.E., F. Lauginie and G. Rondeau (eds.). 2005. A Rapid Biological Assessment of Two Classified Forests in Southwestern Côte d'Ivoire. RAP Bulletin of Biological Assessment 34. Conservation International, Washington, DC.

Democratic Republic of the Congo: Lokutu. Butynski, T.M. and J. McCullough (eds.). 2007. A Rapid Biological Assessment of Lokutu, Democratic Republic of Congo. RAP Bulletin of Biological Assessment 46. Conservation International, Arlington, VA.

Ghana: Draw River. McCullough, J., J. Decher and D.G. Kpelle (eds.). 2005. A Biological Assessment of the Terrestrial Ecosystems of the Draw River, Boi-Tano, Tano Nimiri and Krokosua Hills Forest Reserves, Southwestern Ghana. RAP Bulletin of Biological Assessment 36. Conservation International, Washington, DC.

Ghana: Atewa Range Forest Reserve. McCullough, J., L.E. Alonso, P. Naskrecki, H.E. Wright and Y. Osei-Owusu (eds.). 2007. A Rapid Biological Assessment of the Atewa Range Forest Reserve, Eastern Ghana. RAP Bulletin of Biological Assessment 47. Conservation International. Arlington, VA.

Ghana: Atewa Range Forest Reserve. Rapid Assessment Program. 2007. Biodiversity in the Atewa Range Forest Reserve, Ghana. Conservation International, Arlington, VA.

Ghana: Ajenjua Bepo and Mamang River. McCullough, J., P. Hoke, P. Naskrecki and Y. Osei-Owusu (eds.).2008. A Rapid Biological Assessment of the Ajenjua Bepo and Mamang River Forest Reserves, Ghana. RAP Bulletin of Biological Assessment 50. Conservation International, Arlington, VA.

Guinea: Pic de Fon. McCullough, J. (ed.). 2004. A Rapid Biological Assessment of the Forêt Classée du Pic de Fon, Simandou Range, Southeastern Republic of Guinea. RAP Bulletin of Biological Assessment 35. Conservation International, Washington, DC.

Guinea: Southeastern Guinea. Wright, H.E., J. McCullough, L.E. Alonso and M.S. Diallo (eds.). 2006. A Rapid Biological Assessment of Three Classified Forests in Southeastern Guinea. RAP Bulletin of Biological Assessment 40. Conservation International, Washington, DC.

Guinea: Boké Préfecture. Wright, H.E., J. McCullough and M.S. Diallo (eds.). 2006. A Rapid Biological Assessment of Boké Préfecture, Northwestern Guinea. RAP Bulletin of Biological Assessment 41. Conservation International, Washington, DC.

Liberia: North Lorma, Gola and Grebo National Forests. Hoke, P., R. Demey and A. Peal (eds.). 2007. A Rapid Biological Assessment of North Lorma, Gola and Grebo National Forests, Liberia. RAP Bulletin of Biological Assessment 44. Conservation International, Arlington, VA.

Madagascar: Ankarafantsika. Alonso, L.E., T.S. Schulenberg, S. Radilofe and O. Missa (eds.). 2002. A Biological Assessment of the Réserve Naturelle Intégrale d'Ankarafantsika, Madagascar. RAP Bulletin of Biological Assessment 23. Conservation International, Washington, DC.

Madagascar: Northwest Coral Reefs. McKenna, S.A. and G.R. Allen (eds.). 2005. A Rapid Marine Biodiversity Assessment of the Coral Reefs of Northwest Madagascar. RAP Bulletin of Biological Assessment 31. Conservation International, Washington, DC.

Madagascar: Mantadia-Zahamena. Schmid, J. and L.E. Alonso (eds.). 2005. A Rapid Biological Assessment of the Mantadia-Zahamena Corridor, Madagascar. RAP Bulletin of Biological Assessment 32. Conservation International, Washington, DC.

ASIA-PACIFIC

China: Sichuan Province. Alonso, L.E., L. Shaoying, S. Xiaoli and J. McCullough (eds.). 2010. A Rapid Biological Assessment of Three Sites in the Mountains of Southwest China Hotspot, Ganzi Prefecture, Sichuan Province, China. RAP Bulletin of Biological Assessment 52. Conservation International, Arlington, VA.

Fiji: Nakauvadra Mountain Range. Morrison, C. (ed.). 2010. A Rapid Biodiversity Assessment of the Nakauvadra Range, Ra Province, Fiji. RAP Bulletin of Biological Assessment 57. Conservation International, Arlington, VA.

Indonesia: Wapoga River Area. Mack, A.L. and L.E. Alonso (eds.). 2000. A Biological Assessment of the Wapoga River Area of Northwestern Irian Jaya, Indonesia. RAP Bulletin of Biological Assessment 14. Conservation International, Washington, DC.

Indonesia: Togean and Banggai Islands. Allen, G.R., and S.A. McKenna (eds.). 2001. A Marine Rapid Assessment of the Togean and Banggai Islands, Sulawesi, Indonesia. RAP Bulletin of Biological Assessment 20. Conservation International, Washington, DC.

Indonesia: Raja Ampat Islands. McKenna, S.A., G.R. Allen and S. Suryadi (eds.). 2002. A Marine Rapid Assessment of the Raja Ampat Islands, Papua Province, Indonesia. RAP Bulletin of Biological Assessment 22. Conservation International, Washington, DC.

Indonesia: Yongsu - Cyclops Mountains and the Southern Mamberamo Basin. Richards, S.J. and S. Suryadi (eds.). 2002. A Biodiversity Assessment of Yongsu - Cyclops Mountains and the Southern Mamberamo Basin, Papua, Indonesia. RAP Bulletin of Biological Assessment 25. Conservation International, Washington, DC.

New Caledonia: Mont Panié. McKenna, S.A., N. Baillon, H. Blaffart and G. Abrusci (eds.). 2006. Une Évaluation Rapide de la Biodiversité Marine des Récifs Coralliens du Mont Panié, Province Nord, Nouvelle Calédonie. RAP Bulletin of Biological Assessment 42. Conservation International, Washington, DC.

New Caledonia: Province Nord. McKenna, S.A., N. Baillon and J. Spaggiari (eds.). 2010. A Rapid Marine Biodiversity Assessment of the Coral Reefs of the Northwest Lagoon, between Koumac and Yandé, Province Nord, New Caledonia. RAP Bulletin of Biological Assessment 53. Conservation International, Arlington, VA.

Papua New Guinea: Lakekamu Basin. Mack, A.L. (ed.). 1998. A Biological Assessment of the Lakekamu Basin, Papua New Guinea. RAP Working Papers 9. Conservation International, Washington, DC.

Papua New Guinea: Milne Bay Province. Werner, T.B. and G. Allen (eds.). 1998. A Rapid Biodiversity Assessment of the Coral Reefs of Milne Bay Province, Papua New Guinea. RAP Working Papers 11. Conservation International, Washington, DC.

Papua New Guinea: Southern New Ireland. Beehler, B.M. and L.E. Alonso (eds.). 2001. Southern New Ireland, Papua New Guinea: A Biodiversity Assessment. RAP Bulletin of Biological Assessment 21. Conservation International, Washington, DC.

Papua New Guinea: Milne Bay Province. Allen, G.R., J.P. Kinch, S.A. McKenna and P. Seeto (eds.). 2003. A Rapid Marine Biodiversity Assessment of Milne Bay Province, Papua New Guinea - Survey II (2000). RAP Bulletin of Biological Assessment 29. Conservation International, Washington, DC.

Papua New Guinea: Kaijende Highlands. Richards, S.J. (ed.). 2007. A Rapid Biodiversity Assessment of the Kaijende Highlands, Enga Province, Papua New Guinea. RAP Bulletin of Biological Assessment 45. Conservation International, Arlington, VA.

Philippines: Palawan Province. Werner, T.B. and G. Allen (eds.). 2000. A Rapid Marine Biodiversity Assessment of the Calamianes Islands, Palawan Province, Philippines. RAP Bulletin of Biological Assessment 17. Conservation International, Washington, DC.

INDEX OF RAP SURVEY PROFILES

CENTRAL AND SOUTH AMERICA

AFRICA & MADAGASCAR

ASIA-PACIFIC

Recent RAP Staff

RAP staff 2006: Leslie Kasmir, Leeanne Alonso, Peter Hoke, Heather Wright

RAP staff 2007: Leeanne Alonso, Peter Hoke, Jennifer McCullough, Edward Lohnes